FDI IN INDIA
Issues and Challenges

FDI IN INDIA
Issues and Challenges

Edited by

N. PRASANNA

REGAL PUBLICATIONS
New Delhi - 110 027

FDI IN INDIA: Issues and Challenges

ISBN 978-81-8484-319-4

© 2014 N. PRASANNA

All rights reserved with the Publisher, including the right to translate or to reproduce this book or parts thereof except for brief quotations in critical articles or reviews.

Typeset by
THE LASER PRINTERS
8/15, 3rd Floor, Subhash Nagar, New Delhi-110027

Printed in India at
MAYUR ENTERPRISES,
WZ Plot No. 3, Gujjar Market, Tihar Village, New Delhi-110018

Published by
REGAL PUBLICATIONS
F-159, Rajouri Garden, New Delhi-110027
Phones : 45546396, 25435369
E-mail : regalbookspub@yahoo.com, regaldeepbooks@yahoo.com

Contents

	Preface	vii
	List of Contributors	ix
	Introduction	xi
1.	Issues of FDI in India *Vinish Kathuria*	1
2.	Effects of Foreign Direct Investment in India *S. Iyyampillai*	19
3.	An Analysis of FDI Inflows—Economic Growth Causality in India *N. Prasanna*	26
4.	Impact of Capital Flows on Economic Growth in India *A.B. Angappapillai and C.K. Muthu Kumaran*	52
5.	The Role of FDI on the Economic Growth of Indian Economy *S.R. Keshava*	67
6.	Foreign Direct Investment and Economic Growth: Issues in Attracting FDI into India *S. Preethi and K.T. Geetha*	77
7.	Foreign Direct Investment, Non-Oil Export and Economic Growth in India: An Empirical Investigation *J. Srinivasan and M. Shanmugam*	88
8.	Foreign Direct Investment and Economic Growth *M. Thahira Banu and R. Vaheedha Banu*	97

9. Foreign Direct Investment and Economic Growth in India 112
   Tripura Sundari, C.U. and Balaji, B.

10. FDI in Multi-Brand Retail Business—Opportunities and Challenges 122
    P.G. Arul

11. Foreign Direct Investment in Telecom Sector 136
    Fayaz Ahamed

12. Foreign Direct Investment and Indian Manufacturing Industry Output Growth 147
    Pesala Busenna

13. Productivity Growth of Foreign and Domestic Firms in the Indian Iron and Steel Industry: A Decomposition Analysis 170
    T. Sampathkumar

14. Foreign Direct Investment and Export Performance 182
    K. Kalaichelvi

15. FDI and Export Performance in India 193
    S. Saravanan and G. Saravanan

16. A Study of Role of FDI in Economic Growth and Employment Generation in India 211
    K.S. Santha Kumar

17. Effect of FDI on Spillovers and Productivity: Evidence from India 221
    Suman Sharma

Index 236

Preface

All countries, particularly developing, seek to attract FDI for the package of benefits it brings along with it into the host country's economy. FDI, not only supplements domestic investment resources but also acts as a source of foreign exchange and can relax Balance of Payments (BoP) constraints on growth. Considering the economic benefits and importance of FDI for promoting economic growth, most of the countries have formulated wide-reaching changes in national policies to attract FDI. India has been no exception to this spectacle. During 1991, the government of India introduced full-fledged macroeconomic reforms and structural adjustments under the IMF and World Bank adjustment programmes and is since continuing on the same path. These reforms include liberalising the approval procedures, the investment restrictions, the limitation on foreign equity participation, the restrictions on acquisitions and take-over by foreign investors, the local content requirement, the restrictions on remittance of funds abroad and the special incentives to the foreign investors, among others. All these initiatives resulted in a phenomenal rise in the FDI inflows into India.

But, the empirical literature on the impact of FDI on the host economy is plagued by inconclusive evidences. Some studies suggest that FDI raises national welfare by increasing the volume and efficiency of investment through improved competitiveness, technological diffusion, accelerated spillover effects and the accumulation of human capital. Overall, the flow of FDI to developing countries contributes to growth through two mechanisms, i.e., increasing total investment in the host country and increasing productivity through technology and management spillover. China and East/South-east Asian countries have made rapid improvement in their macro-economic situations, investment, exports and employment over the decades of 1980s and 1990s through the use of large amounts of FDI.

While others argue that the MNCs and TNCs bringing FDI

generally monopolise resources, supplant domestic enterprises, introduce inappropriate technology and create BoP problems through large remittances. Added to this is the reality that India did not move into this reform process wholly for the benefits which it could reap, but due to the fact that the external sector in particular and whole economy in general were facing economic disaster. That is, the government of India had no option, but to resort to full-fledged macro-economic reforms and structural adjustments in order to bring the economy back on rails. Yet another fact is that the process of reforms was a part of the conditionality of IMF and World Bank to bail India out of the severe economic crisis which it was facing at that time.

In this context, this book analyses whether the increased inflows of FDI into the Indian economy have in any way benefited India. Have the increased FDI inflows led to higher economic growth or at least increased investment opportunities. Further, the change in the trade policy from import substitution to export promotion is looked upon as export-oriented growth strategy. In this connection the linkages between higher FDI inflows and trade ratios has been advocated by economists like Bhagwati and Srinivasan, and the World Bank. Hence, another issue analysed in this study is whether the increased FDI has led to improvement in the export competitiveness or performance of India.

N. PRASANNA

List of Contributors

Vinish Kathuria, Associate Professor, SJM School of Management, IIT, Powai, Mumbai.

S. Iyyampillai, Professor of Economics, Bharathidasan University, Tiruchirapalli.

N. Prasanna, Assistant Professor, Department of Economics, Bharathidasan University, Tiruchirappalli.

A.B. Angappapillai, Assistant Professor in Economics, A.A. Govt. Arts College, Musiri, Tiruchy District, Tamilnadu.

C.K. Muthu Kumaran, Head of the Department, Department of Management Studies, Kurniji College of Engg. & Tech., Manpparai, Tamilnadu.

S.R. Keshava, Faculty, Post-Graduate Department of Economics, Bangalore University, Bangalore-560056.

S. Preethi, Assistant Professor, Department of MBA, Dr. SNS Rajalakshmi College of Arts and Science, Coimbatore.

K.T. Geetha, Professor of Economics, Avinashilingam Deemed University, Coimbatore.

J. Srinivasan, Associate Professor, Department of Economics, Pondicherry University, Pondicherry.

M. Shanmugam, Ph.D. Scholar, Department of Economics, Pondicherry University, Pondicherry.

M. Thahira Banu, Assistant Professor, Department of Economics, M.S.S. Wakf Board College, K.K. Nagar, Madurai.

R. Vaheedha Banu, Assistant Professor, Department of Economics, M.S.S. Wakf Board College, K.K. Nagar, Madurai.

Tripura Sundari, C.U., Ph.D. Scholar, Department of Economics, Pondicherry University, Pondicherry.

Balaji B., Ph.D. Scholar, Department of Economics, Pondicherry University, Pondicherry.

P.G. Arul, Assistant Professor in Department of International Business, School of Management, Pondicherry University, Pondicherry.

Fayaz Ahamed, Ph.D. Research Scholar, Dravidian University, Kuppam, India.

Pesala Busenna, Research Associate, CAS&DM, NIRD, Rajendra Nagar, Hyderabad.

T. Sampathkumar, Assistant Professor, PG and Research Department of Economics, Govt. Arts College, Coimbatore-18.

K. Kalaichelvi, Assistant Professor & Head, Department of Commerce, Bharathidasan University College (W), Orathanad, Tanjore.

S. Saravanan, Assistant Professor of Economics, Indira Gandhi College of Arts and Science, Puducherry.

G. Saravanan, Lecturer in Commerce & Management, Achariya Arts and Science College, Villianur.

K.S. Santha Kumar, M.Phil Research Scholar, Department of Economics, Bharathiar University, Coimbatore.

Suman Sharma, Research and Teaching Assistant, School of Social Sciences, Indira Gandhi National Open University (IGNOU), New Delhi.

Introduction

An important issue in India regarding the development policy has been whether the economic growth should be promoted by adopting planning and controls or through free market system in which private sector and foreign investors are permitted to play an important role. Prior to 1991 the issue was resolved in favour of planning and controls. However, such policies were not giving the desired results of rapid economic growth and development. In fact in the 1980s, these policies led to slowdown in economic growth, large fiscal deficits, high inflation rates and huge deficits in the BoP resulting in heavy indebtedness. To overcome these problems some economists such as Ian Little, Jagdish Bhagwati, Bela Balassa, etc. (see for example Balassa, 1985; Bhagwati, 1993; Joshi and Little, 1996) who had been advisors to the World Bank and IMF argued for the adoption of economic liberalisation by developing countries to promote economic growth, bring down fiscal deficit, check inflation and solve the problem of BoP. Here, it is imperative to mention the Washington Consensus which was also framed by the World Bank and IMF and moved in the direction of reforms for developing countries (Kumar, 2000). In the Indian context economists like Jagdish Bhagwati, T.N. Srinivasan and Kirit Parikh are associated with pressing for economic reforms in 1991 (this subject has been addressed in more detail by Bhagwati, 1993; Bhagwati and Srinivasan, 1993; Desai, 1993; EPW Research Foundation, 1994; Ghosh, 1994; Hanumantha Rao, 1994; Rao, 1994; Wadhva,1994; Parikh, 1999). So a paradigm shift in the economic policy of India took place when the economic reforms were ushered into the Indian economy.

The issue of liberalising the inflow of FDI was part and parcel of the economic reforms programme. But, as observed by Rao (1994) the specific reason behind the encouragement of liberal FDI policies has been the desire to attain 7-8 per cent annual growth in GDP which requires higher investment rates and ICORs. In the presence of a sizable gap between the savings and investment rates which has always been around the 3-4 per cent mark since liberalisation, a 7-8 per cent economic growth would be impossible considering FDI Steering Committee Report's (2002) observation that for attaining 7-8 per cent annual growth in GDP, 32 per cent gross investment rate and an ICOR of 4.5 would be required. There was thus, a great need to raise domestic savings and at the same time ensure larger FDI inflows. However, given the low 20-22 per cent savings rate, India's only alternative was to aggressively seek FDI as it is a non-debt creating and reasonably stable source of external finance in the face of IMF and World Bank advising India not to opt for Fiscal Deficit and External Commercial Borrowings (ECBs). In this direction, a series of policy reforms propelling India towards the free market system were undertaken since 1991 by liberalising the approval procedures, the investment restrictions, the limitation on foreign equity participation, the restrictions on acquisitions and take-over by foreign investors, the local content requirement, the restrictions on remittance of funds abroad and the special incentives to the foreign investors.

Indeed, the liberalisation policies being followed in India since 1991 are rapidly picking-up pace and the inflows of FDI through participation by MNCs and TNCs is recording phenomenal growth. Now, India has been ranked at the second place in global Foreign Direct Investment (FDI) in 2010 and will continue to remain among the top five attractive destinations for international investors during 2010-12, according to United Nations Conference on Trade and Development (UNCTAD) in a report on world investment prospects titled, World Investment Prospects Survey, 2009-12. According to Ernst and Young's 2010 European Attractiveness Survey, India is ranked as the 4th most attractive foreign direct investment (FDI) destination in 2010. However, it is ranked the 2nd most attractive destination following China in the next three years. India attracted FDI equity inflows of US$ 1,392 million in October 2010. The cumulative amount of FDI equity inflows from April 2000 to October 2010 stood at US$ 122.68 billion, according to the data released by the Department of Industrial Policy and Promotion (DIPP). The recent financial crises in Asia and Latin America, developing and newly industrialising countries have been strongly advised to rely primarily on foreign direct investment (FDI), in order to supplement national savings by capital inflows and promote economic development.

It can be seen from the discussion that large scale economic reforms were initiated in India since 1991. Among these reforms it is pertinent to note that FDI policies have always received special attention by any political government in India since they viewed in FDI a potential non-debt creating source of finance and a bundle of assets, viz., capital, technology, market access (foreign), employment, skills, management techniques, and environment (cleaner practices), which could solve the problems of low income growth, shortfall in savings, investments and exports, and unemployment. It was argued that FDI would also help India in the expansion of production and trade and increase opportunities to enhance the benefits that could be drawn from greater integration with the world economy. In other words, FDI would broaden the opportunities for India to participate in international specialisation and other gains from trade.

But, recently there has been lot of debate on the impact of FDI on economies. Critics of FDI argue that the MNCs and TNCs bringing FDI generally monopolise resources, supplant domestic enterprises, introduce inappropriate technology and create BoP problems through large remittances. Also, a major argument put forward in favour of FDI is filling the saving investment gap which was wide in India during the 1980s and 1990s. But now, the argument of the gap between saving and investment does not fit the frame of the Indian Economy as the saving has increased to meet the investment. Still the Government of India seems to be in a liberal mood vis-à-vis FDI. Therefore, the main issue discussed in this volume is whether the increased inflows of FDI into the Indian economy in the last 20 years have in any way benefited India. Have the increased FDI inflows led to higher economic growth or at least increase investment opportunities. Further, the change in the trade policy from import substitution to export promotion is looked upon as export-oriented growth strategy. In this connection the linkages between higher FDI inflows and trade ratios has been advocated by economists like Bhagwati and Srinivasan (1993) and the World Bank (1989). Hence, another issue is to know whether increased FDI has led to improvement in the export competitiveness or performance of India.

In this context, this book attempts to examine the impact of FDI on the economic performance of India and sheds some light on the issues and challenges of FDI in India. In this direction Vinish Kathuria firstly analyses what are the different concerns and benefits of FDI in the Indian context and secondly sees whether increased competition through entry of FDI is also matched by enhanced competitiveness. Iyyampillai considers some important aspects relating to FDI in India, both positive and negative and argues that instead of discussing the size of FDI, the nature of FDI, aims and motives of the investors have to be understood; and their operations have to be strictly supervised and regulated wherever necessary. Prasanna probes the impact of FDI on the economic growth of India and also analyses the causality between FDI and Economic Growth of India in a growth accounting framework. Angappapillai and Muthukumaran focus on the trends in the growth of foreign exchange reserves and its components and estimate the impact of capital flows on economic growth by analysing FII, FDI and FPI inflows into India. Keshava analyses the growth of FDI and its impact on economic growth, exports, GDI, foreign exchange and other macro-variables in India. Preethi and Geetha examine the impact of FDI on economic growth and nexus between FDI and economic growth theoretically. They also discuss the issues and challenges which make India a less lucratic destination for FDI. Srinivasan and Shanmugam focus on analysing the role of FDI on export growth and economic growth and investigate the export-led growth (ELG) hypothesis in India, using Vector Error Correction Mechanism. Sundari and Balaji analyse the causal nexus between FDI and economic growth with respect to India using Granger Causality Test. Arul examines various aspects of allowing FDI in organized retail business especially the existing policy on FDI in retail trade, impact of FDI in India in terms of opportunities and challenges for organized retail business and the global experience on allowing FDI in retail trade. Ahamed discusses and analyzes the challenges and opportunities faced by FDI inflow and the future outlook towards FDI in the Telecom Retail Sector in India. Busenna probes the role of FDI in Indian manufacturing sector growth using Granger Causality Test in eight manufacturing industries, viz., Chemical and allied, Food and beverages, Machinery industry, Textile, Metal, Non-Metal, Transport, Miscellaneous industries and total Indian Manufacturing Industry. Sampathkumar compares the total factor productivity change of domestic and foreign firms in the Indian iron and steel industry by applying the stochastic frontier production function technique and decomposes the productivity growth into technical progress and technical efficiency change. Kalaichelvi analyses the influences of FDI on firm-level export outcomes in India and other transition economies. Saravanan and Saravanan have analysesd the impact of FDI on export performance in India. Kumar analyses the role of FDI in economic growth and employment generation in India. Sharma investigates the FDI spillover hypothesis at the firm level using frontier production function, (to estimate firm specific productive efficiency growth for domestic firms) of Indian Drugs and Pharmaceutical industry.

REFERENCES

Balassa, B. (1985), "Exports, Policy Choices, and Economic Growth in Developing Countries After the 1973 Oil Shock", *Journal of Development Economics*, Vol. 18: 23-35.

Bhagwati, J.N. and Srinivasan, T.N. (1993), "India's Economic Reforms", New Delhi: Ministry of Finance, Government of India.

Bhagwati, J.N. (1993), "India in Transition: Freeing the Economy", Oxford: Clarendon Press.

Desai, Ashok (1993), "My Economic Affair", New Delhi: Eastern.

EPW Research Foundation (1994), "What Has Gone Wrong with the Economic Reforms?", *Economic and Political Weekly*, Vol. 29 (18): 1049-53.

Joshi, Vijay and Ian Little (1996), "India's Economic Reforms, 1991-2001", Oxford: Clarendon Press.

Kumar, Nagesh (2000), "Explaining the Geography and Depth of International Production: The Case of US and Japanese Multinational Enterprises", *Weltwirtschaftliches Archiv*, Vol. 136(3): 442-76.

Ghosh, Arun (1994), "1994-95 Budget: A Total Surrender", *Economic and Political Weekly*, Vol. 29 (16 & 17): 889-92.

Rao, C. Hanumantha (1994), "Reforming Agriculture in the New Context", *Economic and Political Weekly*, Vol. 29 (16 & 17): 1005-10.

Rao, V.M. (1994), "Agriculture and Liberalization: Some Implications for Development Policies", *Economic and Political Weekly*, Vol. 29 (16 & 17): 999-1003.

Parikh, Kirit (ed.), (1999), "India Development Report, 1999-2000", Delhi: Oxford University Press.

Wadhva, Charan D. (1994), "Economic Reforms in India and the Market Economy", New Delhi: Allied Publishers for Economic and Scientific Research Foundation.

World Bank (1989), "India's Trade Logistics", Washington, D.C.: The World Bank.

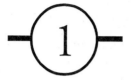

Issues of FDI in India

VINISH KATHURIA

1. Introduction

Technological advancement is an important contributor to economic growth. A number of well-known economists have endorsed this view including Marx, Schumpeter, and Solow. However, it was only after the work of Solow in 1957 that the literature appreciated the full import of technology and technological development in economic growth of a country. Kuznets (1966) moved a step further and argued that economic growth of all the nations depends on successful application of transnational stock of knowledge. Historical evidence also support the role of transnational stock of knowledge, as followers capitalised on the inventions of the leaders. This can be seen from the growth of nations who grew later, as their growth was faster than that of countries which industrialised first.

The historical evidence shows that late starters, capitalizing on the inventions of the leader(s) have grown faster, as there is an 'advantage of backwardness'.[1] England and France, the two nations in which industrialization took place first, grew at a rate of 1.2-1.4 per cent per annum, whereas Germany, Denmark, Switzerland and USA had a growth rate of 1.6-1.8 per cent. These countries were followed by Norway, Sweden and Japan with a growth rate of 2.1-2.8 per cent. These historical evidences were further reinforced by the examples of the erstwhile USSR and the newly industrializing countries (NICs)—South Korea, Taiwan and Singapore—which grew at more than 4 per cent and 8 per cent per annum respectively after they capitalized on the inventions of the already advanced nations (Kathuria, 2011). In absence, countries have to spend huge resources and time to develop their own technology. In other words, this implies 'reinventing the wheel.' The two interesting examples in this context are the development of cryogenic technology which India had to develop after 1998 Pokharan nuclear blasts as the U.S. declined to part the technology under the sanctions. India took nearly 7-8 years to develop it. Similarly, after the U.S. firm 'Cray' refused supercomputers to India in late 1980s and not being impressed with Russian supercomputers. India decided to build its own. It took nearly 9 years to built 100-gigaflop machines—'param 1000' (Mashelkar, 2008).

Sufficient literature also exists suggesting that one of the key determinants of international differences in per-capita income is barriers to technology adoption (see for example, Parente and Prescott, 1994). Multinational corporations (MNCs) are an important conduit for this technology transfer. Statistics show that MNCs undertake major part of world's private R&D; MNCs produce, own, and control most of the world's advanced technology. This implies MNCs are vital for international dissemination of knowledge.

Role of MNCs in technology transfer is always under scrutiny. In the recent past, pro-MNCs have gained upper hand as is evident from the open door policy in large number of countries including India which has been given way from the 'selective policies' of the past. The proponents also argue that a larger share of host countries benefits from FDI/MNCs may come in the form of external effects or spillovers of knowledge to domestically owned firms that are competitors, suppliers, customers or to those firms which have some point of economic contact with MNCs.

The rest of the paper is organized as follows: Section 2 gives the two key features of FDI. Section 3 discusses in brief the issues of FDI. Since FDI has become synonyms with the reform process, there may not be any reversible policy change in near future. In that situation, the next pertinent question is how to benefit from FDI. Section 4 delves into it. The paper concludes with Section 5.

2. Features of FDI

Among various policy reforms in developing countries, allowing Foreign Direct Investment (FDI) is often keenly debated due to its direct influence on industry structure and on product and labor markets. FDI, in general, brings in new technology, improved managerial practices, efficient processes, and better products; and all these in turn facilitate improvement in the competitiveness of the industries (Kathuria, 2002). Apart from the direct role of FDI in bringing technology, there are various indirect sources of inflow of technology involving FDI. These include trade contacts, licensing arrangements, technical assistance, advice for the purchase of capital equipment, construction of plants, quality controls, etc. (Sjoholm, 1999; Kathuria, 1999a).

FDI is the long-term capital flows that also brings technology and is different from volatile short-term capital flows—termed as foreign institutional investments (FII). Post-1990s, FDI is not only the most visible dimension of globalization, but also has outshone any other inflow to the developing countries. This is illustrated in Figure 1. The share of FDI in total resource inflow to developing countries which was nearly 25 per cent in 1990 increased to over 80 per cent in 2001, thereafter fell to over 50 per cent in 2005. In value terms, it is still the most significant but its share has declined due to rise in other source of inflows. (Fig. 1)

However, linking with globalization makes FDI highly contentious as can be seen from what happened to different WTO meetings starting with Seattle in 2000 and Geneva in 2001. Perhaps that might be the reason, why some authors consider FDI to be pernicious to national development (see for example, Addison et al. 2006).

Why to Invite FDI?

There are two reasons to invite FDI—first—they bring technology, which is better than the one available in the developing countries; and second—they bring finance, which developing countries often lack. Incidentally, for finance, other avenues are also available such as stock-market, official development assistance, loan, etc. but for technology, foreign firms are the sole owners. This is well demonstrated by some summary statistics. Between 1981-86 World's 686 largest firms registered 49 per cent of all patents in US (Patel and Pavitt, 1992). Over 4/5th of FDI Global Stock originates from 6 OECD countries—also dominate World's R&D (Kokko, 1992) (US, UK, Japan, Germany, Switzerland, Netherlands). In early 1970s, 30-50 per cent of all spending on R&D in 8 most developed countries was by just top 8 firms. With regard to international technology transfer between 1986 to 1990 more than 75 per cent of all receipts came from foreign subsidiaries in USA and 90 per cent in Germany. This role of MNCs is growing. As of now there are more than 60,000 MNCs and mover 800,000 foreign affiliates. The MNCs account for nearly two-third of world exports and one-third of world trade is intra-firm. The influence of MNCs is

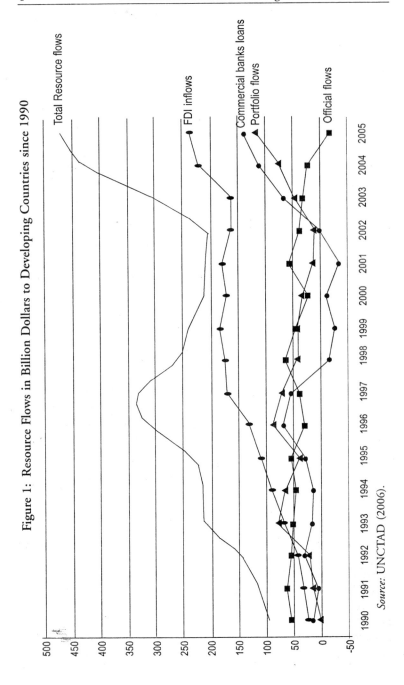

Figure 1: Resource Flows in Billion Dollars to Developing Countries since 1990

Source: UNCTAD (2006).

well illustrated from the fact that the value added by some of the MNCs is as big as the GDP of several countries (Figure 2).

Channels of Technology Transfer

There are several channels—both market mediated and non-market mediated—through which technology can be transferred. FDI and licensing are the two prominent channels where the MNCs play a direct and active role in technology transfer. There are channels like exhibitions, trade fairs or scientific exchange of people where the role of MNCs is not only indirect but also passive. Fransman (1985) argues that even if they don't play a direct and active role in dissemination of technology, their indirect and passive role is sufficient so as to conclude that much of the international transfer of diffusion of technology is connected to FDI. Figure 3 illustrates this connection and the various roles of MNCs leading to the transfer of technology.

From figure 3, it is clear that not all the channels of technology transfer are market-mediated. Channels in the North-West corner (and also goods purchase in North-east corner), where there are formal contracts and direct involvement of foreign firms are the ones for which market exists. For channels like imitation, scientific exchange, exhibitions etc. there does not exist any functioning market.

There are two key features of FDI: first, the character and pattern of FDI is constantly evolving. More changes are expected due to ICT revolution. Historically, most FDI has been directed at the developed nations of the world, as firms based in advanced countries invested in other markets. The US has been the favorite target for FDI inflows. While developed nations still account for the largest share of FDI inflows, FDI into developing nations have increased as can be seen from Figure 4. The most recent inflows into developing nations have been targeted at emerging economies of South (mainly India), East, and Southeast Asia.

Second, FDI has many effects—positive as well as negative—but not consistent. These effects vary significantly by the sector in which FDI is made and by the type of host country.

Typology of Types of FDI

FDI in developing countries can be of four types (UNCTAD, 2006). In 'natural resource-seeking' type, foreign firms invest to seek access to natural resource. The key industries for this are oil and gas extraction, mining, forestry, fisheries etc. In 'market-seeking' FDI also termed as horizontal FDI, the aim is to access a domestic or regional such as EU,

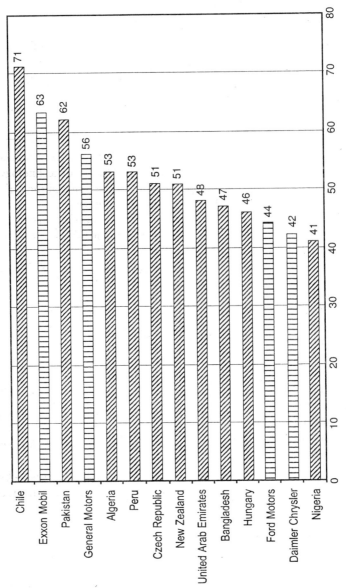

Figure 2: Value Added or GDP in 2000 (US$ billion)

Source: UNCTAD (2006).

Figure 3: Channels of Technology Transfer

	Active	Passive
Formal	**FDI** (Hyundai, Honda), **Turkey Project**, **Collaboration** (Fiat Palio), **Mgmt. Contract**, **JV** (Maruti-Suzuki), **Licensing** (Piaggio-LML)	**Machinery Purchase** (For Narmada Dam—Turbines from Mitsubishi Corpn.
Informal	**Imitation** (Reverse Engg.) (MT Industry—Ludhiana Or Silicon Valley), **Learning by Export** (CNC Control System or CNC M/c Tools	**Trade Journals, Visits, Scientific Exchange** (People Trained in MNCs), **Trade Fairs** (Hanover auto fair, Auto expo, IMTEX)

Source: Kathuria (2011).

NAFTA, or ASEAN market. The third type of FDI is 'efficiency-seeking (also termed as vertical FDI. In this kind, the purpose of MNCs is to specialize and divide production in line with the comparative advantages of different locations; lastly, we have 'strategic-asset seeking' (primarily through M&As) where aim is to access specific (created) assets such as technology, brand name, specialized skills. Besides these we can have export-oriented FDI where foreign firms set-up plants only for export purposes.

In this context, it is important to note that horizontal FDI i.e., to produce same product—in developing countries is less significant than vertical FDI. This is because foreign firms relocate the intermediate stages of production to take advantages of lower costs. The data indicates that only 4 per cent of production by affiliates of US MNCs in EU sold back to US in 2000, whereas this was 18 per cent for developing countries.

3. Issues of FDI—Benefits and Concerns

There are two analytical perspectives on FDI impact on host country. These are financing *versus* micro and macro-impacts. Since FDI provides valuable external financing. A simplistic financing version is that the more FDI means more financing. This implies that more FDI is good. The other perspective is about micro and macro-impacts. According to this, FDI may have important impacts (positive and

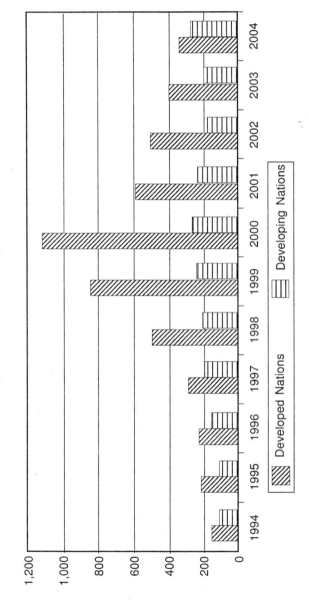

Figure 4: FDI Flows by Region (US bn $)

Source: World Investment Report (2004).

negative) on the host economy—at both micro- and macro-economic level. The remaining section talks about these impacts.

Potential Benefits

The literature has indicated large number of potential benefits from FDI. The key among these are: providing external financing; transfer of technology especially in automobile, steel, medical equipment, telecommunication, etc. transfer of "soft technology" such as knowledge, management skills, organizational methods—the use of JIT, QC, QA, TPM in Indian context started after the Japanese FDI in mid 1980s. FDI also promote exports when it is efficiency-seeking. FDI can be used as an export platform. For instance, Sony, IBM use China as exports base, similarly Intel uses Malaysia for the purpose and Nokia and Hyundai are using India as export base for their products. FDI like any other investment can create employment (provided foreign firms do not use M&A route), besides promoting local skills development through training. There are studies which demonstrated that foreign firms have provided training about environmental management system (EMS), which led to better housekeeping in small local firms.

Other perceived benefit of FDI is improvement in the quality of local services through better technology, overall philosophy, supply-chain, and image. Foreign firms, many a times, introduce new goods and services and force other firms to do so also. The use of multi-point fuel injection system by Maruti-Suzuki is one such example. FDI also spurs local competitive forces. FDI contributes to local enterprise development via spillovers and directly. Foreign firms also provide access to international markets or at least show to local firms the possible exporting channels. The export industry of Mauritius, Bangladesh and Sri Lanka can owe their development to activity of few foreign firms. FDI can also spur innovative activity through enhanced competition.

Potential Negative Impacts

- Balance of Payments problems (potentially large future remittances, possibly high import content of FDI projects).
- Crowding out local enterprises (sometimes via unfair competition *vs.* via higher efficiency and better performance).
- Lack of local linkages (enclave activities using few local inputs).
- Low level of local processing (and low local value added).
- Environmental degradation (from certain activities such as mining etc.).

- Limited transfer of technology (an important aspect of linkages).
- Employment destruction (if route is through mergers and acquisitions, M&As).
- Footloose operations (in industries like garments, IT).
- Excessive use of incentives/race to the top (many countries compete for FDI).
- Anticompetitive practices (abuse of dominant position).
- Transfer pricing (low tax contribution locally).
- Socio-cultural effects.

Of late few new concerns have also emerged. For example, MNCs now primarily resort to M&A rather than investing in Greenfield ventures. This precludes any possibility of capital formation and technology transfer. The data indicates that nearly 40-50 per cent FDI in India during 1995-1999 came through M&A (Kumar, 2000). Another concern irrespective of the origin of technology is that the imports of technology may reduce the R&D efforts of local firms. This is because R&D being a costly and an uncertain activity with gestational lag, in order to remain competitive, the local firms may procure technology from outside rather than investing in R&D. Refer Kathuria, 2008 and Sasidharan and Kathuria, 2011 for evidence on this.

Another major concern is non-creation of capabilities as and when inappropriate technology is transferred. Type of capabilities acquired will be determined by the content of TT. There are three types of technological flow through TT: (a) flow of engineering, managerial service and capital goods; (b) flow of skill, and know-how for operations and maintenance; and (c) flow of knowledge, expertise, and experience for generating and managing technical change. If foreign firms form enclaves and do not engage in vertical linkages, local capabilities won't be generated.

Spillovers

From the list of the potential benefits and negative impacts, it can be seen that many of the positive benefits such as spread of soft technology, knowledge about foreign markets, spurring competition and also the negative impacts like employment destruction, less linkages, etc. are unintentional. These unintentional impacts are termed in literature as Externalities or Spillovers from entry and presence of foreign firms.

Externalities or Spillovers occur/exist when the output of a firm is not only affected by its own market activities, but also by the activities of other economic agents (producers or consumers) (Stewart and Ghani, 1991). If y_i is the output of a firm, then

$$y_i = f(x_1, x_2, x_3,..., z_1, z_2,....)$$

where $x_1, x_2, x_3, ...$ are inputs by the producers; and $z_1, z_2, z_3, ...$ are activities of other agents termed as spillovers.

To give an example, the fuel efficiency of a vehicle depends not only on the Age, model, maintenance frequency of the vehicle, no. of redlights on the road, but also on other vehicles on the road. Similarly, a firm's Profit is a function of its Skill content, Age, type of Ownership, R&D intensity, etc. but also the market share of other firms. The number of other vehicles and market share of other firms are called as externalities or spillovers.

These spillovers facilitate improvement in the productivity and can be within a given industry (termed as intra-industry spillovers) or across the industry (e.g., improved design in automobile forcing quality improvement by the suppliers). They can also influence exporting behaviour—termed as export related spillovers (Figure 4). There are different channels such as enhanced competition, demonstration effect, labour turnover, etc. through which spillovers can occur as can be seen from Figure 5.

Relevance of Spillovers

Of all the arguments in support of inviting in foreign firms, their role and relevance in spillovers to domestic firms is the most significant. The spillovers occur when the knowledge/technology transferred from

Figure 5: Types of Spillovers

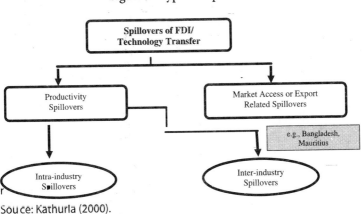

Souce: Kathuria (2000).

the parent firms to the affiliates leaks out to local firms in the host country. Technical assistance and support to suppliers and customers, labour mobility from foreign-owned firms to local firms and the demonstration effect on domestic firms in issues such as managerial practices, choice of technology, product development and export behaviour etc. are some of the suggested channels through which spillovers occur (Blomstrom and Kokko, 1998; Kathuria, 2000a).

Evidence of Spillovers

Before we discuss with evidence of spillovers, we would like to mention that for most other benefits and also concerns, there is not much statistical evidence. The few issues that have been researched pertaining to FDI are—their impact on growth, on exporting activity, and spillovers. This leaves sufficient scope for research so as to quantify

Figure 6: Productivity Spillovers—Types and Channels

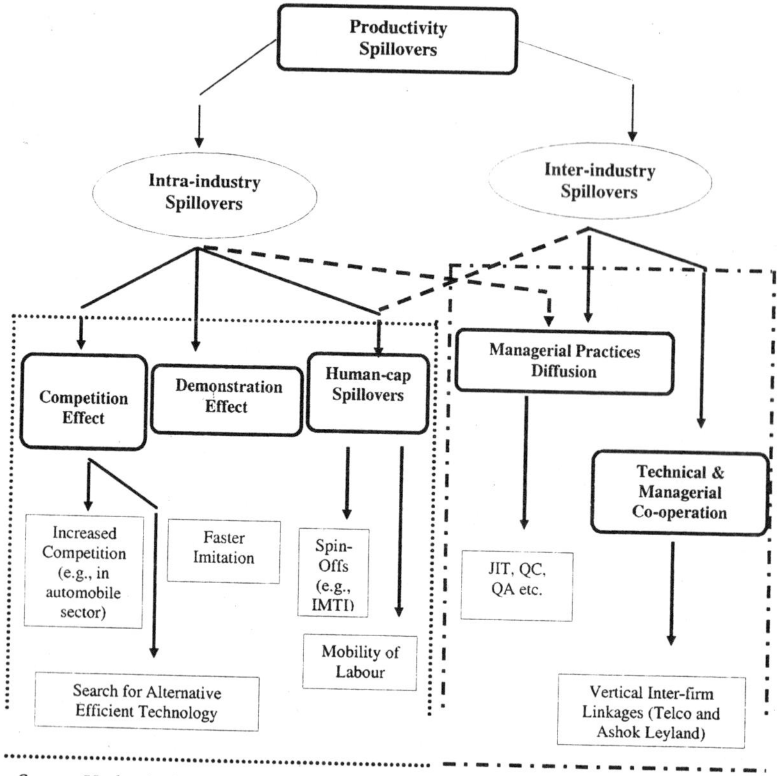

```
                        Productivity
                         Spillovers
                      /             \
          Intra-industry          Inter-industry
            Spillovers              Spillovers
```

- Competition Effect
- Demonstration Effect
- Human-cap Spillovers
- Managerial Practices Diffusion
- Technical & Managerial Co-operation

- Increased Competition (e.g., in automobile sector)
- Faster Imitation
- Spin-Offs (e.g., IMTD)
- JIT, QC, QA etc.
- Mobility of Labour
- Search for Alternative Efficient Technology
- Vertical Inter-firm Linkages (Telco and Ashok Leyland)

Source: Kathuria (2000).

the different impacts of FDI, thereby to conclude whether foreign firms really benefit local firms and industry or not.

Regarding evidence of spillovers, Hindustan Motors moving into CNG bus making—competition effect/search for alternate technologies. Maruti-Suzuki first introducing multi-point fuel injection system forced other players to search for alternate technologies. Among all channels, the most significant channel is human capital spilllovers. This is because people trained in foreign firms when they leave their respective organisations and join a local firm, can add significant value to the local firm. This is because (s)he is one among many working in MNC, but may bring with them lot of tacit knowledge and help in the growth of local firms. There are lot of examples of these kinds of spillovers. The growth of Indian machine tool industry (IMTI) can be attributed to these spin-offs. People trained in HMT, which had over 60 collaborations was a fertile ground for people to learn, they are now working with ACE Designer, Batliboi, MKL, etc., which are leaders in their respective fields (Kathuria, 1999a). Similarly, in the computer chip industry, INTEL is a spin-off from Fairchild and AMD is a spin-off from INTEL.

Many-a-times local suppliers are forced to upgrade technology to meet requirement of the downstream firm. There is evidence that in the initial years, Maruti-Suzuki asked several of its vendors such as Gabriel (producing shockers), Sona Steering (producing steering) etc. to produce components of desired quality. The GM (General Motors) has been instrumental in upgrading local technological capabilities in Australia by demanding better quality products. Such kind of benefits are inter-industry and are termed as vertical linkages. There are evidence (see Lall, 1980) that in 1970s Telco (having collaboration with Benz) and Ashok Leyland (collaboration between British Leyland) crated vertical linkages in HCV market.

According to Dunning (1993) the most important spillover benefit from MNCs entry is intermingling of different business philosophies. Terms like Quality Control (QC), Quality Assurance (QA), Just-in-time (JIT), etc. were virtually unknown in India till 1985. A few Japanese collaborations—Maruti with Suzuki, Eicher with Mitsubishi, Swaraj with Mazda, Hero with Honda, DCM with Toyota, Escorts with Yamaha and Allwyn with Nissan though brought these concepts in India during 1985-89, other firms adopted in due course. Japanese way of doing business is intra-firm consensus of Ideas and opinion, whereas American way thrives on intra-firm interactions with pragmatism, professional, assertive and based on law of contracts.

4. Benefiting from FDI—What Needs to be Done?

With all the potential dangers stated above, economic reforms cannot be consigned to the simple formula where the state assumes a limited role. Liberalization and globalization can only be considered a success from the social point of view if they improve effective competition in the system i.e., enhance contestability, otherwise there won't be any lasting gains (Sikdar, 2002).

Another factor that requires a more proactive role of the state is building of absorptive capacity so as to benefit from entry of foreign firms openness and globalization. The external liberalization since 1991 has resulted in significant FDI to the country, however, a question remains—is there a commensurate increase in the competitiveness of the industry? In other words, has sufficient care been taken to increase the absorptive capacity of the firms/country in the past 20 years after the 1991 liberalisation?

Absorptive Capacity—Investment in Broad Capital[2]

The absorptive capacity at the country level can only be increased with investment in 'broad capital' that comprises of— (i) physical capital (Gross Fixed Capital Formation); (ii) R&D (domestic expenditure on Research & Development); and (iii) human capital (expenditure on Education). Table 1 and Figure 6 give the trend of different indicators of broad capital and FDI inflow from 1990-91 onwards.

Table 1: Trend in FDI and Broad Capital Indicators

Year	FDI Inflow (bn Rs.)	GFCF/GDP	DERD/GDP	EE/GDP
1990-91	3.53	22.93	0.79	3.84
1991-92	6.91	22.03	0.78	3.8
1992-93	18.62	22.45	0.76	3.72
1993-94	31.12	21.45	0.79	3.62
1994-95	64.85	21.94	0.73	3.56
1995-96	87.52	24.36	0.71	3.56
1996-97	129.9	22.79	0.72	3.53
1997-98	132.7	21.70	0.77	3.49
1998-99	101.7	21.50	0.79	3.85
1999-00	123.5	21.78	0.82	4.19
2000-01	167.8	21.20	0.86	4.28
2001-02	181.9	21.46	0.82	3.80
2002-03	116.2	22.15	0.8	3.77
2003-04	172.7	23.15	0.84	3.49
2004-05	193.0	24.52	0.8	3.66 (P)

Source: Economic Survey, SIA Newsletter, www.education.nic and other sources.

It is clear from the table and the figure that after 1991, the quantum of FDI inflow has increased. However, the investment in two of the broad capital indicators (R&D and human capital) reflects a sorry state of affairs. The R&D intensity is continuously on the decline. Though in 1991 itself it was well below the international norm of 2 per cent, it has shown a steady decline in the next 7-8 years and was close to 0.7 per cent in 1997-98. The recent period has witnessed a slight increase but nowhere near the norm. Similarly, the human capital expenditure intensity fell continuously till 1997-98 to 3.49 per cent and then reached a peak of 4.28 per cent in 2000-01. Thereafter, it is declining continuously.

This decline of knowledge creating and human capital investment seems to be getting clearly reflected in loss of competitiveness of India. India's rank, which was 43rd in 2005-06 has fallen to 48th as per 2006-07 ranking of Global Competitiveness Report of World Economic Forum.

The policies do not exist in vacuum or emerge at random, they are grounded on a wider set of beliefs. The non-increasing R&D and human capital investment partly reflects the belief of the government that social sectors are no longer priority areas. The belief or philosophy negates the fact that development is much more than providing physical infrastructure. It is about building capabilities, especially investing in people (through literacy and health programmes) and at the industry level by investing in R&D activities.

5. Concluding Remarks

There is a difference between competition and competitiveness. Measures like allowing FDI, or reduction in import duties, etc., though enhance the contestability at the level of firm (or industry), they do not result in improved efficiency or competitiveness (Kathuria, 1999b). Competitiveness encompasses a much wider landscape than merely ensuring free markets. Unless there is an investment in all the components of 'broader capital—physical, R&D and Human', the enhanced competition through increased MNCs entry and FDI will rather wipe out the Indian firms in the long-run. According to Patel (1992: 43) "... efficiency transcends the domain of micro-economics as narrowly and traditionally conceived, and requires something more than competitive markets."

Thus, only allowing FDI *per se* is not sufficient to ensure that it will result in increased learning for the Indian industry. The aim should be to build absorptive capacity—whose critical elements are investment in R&D and human capital.

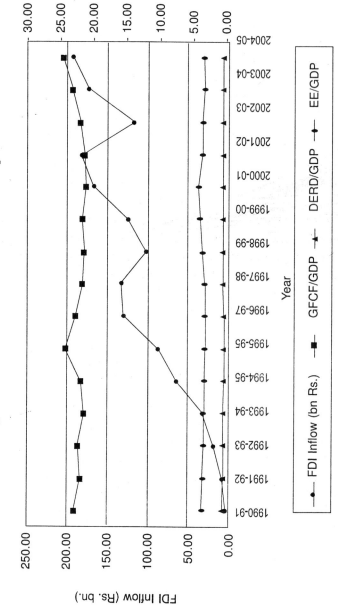

Figure 7: FDI Inflow and Investment in Broad Capital

Notes and References

1. The phrase was coined by Gershenkron (1962: 8).
2. This subsection builds on Kathuria (1999b).

References

Addison, T., Khansnobis, G.B., and G. Mayrotas (2006I), "Introduction and Overview," *World Economy*, 29(1), 1-8.

Dunning, J.H. (1993), *Multinational Enterprises and the Global Economy*, Addison-Wesley, Reading.

Fransman, M. (1985), Conceptualizing Technical Change in the Third World in the 1980s: An Interpretive Survey, *Journal of Development Studies*, 21(4): 572-652.

Gerschenkron, A. (1962), *Economic Backwardness in Historical Perspective: A Book of Essays*, Cambridge: Harvard University Press.

Jensen, O.W. and C.A. Scheraga (1998), "Transferring Technology: Costs and Benefits", *Technology in Society*, 20(1): 99-112.

Kathuria, V. (2011), "South-South Technology Transfer: Facilitating Market Mechanism", *Technology Monitor*, May-June: 12-19 (http://www.techmonitor.net/tm/images/7/77/11may_jun_sf1.pdf).

Kathuria, V. (2010), "Does the Technology-gap influence Spillovers? —A post-liberalisation analysis of Indian Manufacturing Industries", *Oxford Development Studies*, 38(2): 145-70.

Kathuria, V. (2008a), "The Impact of FDI Inflows on R&D Investment by Medium- and High-tech Firms in India in the Post-Reform Period", *Transnational Corporations*, 17(2): 45–66.

Kathuria, V. (2008b), Technology and Human Development in India, in: Human Development in South Asia, 2008—Technology and Human Development (Karachi: Oxford University Press).

Kathuria, V. (2002), "Liberalisation, FDI and Productivity Spillovers—An Analysis of Indian Manufacturing Firms", *Oxford Economic Papers*, 54, 688-718.

Kathuria, V. (2000), Technology Transfer, Productivity Spillovers and Technical Change—A study of Indian Manufacturing Industry. Ph.D. Thesis, Indira Gandhi Institute of Development Research, Mumbai.

Kathuria, V. (1999a), "Role of Externalities in Inducing Technical Change—A Case Study of Indian Machine Tool Industry", *Technological Forecasting and Social Change*, 61(1), 25-44.

Kathuria, V. (1999b), "Competition *sans* Competitiveness: Need for a Policy", *Economic and Political Weekly*, 34(45), Nov. 6: 3175-77.

Kumar, N. (2000), "Multinational Enterprises and M&A in India: Patterns and Implications", *Economic and Political Weekly*, 35: 2851-58.

Kuznets, S. (1966), *Modern Economic Growth*, New Haven, CT: Yale University Press.

Lall, S. (1980), "Vertical Inter-Firm Linkages in LDCs: An Empirical Study", *Oxford Bulletin of Economics and Statistics*, 42, 203-26.

Mashelkar, R.A. (2008), "Indian Science, Technology and Society: The Changing Landscape", *Technology in Society*, 30: 299-308.

Sasidharan, S. and V. Kathuria (2011), "Foreign Direct Investment & R&D: Substitutes or Complements—A Case of Indian Manufacturing After 1991 Reforms", *World Development*, 39(7): 1226-39.

Sikdar, S. (2002), *Contemporary Issues in Globalization: An Introduction to Theory and Policy in India*, Delhi and Oxford: Oxford University Press.

Sjoholm, F. (1999), "Technology—Gap, Competition and Spillovers from DFI: Evidence from Establishment Data", *The Journal of Development Studies*, 36(1), pp. 53-73.

Stewart, F. and E. Ghani (1991), "How Significant are Externalities for Development?," *World Development*, 19(6): 569-94.

UNCTAD (2006), World Investment Report, 2006, New York and Geneva: United Nations.

UNCTAD (2004), World Investment Report, 2004, New York and Geneva: United Nations (Figure 7.2, p. 241).

Effects of Foreign Direct Investment in India

S. IYYAMPILLAI

Introduction

Owners of the capital are observed to be enjoying a greater freedom in the recent years as compared to that of land and labour. This is so due to (a) the easy mobility of capital, compared to the other two factors; (b) the policies designed in favour of owners of the capital, who are now able to control political power and influence the policy-makers and also governments at all levels. Almost free and easy flow of capital across the borders on the one hand and strictly restricted and rigid labour flows on the other hand may cause imbalances (Patnaik, 1996) in the mix of factors required for production of goods and services. This problem may look to be simple at initial stage. However, this problem is more likely to continue and invite many more problems in the long-run. The capitalists, once tasted more profit, would be tempted in the production process to increase the share of profit and reduce the share of wage payments. This kind of neglect of labour welfare would reduce the overall purchasing power in an economy; the effective demand would shrink; there will be market glut followed by recession and depression. This has already happened before the II World War. For achieving sustainable development in the long-run, there needs to be a balance between labour and capital. However, currently the things are moving in a haphazard manner.

Capital Movements

It refers to the movement of capital from one country to another. Of this, speculative short-term capital movements, aiming at obtaining a higher rate of interest or safeguarding the capital from currency depreciation are more dangerous to the host countries. This portion is however increasing nowadays, as compared to the other component namely long-term investment oriented capital flows. More dangerous is the participatory notes (PN) transaction, which accounted for 60 per cent of the foreign institutional investor (FII) funds in the stock market in India in 2008. It was almost zero in the year 2003. This increase was enabled only by the policy changes made by the Securities and Exchange Board of India (SEBI) and Reserve Bank of India (RBI). Such changes have happened though the S.S. Tarapore Committee on Financial Reforms had strongly condemned the PNs and wanted the system scrapped. National Security Advisor M.K. Narayanan had warned that the terrorists too were earning on the Indian stock market via anonymous PNs. Since large amount of PNs come via Mauritius, the speculators do not have to pay capital gains tax nor do they need to report to the Income Tax department (Subramanian Swamy, 2010).

Importance of Capital Movements

Countries are differently endowed with different kinds of resources. But human wants are endless and borderless. Even if the size of human population stops growing, the demand will ever bulge making the resources always scarce. Since labour movements are difficult and are very much restricted by the policies of developed countries due to the fear of catching diseases and terrorism, the capital movement is advocated in the place of labour to satisfy the growing greed of the people. Besides International Monetary Fund (IMF) and World Bank (WB), the two high-powered groups on banking and finance (both set-up by the government of India, not the RBI) —the Raghuram Rajan and Percy Mistry Committees—also called for a significant liberalization of the financial sector in a number of areas (Rammanohar Reddy, 2009). These recommendations are described as a "market fundamentalist" by Rammanohar Reddy.

Full capital account convertibility was advised as a development strategy, though some of the countries who adopted this strategy faced problems in different points of time (e.g. Mexico in 1991, ASEAN in July 1997). Fortunately, the Indian monetarists, including S.S. Tarapore, suggested the delay of capital account convertibility proposal, till lower inflation, fiscal deficits and higher GDP growth were achieved.

In the recent years, the reverse flows have taken place. India purchased 403 tonnes of gold (worth US$13 billion) from the IMF in September 2009 (*The Hindu*, 20.9.2009, p. 20). In the middle of March 2010, the RBI entered into an agreement with the IMF to buy up US$ 10 billion worth notes for assisting the countries hit by global financial/economic crisis (*The Hindu*, 2010).

Capital Controls

Received literature has reported both positive and negative aspects of foreign direct investment. However, instead of uncontrolled free flow of capital, the controlled flow of capital is appreciated. Even the International Monetary Fund (IMF), which was once forcing the countries to go for free flow of capital, has recently advocated the capital controls, after experiencing the pains of financial crisis in the United States of America (USA). Gallagher (2011) has stated, "the IMF has now formally suggested that there may be situations when developing countries can gain from placing regulations on the inward flow of foreign capital". The IMF has authored three reports showing that capital controls can be effective. In a Staff Position Note released in February 2010, the IMF has declared that there are "circumstances in which capital controls can be a legitimate component of the policy response to surges in capital flows" (Chandrasekhar, 2010). Both John Maynard Keynes and Harry Dexter White saw controls as a core component of the Bretton Woods system. Indeed Keynes argued that, "control of capital movements, both inward and outward, should be a permanent feature of the post-war system" (Helleiner, 1994).

India has generally been following an open door policy in FDI, barring a few sensitive areas which are still subject to caps on FDI. However, it is argued (Chalapati Rao & Biswajit Dhar, 2011) that control over enterprises in sensitive sectors cannot be achieved through setting limits on percentage of equity holding, or proportion of directors in the board. Suggestions made to control the enterprises are (i) disallowing veto powers, (ii) withdrawing the "automatic route" option for such sectors and following a case-by-case approach, and (iii) holding golden shares in all companies operating in sectors considered highly sensitive from national security and public health point of view.

FDI in India

The Indian economy was opened to the world in 1990s. Thereafter foreign capital has started flowing into the country in the form of foreign direct investment (FDI) and foreign institutional investment (FII).

About the size of FDI, there is also a view that in India this figure is over-estimated (Smitha, 2010). The FDI was initially restricted in certain sensitive sectors like agriculture, railways, atomic energy, retail, etc. Now, gradually many sectors are being opened to FDI. FDI up to 51 per cent is permitted in single-brand product retailing, with prior government approval, from 2006 onwards. In effect, the government proposes to relax the norms with regard to foreign participation retail business. Countries like China, Malaysia, Thailand, Indonesia and Brazil have gone for higher level of FDI in this sector. Here such positive effects as productivity enhancement, greater integration, price reduction and improved selection are reported. On the other hand, displacement of traditional retailers is also highlighted (Kumar & Singh, 2011).

In India, foreign investment in multi-brand retail is being pushed as an important tool for controlling food prices. However, a survey of the literature (Sukhpal Singh, 2011) shows that (i) FDI in retail often has the opposite effect; and (ii) the impact on low-income consumers in low-income areas has been particularly adverse. Another survey by Sukhpal Singh (2010) on the global and Indian experience with foreign investment in retail supermarkets highlights malpractices due to buying power, employment loss in the value chain and an unwillingness to share the risk of the growers.

RBI's Activities

Subbarao, the RBI governor on 7th September (*The Hindu*, 2011) has said that managing monetary policy was a key challenge, given the increased interconnectedness between the world economies and mushrooming of trouble spots in different regions. The RBI is described in the text-books as the apex bank that is responsible for controlling the money supply, prices and exchange rates through the instruments available with it. To a large extent, it has discharged its duties and saved India from the recent financial/economic crisis of September 2008. Indian Rupee's value against US $ is to some extent safeguarded through the sale and purchase of foreign currencies. The Committee for Financial Sector Assessment noted that going by a number of "financial soundness indicators"- capital adequacy, asset quality and profitability—banks in Indian were in good shape at the end of 2009 (Rammanohar Reddy, 2009). However, in the recent years, the RBI appears to be growingly becoming inefficient in controlling the inflationary pressures and frauds in retail banking. It appears as though the speculators have taken up the price controlling mechanism with them. In his special address at the Triplicane Cultural Academy on January 27th, 2010, Y.V. Reddy, former Governor of RBI, said, "too much foreign investment was too difficult to digest both qualitatively and quantitatively". He suggested a closer look at the qualitative aspects of FDI. He felt that too much integration with the global economy also had its negative consequences in the form of higher risk exposure and global uncertainties (*The Hindu*, January 28, 2010, p.16). With regard to frauds in retail banking, the RBI in its notification to chairmen and chief executives of all commercial banks stated that the incidence of frauds in the banks has been showing increasing trend over recent years, both in terms of number of frauds and the amounts involved. He further added that the trend is more disquieting in retail segment especially in housing and mortgage loans, credit card dues, internet banking and the like. Moreover, it is a matter of concern that instances of frauds in the traditional areas of banking such as cash credit, export finance, guarantees and letters of credit remain unabated. Citing the reasons for frauds, the RBI stated, "adoption of aggressive business strategies by the banks for quick growth and expansion without ensuring that adequate and appropriate internal controls are in place could incentivise operating staff to lower the standards of control while attempting to meet business targets". However, the steps taken by banks in investigating the frauds and identifying the fraudsters from eventual criminal prosecution and appropriate internal punitive action for the staff members involved in the frauds have not been adequate, the RBI felt. "While discussing certain cases of frauds of exceptionally large amounts, the Board of Financial Supervision has expressed grave concern that fraudsters with the involvement of bank officials could engineer system-wide break-down of controls across months while putting through fraudulent transactions", the RBI noted (*The Hindu*, 17 September 2009, p. 16).

In order to control inflationary pressures during 2010-11, the RBI frequently increased four ratios[1], namely statutory liquidity ratio (SLR), cash reserve ratio (CR), repo rate (RR) and reverse repo rate (RRR). There is no such precedent in the history. However, the inflation rate has continued to be high or increased in 2010-11.As per the information available on 7 September 2011, the SLR was 24 per cent and CRR was 6 per cent, meaning that the banks have to keep about 30 per cent of their deposits aside. These rates are considered to be high and decrease the credit availability and crowd out the private sector from raising funds in the public. The RBI miserably failed on this account may be because of circulation of counterfeit currency, black-money and uncontrolled FDI through different routs. For instance, the Naik Committee, appointed to assess the menace of fake currency, estimates the total amount of counterfeit money in circulation in India to the tune of Rs. 1.69 lakh crores. According Government figures during 2006-09, 7.34 lakh of Rs.100 notes, 5.76 lakh of Rs. 500 notes and 1.09 lakh of Rs.1000 notes, all fakes, were seized (Manoharan, 2009). Sainath (2010) observes, quoting a study by Global Financial Integrity, that India has lost US$ 213 billion in illegal capital flight between 1948-2008; and these illicit financial flows were generally the product of corruption, bribery and kickbacks, criminal activities and efforts to shelter wealth from a country's tax authorities.[1]

Conclusion

This paper has considered some important aspects relating to FDI in India. The positive as well as negative effects of the FDI have been discussed. It is suggested that instead of discussing the size of FDI, the nature of FDI, aims and motives of the investors have to be understood; and their operations have to be strictly supervised and regulated wherever necessary. The investors are expected to bribe the poor Indian policy-makers to get done all they are intended to. For this also some checks should be designed.

NOTE AND REFERENCE

1. CRR is the portion of deposits that banks required to keep in cash with the RBI, while the SLR is the amount that banks have to part in government securities. Repo rate (RR) is the rate charged by the RBI on the funds borrowed by the commercial banks. Reverse repo rate (RRR) is the rate of interest paid by the RBI for the funds deposited by the commercial banks. Normally the RR is slightly (about 0.5 per cent) higher than the RRR.

REFERENCES

Chalapati Rao, K.S. and Biswajit Dhar (2011), Foreign Direct Investment Caps in India and Corporate Control Mechanisms, *EPW*, Vol. XLVI, No.14, pp. 66-70.

Chandrasekhar, C.P. (2010), The IMF on Capital Controls, *EPW*, Vol. XLV, No. 20, pp.10-11.

Gallagher, Kevin P. (2011), The IMF, Capital Controls and Developing Countries, *EPW*, Vol. XLVI, No.19, pp. 12-16.

Helleiner Eric (1994), *States and the Re-emergence of Global Finance*, Cornell University Press, Ithaca.

The Hindu, 2010, p.16.

Kumar, Vinod and Singh, Mehar (2011), FDI in India's Retail Sector: Problems and Prospects, *Political Economy Journal of India*, Vol. 20, No.1, pp. 20-25.

Manoharan, N. (2009), Countering the Counterfeit Currency, *The Hindu*, December 27, p.12.

Patnaik, Prabhat (1996), Trade as a Mechanism of Economic Retrogression, *The Journal of Peasant Studies*, Vol. 24, No. 12, pp. 211-25, October.

Rammanohar Reddy, C. (2009), Meddling with Public Sector Banks, *The Hindu*, September 17, p. 8.

Sainath P. (2010), Illegal Financial Flows: The Great Drain Robbery, *The Hindu*, November 18, p. 9.

Smitha Francis (2010), Foreign Direct Investment Concepts: Implications for Negotiations, *EPW*, Vol. XLV, No. 22, pp.31-36.

Subramanian Swamy, A Crisis and an Opportunity Ahead, *The Hindu*, March 5, 2010, p. 8.

Sukhpal Singh (2010), Implications of FDI in Food Supermarkets, *EPW*, Vol. XLV, No. 21, pp. 17-20.

Sukhpal Singh (2011), Controlling Food Inflation: Do Supermarkets Have a Role?, *EPW*, Vol. XLVI, No. 18, pp. 19-22.

3

An Analysis of FDI Inflows—Economic Growth Causality in India

N. PRASANNA

Introduction

India, since independence, like several other developing countries, pursued a policy of import substitution and foreign capital restriction, with the public sector playing an important role in the economy. The government managed the BoP through import controls, with exports and FDI playing a very small role. Strains, first, occurred in the BoP in the 1980s and a mild reform was undertaken in the trade policy which led to an increase in the exports and the inflow of FDI. But, the BoP position kept on deteriorating. This problem was further worsened by a combination of many other factors such as, increase in the burden of debt repayment, stagnation in tourism earnings, collapse of the largest trading partner of India (the former Soviet Union) and increase in the crude oil prices due to the Gulf War.

This resulted in a severe economic crisis at the beginning of the 1990s. The crisis had its root in the persistent deficits in the BoP in the previous several years. The Gulf War of 1990 added to the problem as it resulted in the shooting up of oil prices which required enhanced spending in terms of foreign exchange. By March 1991, current account deficit in the BoP reached a record level of about 10 billion US dollars or over 3 per cent of GDP. Exports were declining and foreign debt to foreign exchange ratio was very high at about 147 per cent. This led to the depletion of foreign exchange reserves and India did not possess sufficient reserves to meet the next few weeks of imports. A default on payments for the first time in history became a distinct possibility in June 1991. Foreign capital was flying away from India and the international community was not willing to give any loans. The severe economic crisis forced the Indian policy-makers to make drastic reforms in the economic policy regime of India as part of the conditionality of IMF and World Bank structural adjustment programmes (UNCTAD, 1999).

But, as mentioned earlier, an important issue in India regarding the development policy has been whether the economic growth should be promoted by adopting planning and controls or through free market system in which private sector and foreign investors are permitted to play an important role. Prior to 1991 the issue was resolved in favour of planning and controls. However, such policies were not giving the desired results of rapid economic growth and development. In fact in the 1980s, these policies led to slowdown in economic growth, large fiscal deficits, high inflation rates and huge deficits in the BoP resulting in heavy indebtedness. To overcome these problems some economists such as I.M.D. Little, Jagdish Bhagwati, Bela Balassa, etc. (see for example, Balassa, 1985; Bhagwati, 1993; Joshi and Little, 1996) who had been advisors to the World Bank and IMF argued for the adoption of economic liberalisation by developing countries to promote economic growth, bring down fiscal deficit, check inflation and solve the problem of BoP. Here, it is imperative to mention the Washington Consensus which was also framed by the World Bank and IMF and moved in the direction of reforms for developing countries (Kumar, 2000). In the Indian context economists like Jagdish Bhagwati, T.N. Srinivasan and Kirit Parikh are associated with pressing for economic reforms in 1991 (this subject has been addressed in more detail by Bhagwati, 1994; Bhagwati and Srinivasan, 1993; Desai, 1993; EPW Research Foundation, 1994; Ghosh, 1994; Hanumantha Rao, 1994; Rao, 1994; Wadhva,1994; Parikh, 1999). So a paradigm shift in the economic policy of India took place when the economic reforms were ushered into the Indian economy.

Coming to the context of FDI, the issue of liberalising the inflow of FDI was part and parcel of the economic reforms programme. But, as observed by Rao (1994) the specific reason behind the encouragement of liberal FDI policies has been the desire to attain 7-8 per cent annual growth in GDP (now the desire is in double digits) which requires higher investment rates and ICORs. In the presence of a sizable gap between the savings and investment rates which has always been around the 3-4 per cent mark since liberalisation, a 7-8 per cent economic growth would be impossible considering FDI Steering Committee Report's (2002) observation that for attaining 7-8 per cent annual growth in GDP, 32 per cent gross investment rate and an ICOR of 4.5 would be required. There was thus, a great need to raise domestic savings and at the same time ensure larger FDI inflows. However, given the low 20-22 per cent savings rate, India's only alternative was to aggressively seek FDI as it is a non-debt creating and reasonably stable source of external finance in the face of IMF and World Bank advising India not to opt for Fiscal Deficit and External Commercial Borrowings (ECBs).

In this direction, a series of policy reforms have been taken since 1991 regarding liberalising the approval procedures, the investment restrictions, the limitation on foreign equity participation, the restrictions on acquisitions and take-over by foreign investors, the local content requirement, the restrictions on remittance of funds abroad and the special incentives to the foreign investors. All these initiatives have resulted in phenomenal rise in FDI inflow in India. It can be seen from Table 1 that after the introduction of the New Economic Policy in 1991, FDI inflows have leaped to more than 100 times over the last 17 years, i.e., from just Rs. 316 crores in 1991-92 to Rs. 22,826 crores in 2006-07.

Table 1: Annual Inflows of FDI into India (In Rupees Crores)

Year	FDI	Percentage Growth	As a Percentage of GDP
1991-92	316.00	–	0.05
1992-93	965.00	205.38	0.13
1993-94	1838.00	90.47	0.24
1994-95	4126.00	124.48	0.49
1995-96	7172.00	73.82	0.80
1996-97	10015.00	39.64	1.03
1997-98	13220.00	32.00	1.30
1998-99	10358.00	-21.65	0.96
1999-2000	9338.00	-9.85	0.81
2000-01	18406.00	97.11	1.54
2001-02	29235.00	58.83	2.31
2002-03	24367.00	-16.65	1.85
2003-04	19860.00	-18.50	1.39
2004-05	25395.00	27.87	1.66
2005-06	34316.00	35.13	2.07

Source: FDI Data: RBI's Online Database, Others: Computed.

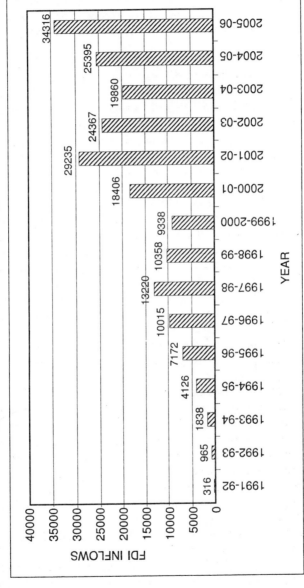

Figure 1: FDI Inflows into India (1991-92 to 2005-06)

The economic growth in terms of growth rate of GDP in the last 17 years has improved and in the recent past 7-8 per cent growth in GDP has been achieved. But, in real terms, it needs to seen if the increased FDI inflows have led to higher economic growth.

FDI and Economic Growth

Foreign direct investment can play an important role in the development process (De Mello and Luiz, 1997). However, the objectives of MNCs and TNCs differ from those of host governments: governments seek to spur national development, while MNCs and TNCs seek to enhance their own competitiveness in an international context. (this can be seen from the previous chapter). There can be considerable overlap between the two, but there are also differences. These differences created much suspicion about FDI in the past in developing countries, especially in India. However, perceptions have changed greatly in recent years, (It would be interesting to note that UNCTAD (1999) puts that liberalisation of FDI (and trade) policy is often part of the conditionality in IMF and World Bank adjustment programmes, and is promoted by many leading aid donors rather than the independent choice of the concerned country). The ways in which MNCs and TNCs operate and organise themselves globally have also changed. Both are in response to the new global context: rapid technical progress, shrinking of economic space, improved communication, intensification of competition, new forms of market rivalry, increasingly mobile capital, widespread policy liberalisation and more vocal (and influential) stakeholders.

Hence, most developing countries today consider FDI an important resource for development. However, the economic effects of FDI on various measures of economic performance are almost impossible to measure with precision as it represents a complex package of attributes that vary from one host country to another. These are difficult to separate and quantify. Where its entry has large (non-marginal) effects, measurement is even more difficult. There is no precise method of specifying a counter-factual-what would have happened if FDI had not entered into the host country.

Many long period cross-section studies that include FDI as a variable tend to find some positive relationship between FDI and growth. One study reported a significant relationship between inflows of FDI as a percentage of GDP and the growth of per capita real GDP across all developed countries for the period 1960-85 (Blomstrom *et al.*, 1994). It suggested that although the gap in technology and productivity between foreign-owned firms and locally owned ones is larger in poorer countries than in richer ones, that does not necessarily mean that the poorer countries gain the most from inward FDI. It argued that "the least developed countries may learn little from the multinationals, because local firms are too far behind in their technological levels to be either imitators or suppliers to the multinationals". And it found, in confirmation of this supposition, that inflows of FDI were significant as determinants of growth for the upper half of the distribution of developing countries, by per capita income, but not in the lower half.

A similar conclusion was reached in a study for 69 developing countries of growth in per capita real GDP from 1970 to 1989 (Borensztein et al., 1995). FDI itself was a marginally significant positive influence on growth, but FDI interacting with a measure of average educational attainment was a stronger and more consistent influence. The higher the level of education of the labour force, the greater the gain in growth from a given inflow of FDI (Borensztein, 1998). This view is also supported by Barro and Martin (1999), and Helpman and Grossman (1991) who use endogenous growth theory in explaining the long-run growth rate of the economy by using endogenous variables like technology and human capital. An interaction between FDI and education was also found in a paper on FDI in China that concluded that "Education becomes even more effective when it is associated with foreign knowledge... the interaction between school enrolment rates and foreign investment is significantly positive, suggesting mutual reinforcement between domestic human capital and foreign knowledge that accompanies the investment" (Mody and Wang, 1997). Whereas another study by Lensink and Morrissey (2001) concludes that there is a consistent finding that FDI has a positive effect on growth and that the positive effect of FDI is not sensitive to the level of human capital (as found in some previous studies).

Another mechanism through which the influence of FDI can take effect is through the impact of inward FDI on domestic capital formation. FDI appears to increase investment in a one-to-one ratio or encourages capital formation by domestic firms, so that a one-dollar increase in the net inflow of FDI is associated with an increase in total investment in the host economy of more than one dollar (Borensztein et al., 1995). This does not mean that cases of FDI crowding-out local capital formation can be ruled out.

A few long period cross section studies have included a measure of FDI as a potential source of growth (Blomstrom et al., 1994; and Borensztein et al., 1995). Reflecting this, a comprehensive review of variables used in such studies did not include FDI (Levine and Renelt, 1992). However, some of the variables identified in these studies as factors of growth are typically under the influence of FDI. Like, relatively "robust" relations were found between investment ratios (investment/GDP) and growth and between investment ratios and trade ratios. But, both investment ratios and trade ratios could be affected by FDI flows, and thus, indirectly form a channel for an effect of FDI on growth. Another study refers to the effects on growth of knowledge spillovers (Eaton and Kortum, 1994 and 1995 and Coe and Helpman, 1995). FDI is also a plausible vehicle for these knowledge spillovers, by itself (through R&D, imitation, competition, etc.) and through its relation to the intensity of trade (Lensink and Morrissey, 2001 and Sjöholm, 1999).

The relation of FDI to trade is more generally a possible connection that may blur the relationship of FDI to growth in quantitative studies including both variables. There is evidence that foreign-owned firms in most countries not only trade more with their parent countries, but also trade more in general than locally-owned firms. This is partly explained by their being concentrated in trade-intensive sectors, and partly because their trading propensity in any given sector tends to be greater than that of local or domestic firms (Dunning, 1993). It is likely, therefore, that high foreign ownership, or a large inflow of FDI, will increase the importance of trade for a host country, thus affecting growth indirectly.

Time series studies focused initially on the impact of FDI on domestic investors. An early study made on Canada, showed that "$1.00 of direct investment led to $3.00 of capital formation" (Lubitz, 1966). A later study of FDI into Canada found a positive direct effect on capital formation greater than the amount of the FDI (Van Loo, 1977). That is, there was some complementary effect on fixed investment by domestic firms. However, when indirect effects through impacts on other variables such as exports, imports, and consumption, operating through the accelerator, were added, the addition to total capital formation was much smaller.

Long-period analyses of growth face endogeneity problems, particularly uncertainty about the direction of causation between growth and investment ratios. In an attempt to avoid some of these problems, in one analysis, the period since 1970 was broken into five year sub-periods (Blomstrom *et al.*, 1994). The main conclusion was that there was more evidence that high growth led to high subsequent investment ratios than for the opposite relationship. In analyses using previous period investment, FDI appeared as a positive and significant influence on a country's rate of growth. The study suggested that FDI in one period may have affected host country capital formation in the following period.

The results by Borensztein *et al.* (1998) and Carkovic and Levine (2002) found a little support for FDI having an exogenous positive effect on economic growth. These results are robust to the inclusion of other growth determinants such as human capital measures, domestic financial development, and institutional quality along with the use of lagged values of FDI.

Time series as well as panel data estimation conducted by De Mello (1999) for a sample covering 15 developed and 17 developing countries for the period 1970-90 to understand the relationships between FDI, capital accumulation, output and productivity growth reveal mixed results. The time series estimations suggest that the effect of FDI on growth or on capital accumulation and total factor productivity (TFP) varies greatly across countries. The panel data estimation suggests a positive impact of FDI on output growth for developed and developing country sub-samples. However, the effect of FDI on capital accumulation and TFP growth varies across developed (technological leaders) and developing countries (technological followers). FDI has a positive effect on TFP growth in developed countries but a negative effect in developing countries but the pattern is reversed in case of effect on capital accumulation. De Mello infers from these findings that the extent to which FDI is growth-enhancing depends on the degree of complementarity between FDI and domestic investment. The degree of substitutability between foreign and domestic capital stocks appears to be greater in technologically advanced countries than in developing countries. Developing countries may have difficulty in using and diffusing new technologies of MNEs. Findings of Xu (2000) for US FDI in 40 countries for the period 1966-94 also corroborate the finding of De Mello that technology transfer from FDI contributes to productivity growth in developed countries but not in developing countries, which he attributes to lack of adequate human capital.

The coefficient of the FDI-GDP ratio turned out to be negative, though not significant in a fixed effects model based on pooled data for five South Asian host countries, among which India figures prominently in the period 1965-96 (Agrawal, 2005). Similar results but significant, were found in a study comprising 73 developing countries (Singh, 1988), and 41 developing countries (Hein, 1992). Another pooled time series cross-section macro-model with 16 developing countries and the period 1966-88 concluded FDI to be having an immiserizing growth effect on the host countries (Fry,1992). However these approaches ignored that FDI is endogenous. Similar qualifications apply to Pradhan (2002) who estimated a Cobb-Douglas production function with FDI stocks as additional input variable. FDI stocks had no significant impact when considering the whole period of observation (1969-97). In an earlier study Pradhan (2001) found a significant positive effect of lagged FDI inflows on growth rates only for Latin American countries in a panel data estimation covering 1975-95 period for 71 developing countries. The effect of FDI was not significantly different from zero for the overall sample and for other regions.

The Granger causation test provides another measure to corroborate the positive relation between FDI inflows and growth. Using aggregate data for 1974-96 Chakraborty and Basu (2002) explored the two–way link between FDI and growth. It suggested that FDI plays no significant role in the short–run adjustment process of GDP, though it is positively related to GDP and openness to trade in the long-run. In an earlier study, Dua and Rashid (1998) report that FDI inflows do not granger cause industrial output. Kumar and Pradhan (2002) in a cross section study of 107 developing countries consider the FDI-growth relationship to be Granger neutral in the case of India as the direction of causation was not pronounced, and Sahoo and Mathiyazhagan (2002) corroborate these results.

Thus, conclusions of the empirical analyses of FDI and economic growth remain unclear, especially as regards the causality within the relationship. Some show a positive impact of FDI on economic growth (Rodan, 1961; Chenery and Strout, 1966; Caves, 1974; Kokko, 1994; Markusen, 1995; Caves, 1996; Sahoo et al., 2001) others a negative impact (Singer, 1950; Griffin, 1970; Weisskof, 1972; Fry, 1992; Dua and Rashid, 1998; Agosin and Mayer, 2000); yet others have found growth to be a determinant of FDI rather than the other way round (Kasibhatla and Sawhney, 1996; Chakraborty and Basu, 2002). Since growth depends on many factors whose effects are difficult to disentangle, and since FDI itself affects several of these factors, an indeterminate conclusion is probably the most sensible. But, there is little doubt that fast growth and large FDI go hand in hand in many instances.

Conceptual Framework

Economic growth in any country depends upon the sustained

growth of productive capacity, supported by savings and investment. Low levels of savings and investment, particularly in developing countries like India results in a low level of capital stock and economic growth. The earlier growth models by Harrod (1939) and Domar (1946) explain that capital formation raises the standard of living, which in turn results in higher growth. Criticising the growth models proposed by Harrod and Domar on the ground of the fixed proportion of factors of production and substitutability between labour and capital, Solow (1956) argues that capital formation increases labour productivity in a dynamic process of investment growth. Some of the recent growth theories such as Lucas (1988) and Rebelo (1991) broaden the definition of capital to include human capital and the accumulation of knowledge. Similarly, Romer (1986; 1990) and Helpman and Grossman (1991) incorporate knowledge capital gained through research and development to explain growth along with other variables. Overall theoretical growth literature demonstrates the role of capital or changes in the definition of capital (knowledge capital or human capital) in enhancing economic growth.

The recognition of the role of knowledge capital in economic growth creates a basis for analysing the role of FDI, which brings new technology and knowledge along with capital. In recent years, the need for FDI inflows has increased as MNCs and TNCs have assumed significant importance as a source of economic growth and development (Bajpai and Sachs, 2000). Since FDI may help developing India by providing new knowledge and complementing domestic investment, it is important to analyse the empirical relationship between FDI and economic growth in a growth accounting framework.

Further, the phenomenon of economic growth is complex, and the lines of causation frequently go both from supposed causes to growth and from growth to the supposed causes. So, the causality between FDI inflows and economic growth needs to be seen before proceeding to probe the impact of FDI on the economic growth of India. Furthermore, the various factors that are thought to explain growth are themselves interrelated. These problems face all studies attempting to throw light on whether, in what way, and to what extent a particular factor or group of factors affect growth. They similarly apply to the study of the impact of FDI on growth.

Analytical Framework

This section deals with empirically testing whether the impact of FDI inflows on the economic growth of India is significantly positive or it is the other way round, i.e., economic growth in India is leading to higher inflows of FDI. The Neo-Classical growth accounting framework has been employed for the analysis through the Vector Autoregressive model (VAR).

Economic growth in the Neo-Classical framework is influenced by parameters such as capital, labour and human capital. Similarly, FDI enters into a country based on many criteria; some of them which can be incorporated in the Neo-Classical framework are past economic growth record, investment climate for the operation of private sector, the resource base (mainly labour) and the level of skill of the host country. Considering this, it would be much appropriate to analyse the relationship between economic growth and FDI in this framework rather than relating the two variables in the absence of other influences.

The use of a Neo-Classical framework through the VAR to probe into the relationship between FDI and economic growth would give more correct and true results than many tests reviewed in the past literature using Granger causality test (see for example, Blomstrom, et al., 1994; Dua and Rashid, 1998). The Granger causality test can be used only with two variables. It removes the possibility of testing the relationship between two variables in the presence other variables affecting both these variables. Then the Multiple Linear Regression (MLR) results of the VAR model are used to probe into the details of the impact of FDI inflows on economic growth.

Hence, this study first develops a structure of the Neo-Classical framework to understand the two-way causality between economic growth and FDI. This would help in establishing whether the causality is unidirectional from FDI to growth or unidirectional from growth to FDI or it is bidirectional. If the relationship is unidirectional from FDI to growth or bidirectional further exploring would be needed to understand the relationship more fully.

To develop a structural model for empirical analysis, this study takes the standard Neo-Classical growth accounting framework through the Cobb-Douglas production function. Here, the total capital stock is assumed to comprise two components, viz., domestic and foreign owned capital stock. Further, three variations are made in the model; the first is based on an augmented Solow production function that makes output a function of stocks of capital, labour, human capital and productivity (Mankiw et al., 1992; Benhabib and Spiegel 1994; Kumar and Pradhan 2002; among others); the second and third are based on the review of literature in this study emphasizing that current growth is a function of the past growth (UNCTAD, 1999) and that growth is a function of exports due to the export oriented growth strategy (Wen, 2002). The growth model is algebraically put as follows.

$$Y_t = \beta_1 + \beta_2 Y_{t-1} + \beta_3 I_t + \beta_4 F_t + \beta_5 E_t + \beta_6 L_t + \beta_7 H_t + u_t \quad (1)$$

where, following the established practice in the literature (Blomstrom, Lipsey, and Zejan, 1994; Bosworth and Collins, 1996; Balasubramanyam et al., 1996; Hu and Khan, 1997; Athukorala and Chand, 2000; Wen, 2002), the dependent variable is taken as Growth in Per Capita Real GDP (1993-94 prices). The domestic capital stock is proxied by Gross Domestic Investment-GDP ratio (1993-94 prices) and the foreign capital stock is proxied by FDI inflows GDP (deflated to 1993-94 prices) ratio. Exports (deflated to 1993-94 prices) are taken as the Rate of Growth of Exports, labour is taken as the Growth in the Labour Force Participation Rate and human capital is taken as the growth in Growth in the Total Secondary School Enrolment Rate. (All the variables have been taken in their logarithmic form for the analysis.) The growth model would now be algebraically put as follows.

$$GPRG_t = \beta_1 + \beta_2 GPRG_{t-1} + \beta_3 DINV_t + \beta_4 FDI_t + \beta_5 ROGX_t + b_6 LPR_t + b_7 SER_t + u_t \quad (2)$$

where, GPRG is the Growth in Per Capita Real GDP, DINV is the Gross Domestic Investment-GDP ratio, FDI is the FDI-GDP ratio, ROGX is the Rate of Growth of Exports, LPR is the Growth in the Labour Force Participation Rate and SER is the Growth in the Total Secondary School Enrolment Rate. The subscript 't' stands for the time period, β_1 is the regression constant denoting total factor productivity, $\beta_2, \beta_3, \beta_4, \beta_5, \beta_6$ and β_7 —are the coefficients of the respective regressors and u denotes the standard error.

In the above Equation (2), there may arise a difficulty of two-way interaction between the dependent variable GPRG and independent variables DINV and FDI, i.e., high growth rates may induce high investment rates at least as much as high investment rates induce high rates of Growth in Per Capita Real GDP. To reduce such ambiguities (although without the expectation of completely eliminating them) the above mentioned independent variables are taken in lagged form. That is, only observations for period 't–1' and 't–2' enter the equations for growth in period 't'. The optimal lag structure would be determined with the help of information criteria AIC, SIC and HQC (see Appendix for details). Therefore, the final form of the equation is written as follows:

$$GPRG_t = \beta_1 + \beta_2 GPRG_{t-1} + \beta_3 GPRG_{t-2} + \beta_4 DINV_{t-1} + \beta_5 DINV_{t-2} +$$

$$\beta_6 FDI_{t-1} + \beta_7 FDI_{t-2} + \beta_8 ROGX_t + \beta_9 LPR_t + \beta_{10} SER_t + u_t \quad (3)$$

This set of variables may influence investors' choice of country for investing directly as much as they would influence economic growth. Hence, the equation with FDI as a dependent variable would be:

$$FDI_t = \beta_1 + \beta_2 GPRG_{t-1} + \beta_3 GPRG_{t-2} + \beta_4 DINV_{t-1} + \beta_5 DINV_{t-2} +$$

$$\beta_6 FDI_{t-1} + \beta_7 FDI_{t-2} + \beta_8 ROGX_t + \beta_9 LPR_t + \beta_{10} SER_t + u_t \quad (4)$$

In the above Equation (3), the only change from the Equation (4) is the dependent variable, i.e., FDI_t instead of $GPRG_t$. All the independent variables are the same.

The main source of data for the present study is the online database of the Reserve Bank of India (RBI) from which the data on the total FDI inflows, GDP, Gross Domestic Investment, Population, Manufacturing Sector and Exports have been acquired. The data on Sector-wise and Country-wise FDI inflows have been gathered from the Secretariat of Industrial Assistance's (SIA) online data base. The data on the Labour Force Participation Rate and Total Secondary School Enrolment Rate have been compiled from various sources which are the online database of the NSSO, the online database of the World Bank, the website of the Indian Planning Commission and the website of the Economic Survey. The data relating to GDP and Gross Domestic Investment have been taken at 1993-94 prices while the data relating to FDI and exports have been deflated to 1993-94 prices.

For ensuring the consistency of data, the present study uses the Augmented Dickey Fuller Test (ADF) to check for the presence of a unit root so as to confirm that the data sequence of a variable is stationary (see Appendix for details). This study has used the Akaike Information Criterion (AIC), Schwartz Information Criterion (SIC) and Hannan-Quinn Criterion (HQC) to select the appropriate lag length for the VAR model (see Appendix for details).

Results

The results of the ADF tests are displayed in Table 2. It can be seen that the 't' statistic corresponding to all the variables and their corresponding P-values show that all the variables do not have the presence of a unit root and are stationary in their original form. Hence, all the variables are taken in their original form for the analysis.

Table 2: ADF Test Results for Equations (4.1 & 4.2)

Variables	Actual	
	t	P-Value
GPRG	-2.572*	0.098
DINV	-3.027*	0.100
FDI	-5.137***	0.000
ROGX	-2.690*	0.075
LPR	-4.817***	0.000
SER	-3.323***	0.013

*** and * Significance at 1% and 10% level respectively.
P-values based on MacKinnon (JAE, 1996).

Coming to the analysis part, the Equations (3) and (4) have been used in the VAR model. To understand the causality within the relationship between FDI and economic growth and to arrive at a possible conclusion in the Indian context, first the two-way causality is tested. FDI would be considered to cause a change in the Growth in Per Capita Real GDP which has been taken as an indicator of economic growth, only if the lagged values of FDI significantly contribute to the explanation of current growth in the presence of other influencing parameters and the Growth in Per Capita Real GDP would be considered to cause FDI only if the lagged values of GPRG significantly contribute to the explanation of current FDI inflows in the presence of other influencing parameters. Therefore, this test essentially looks at the predictive performance between variables to determine the existence or direction of causality between them in the presence of other parameters. Given the fact that it takes into account the effect of lagged values of the causing variable on the current value of the dependent variable along with current and lagged values of other variables, it takes care of the dynamic nature of FDI's effect on economic growth.

The optimal lag length for the VAR model has been decided based on the three information criteria as mentioned earlier. The results of the lag selection criteria are displayed in Table 3. The lag length with the lowest values of the criteria would be selected. This clearly shows that a two year lag length is optimal for the model. Hence, a model with a lag length of two years is selected for VAR estimations. The VAR analysis is made with the inclusion of robust standard errors so as to give more correct results. The results of the two-way causality test are presented in Table 4.

Table 3: LAG Selection for VAR

Lag Length	AIC	SIC	HQC
1	0.918	1.614	0.775
2	-1.651*	-0.782*	-1.830*

* Lower values indicate better significance.

Table 4: VAR Model: Two-Way Causality Test on FDI and GPRG

Independent Variables	All Lags of FDI on GPRG	All Lags of GPRG on FDI
F-Value	152.36***	1.212
P-value	0.001	0.411

Dependent Variable in Equation 1: Growth in Per Capita Real GDP.
Dependent Variable in Equation 2: FDI
*** Significance at 1% level.

The two-way causality is seen in the VAR framework by inferring to the F-statistic for all the lags of FDI on $GPRG_t$ and all the lags of GPRG on FDI_t. The F-statistic for the corresponding regression coefficients of all the lags of FDI is 152.36 with a corresponding P-value of 0.001. This suggests that there is high significance and so FDI causes Growth in Per Capita Real GDP. All lags of the regressor GPRG have a corresponding F-statistic of 1.212 with a corresponding P-value equal to 0.411. This means it is not significant and therefore, GPRG does not cause FDI.

Hence, the two-way causality test in the VAR framework suggests that the causality between the two variables GPRG taken as a representative for economic growth and FDI-GDP ratio taken as a proxy for foreign capital stock have a 'unidirectional' relationship of FDI causing growth. This puts an end to the search for the answer to the question of whether FDI has positively and significantly contributed to economic growth in India during period of the study. FDI has significantly and positively contributed to growth during the period 1991-92 to 2006-07. For understanding the effect of FDI on the indicator of growth that the present study has employed, viz., Growth in Per Capita Real GDP in a fuller way, the MLR results of the growth equation is explored much in detail. The results of the MLR estimations of the growth equation are summarized in Table 5.

Table 5: MLR Model: The Impact of FDI on Economic Growth

Independent Variables	Beta (β)	T	P-Value
(Constant)	-8.916	-1.404	0.255
$GPRG_{t-1}$	-0.464*	-2.580	0.082
$GPRG_{t-2}$	0.153*	2.346	0.100
FDI_{t-1}	-0.768***	-16.235	0.000
FDI_{t-2}	1.246***	6.059	0.009
$DINV_{t-1}$	2.116**	4.425	0.021
$DINV_{t-2}$	2.468	2.070	0.130
ROGX	-0.120**	-3.723	0.034
LPR_t	-4.880***	-6.177	0.008
SER_t	-0.406***	-6.559	0.007
R-square		0.860	
F-statistic		431.161	
P-value		0.000	

Dependent Variable: Growth in Per Capita Real GDP.
***, ** and * Significance at 1%, 5% and 10% level respectively.

From the MLR analysis it is seen that the R-square coefficient of multiple determination is 0.860 which implies that around 86 per cent of variation in Growth in Per Capita Real GDP is caused by the regressors involved in the model. The corresponding F-statistic is 431.161 and the corresponding P-value is 0.000. This implies high significance and that the model is a good fit for the data.

The student 't' statistic for the corresponding partial regression coefficient of the regressor $GPRG_{t-1}$, i.e., lag order one Growth in Per Capita Real GDP is –2.580 with a corresponding P-value of 0.082. This suggests that the partial regression coefficient for the variable $GPRG_{t-1}$ is significant at the 10 per cent level and that the lag order one Growth in Per Capita Real GDP is a negative determinant of the current Growth in Per Capita Real GDP. The partial regression coefficient corresponding to the variable $GPRG_{t-1}$ is equal to –0.464 which implies its one unit increase will lead to a 0.5 unit fall in the current GPRG.

However, the 't' statistic corresponding to the partial regression coefficient $GPRG_{t-2}$, i.e., lag order two Growth in Per Capita Real GDP is 2.346 with a corresponding P-value of 0.100. This suggests that the partial regression coefficient for the variable $GPRG_{t-2}$ is significant at the 10 per cent level and it is a positive determinant of the current Growth in Per Capita Real GDP. The partial regression coefficient corresponding to the variable $GPRG_{t-2}$ is equal to 0.153 which implies its one unit increase will lead to a 0.2 unit increase in the current GPRG.

'The student 't' statistic corresponding to the partial regression coefficients of the regressors $DINV_{t-1}$ and $DINV_{t-2}$, i.e., lag order one and two of Gross Domestic Investment-GDP ratio are 4.425 and 2.070 with corresponding P-values equal to 0.021 and 0.130 respectively. This shows that the partial regression coefficient of past Domestic Investment $DINV_{t-1}$ is significant and so $DINV_{t-1}$ is a variation which is a positive determinant of the dependent variable $GPRG_t$. The variable $DINV_{t-2}$ is not a very significant determinant of the dependent variable $GPRG_t$, however it is positive. The coefficients corresponding to the variables $DINV_{t-1}$ and $DINV_{t-2}$ are 2.116 and 2.468 which suggest that a one unit change in these variables would produce a two and two and half unit change in the dependent variable $GPRG_t$.

The partial regression coefficients of the regressors FDI_{t-1} and FDI_{t-2}, i.e., lag order one and two of FDI-GDP ratio have corresponding 't' statistic equal to -16.235 and 6.059 with corresponding P-values equal to 0.000 and 0.009 respectively. This shows that the variable FDI_{t-1} with a partial regression coefficient of -0.768 is a significant negative determinant of $GPRG_t$. While the variable FDI_{t-2} with a partial regression coefficient of 1.246 is a significant positive determinant of $GPRG_t$. A one unit change in FDI_{t-1} would lead to a 0.8 unit change in $GPRG_t$ in the opposite direction. While a one unit change in the variable FDI_{t-2} would produce a 1.25 unit change in the current GPRG in the same direction.

The student 't' statistic for the corresponding partial regression coefficient of the regressor $ROGX_t$, i.e., Rate of Growth of Exports is -3.723 with a corresponding P-value of 0.034. This suggests that the partial regression coefficient for the variable $ROGX_t$ is significant and that the Rate of Growth of Exports is a negative determinant of the current Growth in Per Capita Real GDP. The partial regression coefficient corresponding to the variable $ROGX_t$ is equal to -0.120 which implies its one unit increase will lead to only a 0.1 unit fall in the current GPRG.

The remaining two variables, viz., LPR, i.e., Growth in Labour Force Participation Rate and SER, i.e., Growth in Total Secondary School Enrolment Rate show a negative relationship with the dependent variable $GPRG_t$, current Growth in Per Capita Real GDP. The 't' statistic corresponding to the partial regression coefficients LPR and SER are –6.177 and –6.559 with corresponding P-values 0.008 and 0.007 respectively. This shows that the partial regression coefficients for the regressors LPR and SER are highly significant and since the 't' statistic values corresponding to these variables are negative, these variables are negative determinants of the dependent variable $GPRG_t$. The coefficient corresponding to the variable LPR is -4.880 which is the highest coefficient in the equation suggesting a five unit change in the dependent variable $GPRG_t$ would occur with a one unit change in LPR. The coefficient corresponding to the variable SER is -0.4 which shows that a one unit change in the independent variable SER would cause a 0.4 unit change in the dependent variable $GPRG_t$.

Discussions

From the results of the two-way causality test on FDI inflows and the indicator of economic growth, it is made clear that the causality is unidirectional in India from FDI inflows to economic growth during the study period 1991-92 to 2005-06. As this test has been performed in a growth accounting framework with the inclusion of other parameters that influence both these variables, it may be considered to give better results than two-way causality tests such as 'Granger causality'.

But, the unidirectional causality may not be taken as an end in itself. It just reveals the direction of causality between FDI inflows and economic growth. For further probing into the effect of FDI on economic growth, the MLR results are seen. The MLR results from the growth equation suggest that the lag order one FDI variable has a negative impact on growth with a coefficient of -0.768. However, the lag order two FDI variable contributes positively and to a larger extent to the Growth in Per Capita Real GDP in India with a coefficient of 1.246. So, when the net effect of both the lags of FDI is put together it may be said that a one unit change in the past FDI inflows would lead to a half unit change in economic growth in the current year in the same direction.

The other variables in the growth accounting framework, viz., past Growth in Per Capita Real GDP, Gross Domestic Investment ratio, Rate of Growth of Exports, Growth in Labour Force Participation Rate and the Growth in Total Secondary School Enrolment Rate register a significant relationship with the current period's Growth in Per Capita Real GDP. But, the point to be noted here is that all these variables put together have a net negative effect on the Growth in Per Capita Real GDP.

Comparing the average annual Growth Rate of Per Capita Real GDP during the study period would help in knowing the effect of FDI on economic growth. The average annual Growth Rate of Per Capita Real GDP was 2.3 per cent in the early 1990s which has increased to 4.5 per cent during the period 1996 to 2005. This proof is sufficient enough to suggest that FDI inflows is one of the influencing factors that has significantly contributed to promoting economic growth in India during the reform era.

It may be seen from the results of the MLR analysis of the growth framework that the net effect of past Growth in Per Capita Real GDP on its current period is negative. This is due to the fact that the Growth in Per Capita Real GDP has an uneven trend (Prasanna, 2006). In many instances a higher growth is followed by a fall in the Growth of Per Capita Real GDP. This is further corroborated by UNCTAD (1999) that in general, in developing countries a higher Growth Rate of Per Capita Real GDP seem to be associated with lower growth in the following period, an indication that the past growth coefficients reflect cyclical swings rather than long-term influences.

The results of the past investment ratios in the growth framework, with coefficient values 2.116 and 2.468 for the one and two year lags respectively, suggest that past investment have a positive relationship with the current Growth in Per Capita Real GDP. But, the lag order two Domestic Investment variable's significance is lower than the 10 per cent level. This needs some discussion. To explain the cause for the lower significance of the two year lagged Domestic Investment ratio, the results from a study made by Prasanna (2010) would be helpful. The study suggests that the net effect of the past FDI inflows in India is crowding-out of the Domestic Investment in the long-term. This implies that the FDI inflows rather than complementing Domestic Investment are competing with it. This may provide some explanation for the lower significance of the two year lagged Domestic Investment variable.

The Rate of Growth of Exports has been contributing (though not very effectively as its coefficient is only 0.120) negatively to economic growth. The reason for this may be seen form a study made by Prasanna (2011) on the impact of FDI on the Export Performance of India. The study reveals that Per Capita FDI as well as Per Capita Manufacturing Value Added do not effectively contribute to Per Capita Total and Per Capita High-Technology Manufactured Exports as their coefficients are very low. This implies that growth in the manufactured exports is not sufficient in India for attaining the objective of the export-led growth strategy.

An astounding revelation of this study is relating to the results of the Growth in Labour Force Participation Rate and Growth in Total Secondary School Enrolment Rate. Both these parameters which are taken to be granted as positive contributors to economic growth in many studies show high negative influence on the Growth in Per Capita Real GDP. The coefficient of Growth in Labour Force Participation Rate is the highest in the equation at -4.880 while the coefficient of Growth in Total School Enrolment Rate is -0.406. The reason for the huge negative impact of these two factors may be attributed to low social expenditure on the part of the Government of India.

Policy Implications

With the objective of becoming more efficient in the global environment, a number of countries adopted market-oriented reforms. This resulted in a surge of FDI inflows in these countries. India, a late comer on the scene of economic reforms, started liberalising its FDI policy and introduced new institutions for facilitating FDI following a macro-economic crisis in 1991. Subsequently, India has been experiencing increased FDI inflows. This study examines whether this increased inflow of FDI has proved beneficial for India in promoting economic growth, enhancing investment opportunities and improving export performance. Based on the results and discussions in the previous chapter, this chapter spells out some policy suggestions for enhancing FDI's positive impact and minimising its negative impact on the Indian economy. The chapter later provides the scope for further research in this area.

From the results and discussions it can be seen that the effect of FDI on economic growth and domestic investment is negative in the first year, whereas it is positive in the second year. Considering that the second year's positive effect is able to offset the first year's negative effect, the economic performance of India in the short-term may increase many folds if this offset is to a larger extent. This could be done by attracting more FDI in all areas.

(i) One such way of doing this could be increasing the source of FDI, country-wise. The present scenario shows FDI flowing mainly from U.S.A and Mauritius contributing to around 45 per cent of the total FDI inflows into India which means that rest of the 112 countries contribute only a meager share of FDI flows into India. This may be seen as an opportunity by the Government of India and more FDI may be attracted from the remaining countries through Bilateral and Multilateral MoUs.

(ii) Secondly, FDI inflows may be attracted from what are called 'footloose industries.' 'Footloose industries' imply those TNCs that operate only to indulge in the production and export of commodities. Such TNCs just require infrastructural facilities to enter a host country. Hence, attracting such TNCs may lead to increase in FDI as well as exports without causing any damage to the Indian economy.

(iii) Furthermore, the following sector specific policy suggestions related to private sector banking, insurance, airlines, telecommunications, infrastructure, print media, broadcasting, and services may be taken into consideration for increasing FDI inflows into India.

Although FDI has a positive effect on economic growth, its negative impact on domestic investment reduces the effect of domestic investment on economic growth. This leads to a combined reduced effect of both these investments put together on economic growth. It would be much better if FDI had a positive impact on domestic investment so that both FDI and domestic investment added together could cause a larger positive impact on economic growth. The way for achieving this is to have a crowding-in effect of FDI on domestic investment. This could be done in the following ways:

(i) By encouraging more FDI into the infrastructure sectors like telecommunications and transportation through either by relaxing the sectoral cap on the investing companies in infrastructure which is currently at 49 per cent to at least 74 per cent in the first phase and then to 100 per cent or by allowing for full capital account convertibility.

(ii) By decentralising FDI inflows into India instead of concentrating on few metropolitan cities which may lead to the establishment of foreign industries in the areas where there is less scope which would ultimately lead to crowding-in new domestic entrepreneurs.

(iii) By starting backward linkage programmes with TNCs which means starting a dialogue process by the Government of India with the TNCs to train and disseminate knowledge and technology to local manufacturers who would provide a supply chain for the TNCs. In return, the Government of India may offer better incentives for such TNCs.

(iv) By identifying gaps in the domestic manufactures. This could be done by examining the imports of finished goods and analysing whether such goods could be produced domestically just with the help of technology and capital. If so, FDI may be sought in that industry. This may lead to the establishment of a new industrial base which would in turn lead to complementing domestic investment.

These measures may lead to increase the complementary effect of FDI on domestic investment and may ultimately lead to higher economic growth. Simultaneously, these measures may also cause an increase in the inflows of FDI.

FDI as well as domestic investment would give better effect to economic growth if labour force participation rate and secondary school enrolment rate contribute positively to economic growth. But in the Indian case, it can be seen from the results that labour force participation rate and secondary school enrolment rate contribute negatively to economic growth. So, steps may be taken to make labour force participation rate and secondary school enrolment rate to contribute positively to economic growth. This requires labour force participation rate and secondary school enrolment rate to have an increasing trend. Considering that social expenditure on the part of the Government of India has been declining, a Public Private Participation (PPP) may be adopted for improving the labour force participation rate and secondary school enrolment rate. Viewing the knowledge spillover capability of FDI, it may be encouraged in this participation, which may make both the government and private sector more accountable.

Much FDI into India has come seeking the immense size of the domestic market. FDI inflows may be welcome into the Indian domestic market subject to non-displacement of domestic investment in India. Considering that India has the most liberal M&A policy among South/Southeast Asian countries, FDI coming into the Indian domestic market may displace domestic investment. Not only the increase in the quantity of FDI is important, but also its quality. So, a reassessment of the M&A policy in India may be considered.

So, if the Government of India desires to continue on the FDI-led growth strategy and benefit from it in the long-run, it may need to concentrate more on domestic efforts to expand investment opportunities and manufacturing in line with the FDI policy framework. Hence, it is necessary to revise and amend the investment and manufacturing policy framework. Most importantly, the Government of India should recognise that FDI is not a panacea for achieving the national objectives, it can only complement domestic efforts to meet the development objectives. Hence, to achieve faster economic growth and develop India sustainably and dynamically, FDI policies may not be pursued in isolation. Instead, they may be linked with policies in core areas of the economy.

References

Agosin, M.R. and Ricardo Mayer (2000), Foreign Investment in Developing Countries: Does it Crowd in Domestic Investment? *UNCTAD Discussion Paper*, 146. (Geneva: UNCTAD).

Agrawal, P. (2005), Foreign Direct Investment in South Asia: Impact on Economic Growth and Local Investment. in E.M. Graham, ed., *Multinationals and Foreign Investment in Economic Development*. (Basingstoke: Palgrave Macmillan): 94-118.

Athukorala, P. and S. Chand (2000), Trade Orientation and Productivity Gains from International Production: A Study of Overseas Operation of United States TNCs. *Transnational Corporations*, 9(2):1-27.

Bajpai, N. and Jeffrey D. Sachs (2000), Foreign Direct Investment in India: Issues and Problems. *Harvard Institute of International Development*, DDP No.759, March.

Balasubramanyam, V.N., Salisu, M. and D. Sapsford (1996), Foreign Direct Investment and Growth in EP and IS Countries. *The Economic Journal*, 106 (434): 92-105.

Barro, R. and Salai-I-Martin (1999), *Economic Growth* (Cambridge: MIT Press).

Benhabib, Jess and Mark M. Spiegel (1994), The Role of Human Capital in Economic Development: Evidence from Aggregate Cross-Country Data. *Journal of Monetary Economics*, 34: 143-173.

Bhagwati, J.N. and Srinivasan, T.N. (1993), India's Economic Reforms. Ministry of Finance, Government of India, New Delhi.

Bhagwati, J.N. (1993), *India in Transition: Freeing the Economy*. (Oxford: Clarendon Press).

Bhagwati, J.N. (1994), *India in Transition: Freeing the Economy*. (Delhi: Oxford University Press).

Blomstrom, Magnus, Robert E. Lipsey and Mario Zejan (1994), What Explains Developing Country Growth? *Cambridge, MA: National Bureau of Economic Research*, Working Paper.

Borensztein, E., J. De Gregorio and J.W. Lee (1995, 1998), How Does Foreign Direct Investment Affect Economic Growth. *Journal of International Economics*, 45:115-135.

Bosworth, Barry P. and Susan M. Collins (1996), Economic Growth in East Asia: Accumulation *versus* Assimilation in Borrkings, ed., *Papers on Economic Activity*, 1:135-203.

Carkovic, M. and R. Levine (2002), Doesn't Foreign Direct Investment Accelerate Economic Growth? *University of Minnesota Working Paper*, 6 (Minnesota: Edward).

Caves, R. (1974), Multinational Firms, Competition and Productivity in the Host Country. *Economica*, 41: 176-93.

Caves, R. (1996), *Multinational Enterprise and Economic Analysis*, Cambridge. (Cambridge: Cambridge University Press).

Chakraborty, C. and P. Basu (2002), Foreign Direct Investment and growth in India: A Co-Integration Approach. *Applied Economics*, 34(9):1061-73.

Chenery, H.B. and A.M. Strout (1966), Foreign Assistance and Economic Development. *American Economic Review*, 56:679-733.

Coe, David T. and Elhanan Helpmann (1995), International R&D Spillovers, Working paper 4444, (Cambridge, MA: NBER).

De Mello, Jr. and R. Luiz (1997), Foreign Direct Investment in Developing Countries and Growth: A Selective Survey. *Journal of Development Studies*, 34(1): 1-34.

De Mello, Jr. (1999), Foreign Direct Investment-Led Growth: Evidence from Time Series and Panel Data. *Oxford Economic Papers*, 51: 133-54.

Desai, Ashok (1993), *My Economic Affair*. (New Delhi: Eastern).

Domar, E.D. (1946), Capital Expansion, Rate of Growth and Employment. *Econometrica*, 14: 137-47.

Dua, P. and A.I. Rashid (1998), FDI and Economic Activity in India. *Indian Economic Review*, 33(2): 153-68.

Dunning John, H. (1993), *The Globalization of Business* (London and New York: Routledge).

Eaton, Jonathan and Samuel Kortum (1995), Engines of Growth: Domestic and Foreign Sources of Innovation. *Working Paper*, 5207 (Cambridge, MA: NBER).

Economic Survey (2005-06), (New Delhi: Government of India).

Economic Survey (http://www.indiabudget.nic.in).

EPW Research Foundation (1994), What Has Gone Wrong with the Economic Reforms? *Economic and Political Weekly*, 29(18): April 30: 1049-53.

Fry, Maxwell J. (1992), Foreign Direct Investment in a Macroeconomic Framework: Finance, Efficiency, Incentives and Distortions. *PRE Working Paper*, 7, (Washington, DC: The World Bank).

Ghosh, Arun (1994), 1994-95 Budget: A Total Surrender. *Economic and Political Weekly*, 29 (16&17), April 16-23: 889-92.

Granger, C. and P. Newbold (1974), Spurious Regressions in Econometrics. *Journal of Econometrics*, 2:111-20.

Griffin, K.B. (1970), Foreign Capital, Domestic Savings and Development. *Oxford Bulletin of Economics and Statistics*, 32: 99-112.

Harrod, R.F. (1939), An Essay in Dynamic Theory. *The Economic Journal*, 49: 14-33.

Hein, Simeon (1992), Trade Strategy and the Dependency Hypothesis: A Comparison of Policy, Foreign Investment, and Economic Growth in Latin America. *Economic Development and Cultural Change*, 40(3): 4895-521.

Helpman, E. and G.M. Grossman (1991), *Innovation and Growth in the Global Economy*. (Cambridge MA: MIT Press).

Hu, Z.F. and M.S. Khan (1997), Why Is China Growing So Fast? *IMF Staff Papers*, 44(1):103-31.
Indian Planning Commission, Government of India. (http://www.planning commission.nic.in).
Indian Planning Commission (2002), Report of the Steering Group on Foreign Direct Investment. (New Delhi: Academic Foundation).
Joshi, V. and Little, I. (1996), India's Economic Reforms, 1991-2001. Oxford and New York: Oxford University Press, Clarendon Press.
Kashibhatla, K. and B. Sawhney (1996), FDI and Economic Growth in the US: Evidence from Co-integration and Granger Causality Test. *Rivista Internazioriale di Sceinze Economiche e Commerciali*, 43: 411-20.
Kokko, A. (1994), Technology, Market Characteristics and Spillovers. *Journal of Development of Economics*, 43:279-93.
Kumar, N., and J.P. Pradhan (2002), Foreign Direct Investment, Externalities and Economic Growth in Developing Countries: Some Empirical Explorations and Implications for WTO Negotiations on Investment. *Research and Information System for the Non-Aligned and Other Developing Countries (RIS) Discussion Papers*, 27 (New Delhi: RIS).
Kumar, N. (2003), Liberalisation, FDI Flows and Economic Development: An Indian Experience in the 1990s. *RIS Discussion Papers*, 65/2003. (New Delhi: RIS).
Lensink, Robert and Ooliuver Morrissey (2001), Foreign Direct Investment: Flows, Volatility and Growth. *DESG, University of Nottingham*, April 5-7.
Levine, Ross and David Renelt (1992), A sensitivity Analysis of Cross-Country Growth Regressions. *American Economic Review*, 82(4): 942-63.
Lucas, R.E.J. (1988), On the Mechanics of Economic Development. *Journal of Monetary Economics*, 22:3-42.
Mankiw, N. Gregory, David Romer, and David N. Weil (1992), A Contribution to the Empirics of Economic Growth. *Quarterly Journal of Economics*, 107(2): 407-37.
Markusen, J.R. (1995), The Boundaries of Multinational Enterprises and the Theory of International Trade. *Journal of Economic Perspectives*, 9:169-89.
Mody, Ashota and Fung-Yi Wang (1997), Explaining Industrial Growth in Coastal China: Economic reforms... and what else? *World Bank Economic Review*, 11(2) May: 293-325.
National Sample Survey Organisation (NSSO), India. (http://www.mospi.nic.in/nsso_test1.html)
Parikh, Kirit (ed.) (1999), *India Development Report, 1999-2000*. (Delhi: Oxford University Press).
Pradhan, J.P. (2002), Foreign Direct Investment and Economic Growth in India: A Production Function Analysis. *Indian Journal of Economics*, 82 (327): 582-86.
Rao, C. Hanumantha (1994), Reforming Agriculture in the New Context. *Economic and Political Weekly*, 29(16&17), April, 16-23:1005-10.
Rao, V.M. (1994), Agriculture and Liberalization: Some Implications for Development Policies. *Economic and Political Weekly*, 29 (16&17), April, 16-23: 999-1003.

Reserve Bank of India (RBI), Online Database, (http://www.rbi.org.in)
Rebelo, S. (1991), Long-run Policy Analysis and Long-run Growth. *Journal of Political Economy*, 99: 500-21.
Rodan, R.P.N. (1961), International Aid for Underdeveloped Countries. *Review of Economics and Statistics*, 43:107-138.
Romer, P. (1986), Increasing Returns and Long-term Growth. *Journal of Political Economy*, 94: 1002-1037.
Romer, P. (1990), Endogenous Technological Change. *Journal of Political Economy*, 98: S71-S102.
Sahoo, D., and M.K. Mathiyazhagan (2002), Economic Growth in India: Does Foreign Direct Investment Inflow Matter? *Singapore Economic Review*, 48(2): 151-71.
Secretariate of Industrial Assistance (SIA), Directorate of Industrial Policy Promotion (DIPP), Online Database. (http://www.dipp.gov.in/fdi_statistics).
Singer, H. (1950), The Distributions of Gains Between Investing and Borrowing Countries. *American Economic Review*, 9:473-85.
Singh, R.D. (1988), The Multinationals' Economic Penetration, Growth, Industrial Output, and Domestic Savings in Developing countries: Another Look. *The Journal of Development Studies*, 25(1): 55-82.
Sjöholm, Fredrik (1999), Technology Gap, Competition and Spillovers from Direct Foreign Investment: Evidence from Establishment Data. *The Journal of Development Studies*, 36(1): 53-73.
Solow, R. (1956), A Contribution to the Theory of Economic Growth. *Quarterly Journal of Economics*, 70:65-94.
United Nations Conference on Trade and Development (UNCTAD) (1999), World Investment Report, 1999: *Foreign Direct Investment and The Challenge of Development.* (New York and Geneva: United Nations).
Van Loo Land, Frances (1977), The Effects of Foreign Direct Investment on Investment in Canada. *Review of Economics and Statistics*, L9(4), November: 474-81.
Wadhva, Charan D. (1994), *Economic Reforms in India and the Market Economy.* (New Delhi: Allied Publishers for Economic and Scientific Research Foundation).
Weisskof, T.E. (1972), The Impact of Foreign Capital Inflow on Domestic Savings in Underdeveloped Countries. *Journal of International Economics*, 2:25-38.
Wen, Mei (2002), Foreign Direct Investment, Regional Geographical and Market Conditions, and Regional Development: A Panel Study on China. *Australian Economic Review*, 25(1): 10-28
World Bank (1991/1994), World Development Report (Washington, D.C.: The World Bank).
World Bank Online Database. (http://www.worldbank/data).

Impact of Capital Flows on Economic Growth in India

A.B. ANGAPPAPILLAI AND C.K. MUTHU KUMARAN

Introduction

The recent wave of financial globalization and its aftermath has been marked by a surge in international capital flows among the industrial and developing countries, where the notions of tense capital flows have been associated with high growth rates in some developing countries. Some countries have experienced periodic collapse in growth rates and financial crisis over the same period. It is true that many developing economies with a high degree of financial integration have also experience higher growth rate. Low Developing Countries (LDCs) are eager to welcome any kind of foreign capital inflows to overcome the debt crisis situation. They are facing the challenges from the foreign capital and the invisible resource. From the supply side also there are some strong inducing factors, which led the international investors towards the financial market of the developing countries. The correlation between the movements in developed and developing countries financial market, the deceleration in industrial economy markets and high growth prospects of the less developed market are some of the important reasons, which made them an attractive option for portfolio diversification.

It is fact that international capital flows on financial market can be very volatile. However, different countries experienced different degree of volatility of financial market and this may be systematically related to the quality of macroeconomic policies and domestic financial governance. In this context high volatility of capital flows has affected the macro economic variables such as exchange rate, interest rate, money stock (M_3) and inflation negatively. Even in countries where a conductive atmosphere is created for the free flow of capital and authorities don't operate with any current account deficit complicates the assessment of integration in financial market. Capital flows have significant potential benefits for economies around the world. Countries with sound macro-economic policies and well-functioning institutions are their best to reap the benefits of capital flows and minimize the risks. Countries that permit free capital flows must choose between the stability provided by fixed exchange rates and the flexibility afforded by an independent monetary policy.

Capital flows have particularly become prominent after the advent of globalization that has led to widespread implementation of liberalization programme and financial reforms in various countries across the globe in 1990's. This resulted in the integration of global financial markets. As a result, capital started flowing freely across national border seeking out the highest return. During 1991 to 1996 there was a spectacular rise in net capital flows from industrial countries to developing countries and transition economies. This development was associated with greatly increased interest by international asset holders in the emerging market economies to find trend toward the globalization of financial markets. The global financial markets can gradually create a virtuous circle in which developing and transitional economies strengthen the market discipline that enhances financial system soundness. At present, however, there are important informational uncertainties in global market as well as major gaps and inefficiencies in financial system of many developing countries.

Looking at the composition of capital flows, net foreign direct investment represents the largest share of private capital flows in the emerging markets. Net portfolio investment is also an important source of finance in the emerging markets, though these flows were more volatile after 1994. Until 1997 a market shift, in the composition of capital flows to domestic financial market with a significant increase in net private capital inflows to financial markets and a decline in the share of official flows. Foreign Direct Investment (FDI) is the most stable capital. Both net portfolio investment and banking flows were volatile. Portfolio flows are rendering the financial markets more volatile through increased linkage between the domestic and foreign financial markets. Capital flows expose the potential vulnerability of the economy to sudden withdrawals of foreign investor from the financial market, which will affect liquidity and contribute to financial market volatility. One opinion that could be explored in the face of capital inflow surge is absorption by the external sector through capital outflows.

Financial markets are thrown open to Foreign Institutional Investors (FII's) and there is convertibility of the rupee for FII's both on current and capital account. Over the years, Indian capital market has experienced a significant structural transformation. Financial markets are significantly different from other markets; market failures are likely to be more pervasive in these markets and there exists Government intervention. Government interventions in the financial markets that promoted savings and the efficient allocation of capital are the central factor to the efficiency of financial markets.

Importance of the Foreign Capital Flows

The purpose of the flow of capital to underdeveloped countries is to accelerate their economic development upto a point where a satisfactory growth of rate can be achieved on a self-sustaining basis. Capital flows in the form of private investment, foreign investment; foreign aid and private bank lending are the principle ways by which resources can come from rich to poor countries. The transmission of technology, ideas and knowledge are other special types of resource transfer.

When discuss about the constraints of economic growth, one should referred to the saving gap and foreign exchange gap of the country. A net capital inflow contributes to the filling of the both the gaps. The capital flow of countries increases due to the amount of resources available for capital formation above what can be provided by domestic savings. It also raises the recipient economy's capacity to import goods: capital flow provides foreign exchange and eases the problem of making international payments.

Countries in early stages of development assumed to have a primary need for technical assistance and institution building and only limited need for capital assistance chiefly for infrastructure projects. As the need for capital assistance increases, the need for technical assistance shifts from general to more specific skills. The gradual increase in domestic savings and a growing capacity to attract private and other conventional foreign capital on non-concession ally term will progressively reduce the need for foreign aid. The assumption that need for foreign capital is temporary and limited is underlined several recipients in Latin America elsewhere and expected attain rapid development in ten to fifteen years but it is recognized that in Asia and Africa, the need for capital flows will remain for a much longer time.

Theoretical and empirical research on the role of foreign capital in the growth process has generally yielded conflicting results. Conventionally, the two-gap approach justifies the role of foreign capital for relaxing the two major constraints to growth. In the neo-classical framework, however, capital neither explains differences in the levels and rates of growth across countries nor can large capital flows make any significant difference to the growth rate that a country could achieve. In the subsequent resurrection of the two-gap approach, the emphasis has generally laid on the preconditions that could make foreign capital more productive in developing countries. The important preconditions comprised presence of surplus labor and excess productive demand for foreign exchange. With the growing influence of the new growth theories in the second half of the 1980s that recognized the effects of positive externalities associated with capital accumulation on growth, the role of foreign capital in the growth process assumed renewed importance. In the endogenous growth framework, the sources of growth attributed to capital flows comprise the spillovers associated with foreign capital in the form of technology, skills, and introduction of new products as well as the positive externalities in terms of higher efficiency of domestic financial markets, improved resource allocation and efficient financial intermediation by domestic financial institutions. Since the spillovers and externalities associated with different forms of foreign capital could vary, a pecking order approach to the composition of capital flows is often pursued which helps in prioritizing the capital flows based on the growth enhancing role of each form of capital. The dominant view on what drives cross-border capital flows is that marginal productivity of capital is higher in a country where capital is scarce.

Economic Reforms in India and Capital Flows

After independence, India has a comparatively unrestricted financial system until the 1960's when the government began to impose controls for the purpose of directing credit towards development programmes. Over the decade of the 1960's, interest rate restrictions and liquidity requirement were adopted and progressively tightened. Government established the state banks and nationalized commercial banks by the end of the decade. Through the 1970s and into the 1980s directed credit to rising share of domestic lending and interest rate. Subsidies became common for targeted industries, with the start of economic reforms in 1985, the government began to reduce financial controls, which were reinstated, and it began to realm ceiling on lending rates of interest.

Until reforms began in the late 1980s, international capital inflows and outflows were restricted by administrative controls, which had outright prohibition on the purchase of foreign asset by residents, direct investment by foreigners and private external borrowing. After the balance of payment difficulties in 1991, authorities began a gradual relax restriction in inward capital flows and currency convertible for current account transaction.

Over the last several years, restrictions on direct foreign investment, portfolio borrowing and foreign equity ownership have been relaxed. This was significant turn around reform banning foreign investment. Restrictions on the share of foreign enterprise for most sectors have been removed, and the upper bounds for automatic approval of direct and portfolio investment have been progressively raised. Foreign investment income is fully convertible to foreign currency for repatriation. External commercial borrowing has been relaxed but as regulated with respect of maturities and interest rate spreads. Effective restrictions continued on the acquisition of foreign financial assets by residents and on currency convertibility for capital account transaction. Recently these restrictions have been slightly eased to allow domestic resident to investment in foreign equities.

The experience of capital account liberalization elsewhere suggests that opening domestic financial markets to international capital flows exacerbates imprudent practice under weak regulation or regulatory forbearance. The large accumulation of reserves by RBI provides insurance against rapid capital outflows but at the loss of foreign interest earnings.

The rapid liberalization of financially repressed economy often leads to large capital and rapid expansion of domestic financial market followed by a capital account crisis and economic contraction. The elimination of capital controls exposes domestic capital markets and macro-economic policies to discipline of international capital market, starting a race between financial reforms and crash. Indian policy is following a determined gradual path towards economic liberalization and international integration. Following the liberalization of transaction on the current account, restrictions on capital inflows have been relaxed steadily with an emphasis on encouraging long-term investment and saving. The pattern of liberalization capital inflows in India has been the gradual raising of quantitative restriction on inflows and the size of flows that automatically approved. The gradual relaxation on restriction on capital outflows would logically follow, while restriction that discourages short-term inflow, which are the parts of current policy. Capital control means that the Government borrows on captive domestic financial market regardless of financial reforms on date. International financial integration typically leads to both inward and outward gross capital flows. Gross capital flows are indeed are much larger internationally then are net capital flows; with capital account, India could well experience a large outflow of domestic saving from high cost domestic financial intermediaries to international capital markets. The process of opening the Indian economy to foreign capital inflows is not complete and making India more attractive to FDI require more than the relaxation of constraints on inflows and foreign ownership. Domestic policy distortions and regulatory uncertainty can inhibit investment inflows, perhaps significantly. Opening up capital account to outflow could also enhance FDI.

The process was completed by the simultaneous evolution of factors encouraging the flow of private capital across the globe. The developments have stimulated a keen interest in understanding the nature and economic effects of capital flows as well as the appropriate policy responses to safeguard against financial instability that appears to be associated with the global movement of private capital.

Trends and Composition of Capital Flows into India

The 1990's saw a radical transformation in the nature of capital flow into India. From a mere absence of any private capital inflows till 1992 (expect those by Non-Resident Indians), today such inflows represent a dominant proportion of total flows. The official flows shown as external assistance, i.e., grants and loans from bilateral and multilateral sources represented 75-80 per cent of flows till 1991. By 1994, this has come down to about 20 per cent and has further fallen to below 5 per cent by late 1990s. During the last 10 years, India has attracted more than US$ 40 billion of foreign investment (Table 1). At a time, when the flow of private capital to developing countries has shrunk considerably, private flows to India have strengthened, and are currently running at US$ 9 to 10 billion per year, of which more than 55 per cent constitute FDI and portfolio flows. As a matter of fact, there has been limited recourse to bank borrowing or floating of bonds abroad by Indian corporate sector, as RBI and government tried to limit access to such borrowings to few large private companies with high credit ratings, in a policy of limiting debt creating inflow. In some years though, such debt creating flows were significant and constituted about 40 per cent of inflows.

The liberalization of the portfolio investment led to a surge in inflow of capital for investment in the primary and secondary market for Indian equity and corporate (and subsequently sovereign) bond market. About 460 foreign institutional investors (FIIs) have been allowed to enter the Indian market and together have brought in more than US $ 14 billion GDR and ADR floated by Indian corporate sector brought in the remaining portfolio inflows.

Table 1 provides an overview of the total foreign capital that India attracted during the 1992-2006 period. As the Table shows, India has attracted about $ 22 billion in portfolio investments since 1993-94 and more than $18 billion in FDI. These portfolio flows began in 1993 when India attracted more than $5 billion in few months and continued at the level of $ 2-3 billion per year till the Asian crises. The year 1998 witnessed a marginal out flow from the Indian stock market but soon the inflows went back to the US $ 2-3 billion per year level.

The first phase of stock market liberalization also saw many Indian companies issuing GDR and listing them on European exchanges. As Table 2 shows the composition of capital flows during 1993-95 more than half of the portfolio investments were the Global Depository Receipts (GDR) floated by the Indian companies while the other half was FII investments.

The FII investment was initially limited to a selected group of stocks and they were excluded from the growing market for bonds, and government securities. Their entry into the latter was permitted only in the late 1990s. The total amount of funds raised by India through GDR constituted roughly 40 percent of total inflows. However, during the second half of the 1990s there was a sharp declined in the funds raised through GDR and FII investment in the Indian equity (and recently bond market) became the main form of portfolio inflows. Thus, in a span of less than a decade, private foreign investment to India constitute more than 55 per cent of all flows. The total inflow of $ 22 billion as portfolio investment also constitutes a significant proportion of the total market capitalization in India.

The Indian economy faced first time a comfortable foreign exchange position. The rising reserves also reduced the vulnerability of the economy to minor shocks and also brought in large amount of investments from Non-Resident Indians (NRIs). The liberalization of gold imports and over all trade liberalization led to a sharp decline in capital flight and the black market premium on foreign exchange disappeared. This led to a diversion of transfer payments (mainly remittances from workers abroad) from illegal to banking channels. The

Table 1: India's Composition of Capital Inflows

(US$ million)

Variable	1990-91	1991-92	1992-93	1993-94	1994-95	1995-96	1996-97	1997-98	1998-99	1999-00	2000-01	2001-02	2002-03	2003-04	2004-05	2005-06
Total Inflows (net) of which (In %)	7056	3910	3876	8895	8502	4089	12006	9844	8435	10444	10018	10573	12133	22112	31027	24693
1. Non-Debt-creating inflows	1.5	3.4	14.3	47.6	57.9	117.5	51.3	54.8	28.6	49.7	67.8	77.1	46.6	72.5	46.7	81.7
(a) Foreign Direct investment	1.4	3.3	8.1	6.6	15.8	52.4	23.7	36.2	29.4	20.7	40.2	58.0	38.5	21.1	18.0	31.1
(b) Portfolio investment	0.1	0.1	6.2	41	42.1	65.1	27.6	18.6	-0.8	29	27.6	19.1	8.1	51.4	28.7	50.6
2. Debt creating-inflows	83.3	77.5	39.0	21.3	25	57.7	61.7	52.4	54.4	23.1	59.4	9.2	-10.7	1.4	30.6	29.9
(a) External assistance	31.3	77.7	48.0	21.4	17.9	21.6	9.2	9.2	9.7	8.6	4.3	11.4	-20.0	-12.0	6.5	6.2
(b) External commercial Borrowing #	31.9	37.2	-9.2	6.8	12.1	31.2	23.7	40.6	51.7	3	37.2	-14.9	-19.4	-8.4	16.3	7.8
(c) Short-term Credits	15.2	-13.1	-27.8	-8.6	46	1.2	7	-1	-8.9	3.6	1.0	-8.4	8.1	7.1	12.2	6.9
(d) NRI Deposits ($)	21.8	7.4	51.6	13.5	2	27	27.9	11.4	11.4	14.7	23.1	26.0	24.6	16.4	-3.1	11.3
(e) Rupee Debt-Service	-16.9	-31.7	-22.7	-11.8	-11.6	-23.3	-6.1	-7.8	-9.5	-6.8	-6.2	-4.9	-3.9	-1.7	-1.3	-2.3
3. Other Capital@	15.2	19.1	45.8	31.1	17.1	-75.2	-13	-7.2	17	27.2	-27.2	13.7	64.1	26.1	22.7	-11.6
Total (1+2+3)	100	100	100	100	100	100	100	100	100	100	100	100	100	100	100	100
Memo Item: Stable flows*	84.7	112.9	121.6	67.6	53.3	33.7	65.4	82.4	109.7	67.4	68.2	88.1	84.5	85.6	59.1	42.5

\# refers to medium and long-terms borrowings.
$ including NRNR deposits.
@ includes delayed export receipts, advance payment against imports, loans to non-residents by residents and banking capital.
*Stable flows are defined to represent all capital flows excluding portfolio flows and short-term trade credits.
Source: *Report on Currency and Finance, 2005-06, RBI.*

transfer payments rose sharply from $ 2-3 billion in 1991-92 to $ 11-13 billion by the end of the decade 1999-2000.

Table 2: Annual Capital Flows Since 1990s (US$ million)

Year	FDI	FPI	FII	NRI	ADR/GDR	TCF
1990-91	97	6	-	-	-	103
1991-92	129	4	-	-	-	133
1992-93	315	244	1	42	240	559
1993-94	586	3567	1665	89	1520	4153
1994-95	1314	3824	1503	171	2082	5138
1995-96	2144	2748	2009	169	683	4892
1996-97	2821	3312	1926	135	1366	6133
1997-98	3557	1828	979	202	645	5385
1998-99	2462	-61	-390	179	270	2911
1999-00	2155	3026	2135	171	768	5181
2000-01	4029	2760	1847	67	831	6789
2001-02	6130	2021	1505	35	477	8151
2002-03	5035	979	377	N.A.	600	6014
2003-04	4673	11377	10918	N.A.	459	16050
2004-05	5653	9313	8684	N.A.	613	14966
2005-06	7751	12492	9926	N.A.	2552	20243
2006-07P	19531	7003	3776	N.A.	3225	26534

@[1] FIIs, NRI, and GDR are introduced in 1993 September, so data before the 1993 is not available. TCF[2]: Total Capital Flows; P[3]: Projection value.
Source: Hand Book of Statistics on Indian Economy, Reserve Bank of India (RBI)

In this context, our earlier discussion arises the question whether the international capital flows have been successfully increasing the growth of the economy.

Impact of International Capital Flows on India's Economic Growth

The earlier sections provided a detailed discussion on the trends in the growth of foreign exchange reserves and the factors determining them. In the present paragraph it is attempted to examine the impact of capital flows on the economic growth of the Indian economy.

International capital flows have significant potential benefits for economies around the world. Countries with sound macro-economic policies and well-functioning institutions are in the best position to reap the benefits of capital flows and minimize the risks. Countries that permit free capital flows must choose between the stability provided by fixed exchange rates and the flexibility afforded by an independent monetary policy. International capital flows have increased dramatically since the 1980s. During the 1990s gross capital flows between industrial countries rose by 300 per cent, while trade flows increased by 63 percent. Much of the increase in capital flows is due to trade in equity and debt markets, with the result that the international pattern of asset ownership. The integration of debt and equity markets should have been accompanied by a short period of large capital flows as investors re-allocated their portfolios towards foreign debt and equity. After this adjustment period is over, there seems little reason to suspect that international portfolio flows will be either large or volatile. The prolonged increase in the size and volatility of capital flows observed that the adjustment to greater financial integration is taking a very long time, or that integration has little to do with the recent behavior of capital flows.

The nature, volatility and impact of international capital flows are still a debatable issue. In the present paragraph a preliminary attempt is being made to test whether international capital flows has the positive impact on financial market and economic growth with the help of macroeconomic variables in the India economy. Hence, the financial sector reforms to revive the capital markets help to attract the capital flows due to comparative returns. The international capital flow is expected to have a positive contribution on the economic growth of the countries explicitly.

This section presents the empirical results of the impact of international capital flows on India's economic growth after post-liberalization era. The result is based on OLS regression analysis.

Test of Stationarity

Before going to apply OLS technique the first step is test the stationary of the variables. The results of various unit root tests namely (Dicky Fuller) DF, Augmented Dicky Fuller (ADF) and PP (Phillips–Perron) tests are shown in Table 5.3. All the three tests suggest that not all the variables are having unit root at level. That means they are stationary at level. The DF, ADF and PP test are carried out using without trend and with trend option. In both the cases, results suggest that all the variables are stationary. However, the estimates show somewhat a different picture in case of the variable on Index of Industrial Production (IIP). The ADF test for IIP suggest that it is stationary at level with trend, where as DF and PP tests indicate it is stationary. However, DF and PP tests suggest that the IIP variable is stationary at level when trend is allowed, where as ADF test does not support it.

Hence, it can be concluded that IIP is stationary at level as two tests namely; DF and PP indicate that it is stationary when trend is allowed. As the tests of stationarity show that all the variables are stationary at level, the study uses these variables without taking any difference for regression analysis.

Table 3: Unit Root Tests Results

Variable	Without Trend			With Trend		
	DF	ADF	PP	DF	ADF	PP
FDI	-9.278*	-9.278* (12)	-9.759* (6)	-9.274*	-9.274* (12)	-9.759* (6)
FPI	-5.852*	-5.852* (12)	-5.852* (0)	-6.251*	-6.251* (12)	-6.251* (0)
FII	-5.421*	-5.421* (12)	-5.348* (1)	-5.919*	-5.919* (12)	-5.879* (2)
IIP	1.234	2.738*** (12)	-0.388 (6)	-6.456*	1.387 (12)	-6.685* (3)

Notes: *: Significant at 1% level, **: significant at 5% level and ***: significant at 10% level. The critical values for unit root tests are 3.48 per cent, 2.88 per cent and 2.58 per cent without trend and 4.03 per cent, 3.44 per cent and 3.14 per cent with trend at 1 per cent, 5 per cent and 10 per cent level respectively. The numbers in parentheses represent optimal lags, which are selected automatically by E-Views using Schwarz info Criterion for ADF test and newly west method for PP test.

The study regresses IIP on FDI, FPI and FII to find out the impact of capital flows on economic growth of after liberalization. The OLS technique has been used. However, the results of Durbin-Watson (DW) statistic indicate that it is very low implying the presence of auto-correlations. This violates the OLS assumptions. To solve the problem of auto-correlation of error term, the AR(1) term of residual has been allowed. This result is shown in Table 4 in Model-2.

The results show that DW statistics as 2.71 which means that still there is the presence of auto-correlations in the error terms. To get better result, the models allowing for AR (1) and AR (2) terms of the residuals have been estimated and the results are presented in Table 4 in Model-3.

Table 4: Impact of Capital Flows on Growth

Variables	Model-1	Model-2	Model-3
C	184.2699	244.9976	244.9976
	(4.7761)*	(1.2645)*	(1.2645)*
FDI	0.009901	0.010115	0.010115
	(2.2380)*	(2.1250)*	(2.1250)*
FPI	0.016291	0.013070	0.013070
	(4.1530)*	(3.0979)*	(3.0979)*
FII	-0.014096	-0.009313	-0.009313
	(3.2681)*	(-2.0570)*	(2.0570)*
AR (1)	-	0.972040	0.533676
		(34.9807)*	(5.88)*
AR (2)	-	-	0.453423
			(5.0096)*
R^2	-	0.919	0.932
Adjusted R^2	-	0.916	0.928
DW Statistics	-	2.714	
Akaike Info Criterion	-	6.782	6.610

* Indicates the t values are significant at 1 percent level.
Notes: Figure in brackets of table relate to t-value.

The DW statistics is 2.02 in Model-3, which means there is absence of autocorrelation in the error term. The R^2 of this model is comparatively higher (0.93) in Model-3 than the Model-2 (R^2 = 0.91). Also the Akaike Info Criterion (AIC) which is used for the selections of better model suggest this Model-3 as better than the Model-2, as AIC 6.610 for the Model-3 where as AIC = 6.782 for the Model-2. Hence, the Model-3 provided in Table 4 has been considered for the analysis.

The coefficient of the variables shows the effect on economic growth. In Table 4 the coefficient of FDI (α_1), FPI (α_2) and FII (α_3) are statistically significant. The t-values reported in the table to test the significance of α_1, α_2 and α_3 respectively are greater than 2. That means the coefficients are significantly different from zero (0). Therefore, all the independent variables (FDI, FPI and FII) have significant effect on economic growth. FDI and FPI are affecting IIP positively as the coefficients are 0.010 and 0.013 respectively. This supports the theory that capital flows affect economic growth positively. In the case of FII the coefficient is negative that is -0.0093 which means that FII affects IIP negatively and the effect is very negligible.

The empirical analysis showed that FII negatively affect the economic growth, where as FDI and FPI positively affect the economic growth in India. FII are more volatile in nature into Indian capital market. After some years and month FII is negative in India, due to the more volatility in Indian capital market. Volatility of FII flows probably has negative effects on economic growth. Somewhat surprising, the coefficient for the level of total capital flows is significant with negative sign of FII on economic growth in India.

Conclusion

The present study has focused on the trends in the growth of foreign exchange reserves and its components. The analysis suggested that there has been a significant positive growth in the components of reserves. The estimates on the impact of capital flows on economic growth indicated that FII negatively affect the economic growth, where as FDI and FPI positively affect the economic growth in India. Hence, it can be concluded that both the foreign exchange reserves and the macro economic variables have gone hand in hand during the study period.

REFERENCES

Agarwal, R.N. (1997), "Foreign Portfolio Investment in Some Developing Countries: A Study of Determinants and Macro Economic Impact", *The Indian Economic Review*, Vol. XXXII (2), pp. 217-29.

Bhole L.M. (1999), "Financial Market and Institution", Tata McGraw-Hill, 4th Edition.

Brenan, Micheal J. and Henery, H. (1997), "International Portfolio Investment Flows", *Journal of Finance*, Vol. LII. (5), pp. 151-93.

Chakrabarti, Rajesh (2001), "FII Flows to India: Nature and Causes", *Money and Finance*, Vol. 2, Issue 7, Oct.-Dec.

Chakraborty, Indrani. (2001), "Economic Reforms, Capital Inflows and Macro-Economic Impact in India", *CDS Working Paper*, No. 311.

Chakraborty, Indrani (2003), "Liberalization of Capital Flows and the Real Exchange Rate in India: A VAR Analysis", *CDS Working Paper*, No. 351, Sept.

Chitre, Vikas (1996), "Foreign Capital Flows and Financial Market in India", *Journal of Foreign Exchange and International Finance*, Vol. 4, pp. 275-82.

Dicky, D.A. and W.A. Fuller (1981), "Likehood Ratio Statistics for Autoregressive Time Series with a Unit Root", *Econometrica*, 49, July, pp. 1057-72.

Duttaray, Mousami, Dutt, A.K. and Mukhopadhyay, Kajol (2003), "The Relation between Foreign Direct Investment and Growth: Causality and Mechanisms", *Asian Development Review*, Vol, 83, pp. 369-75.

Enders, Walter (1995), *Applied Econometric Time Series*, John Wiley & Sons.
Engle, R.F. and Granger, C.W.J. (1987), "Cointegration and Error-Correction: Representation, Estimation and Testing", *Econometrica*, 55.
Granger, C.W.J. (1981), "Some Properties of Time-Series Data and Their Use in Econometric Model Specification", *Journal of Econometrics*, 16.
Granger, C.W.J. and Newbold, P. (1974), "Spurious Regressions in Econometrics", *Journal of Econometrics*, 2.
Kaminsky, Graciela (2005), "International Capital Flows, Financial Stability and Growth", *DESA Working Paper*, No.10, December
Khanna, S. (1999), "Financial Reforms and Industrial Sector in India", *Economic and Political Weekly*, Nov. 6, pp, 3231-38.
Khanna, Sushil (2002), "Has India Gained from Capital Account Liberalization? Private Capital Flows and Indian Economy in the 1990's", *Paper Presented at the IDEAS Conference*, "International Money and Developing Countries", Dec. 16-19.
Kohli, Renu (2001), "Capital Flows and Their Macro Economic Effects in India", *Working Paper ICRIER*, No. 64, pp. 11-42.
Kohli, Renu (2003), "Capital Flows and Domestic Financial Sector in India", *Economic and Political Weekly*, Feb. 22, pp. 761-68.
Lensik, R. Oliver, M. and Osei, R. (1999), "The Impact of Uncertain Capital Flows on Economic Growth in Developing Countries: An Empirical Analysis For the 1999's", *Paper Presented in University of Groningen*.
Lucas, R.E. (1990), "Why Does Capital Flows From Rich to Poor Countries", *American Economic Review*, Vol. 80, pp. 92-96.
Mazumdar, T. (2005) "Capital Flows into India: Implications for its Economic Growth," *Economic and Political Weekly*, May.
Mckibbin, W.J. (2003), "International Capital Flows, Financial Reform and Consequences of Changing Risk Perception in APEC Economies", *Paper Presented at Economic Studies Program*, Massachusetts.
Mishra, D. Mody, A. and Murshid, A.P. (2001), "Private Capital Flows and Growth", *A Quarterly Magazine of IMF*, Vol. 38, No. (2).
Pal, Parthapratim (1998), "Foreign Portfolio Investment in India Equity Market: Has the Economy Benefited?" *Economic and Political Weekly*, March 14, pp. 589-98.
Phillips, P.C.B. and P. Perron (1988), "Testing for Unit Root in Time Series Regression" *Biometrica*, pp. 335-46.
Prasad, E. Rogoff, K., S.J. Wei and M.A. Kose (2003), "Effects of Financial Globalization on Developing Countries: Some Empirical Evidence", *Economic and Political Weekly*, Vol. 38, Nov./Oct. 11-17, pp. 4319-30.
Rangarajan, C. (2000), "Capital Flows: Another Look", *Economic and Political Weekly*, Dec. 9, pp. 4421-27.
Rakshit, Mihir (1994), "Issues in Financial Liberalization", *Economic and Political Weekly*, Sept. 24, pp. 2547-52.
Reserve Bank of India, RBI (2006), Report on Currency and Finance, Govt. of India, India.

Reserve Bank of India (2006), RBI Annual Report, Govt. of India.

_____,(2006), Report on Currency and Finance.

S.S. Tarapore (2006), Report of Fuller Capital Account Convertibility.

Shah, Ajay and Patnaik, Illa (2004), "India's Experience with Capital Flows", *Paper Published by Ministry of Finance, India*, December.

Singh, A. and Bruce, A.W. (1998), "Emerging Stock Markets, Portfolio Capital Flows and Long-Term Economic Growth: Micro and Macro Economic Perspectives", *World Development*, Vol. 26(4), pp. 607-22.

The Role of FDI on the Economic Growth of Indian Economy

S.R. KESHAVA

Introduction

India is one of the emerging economic giants of the developing world. But few feel India has already risen. Barack Obama, when visited India in 2010 was clear when he said, 'India is not a rising power, but has already risen'. The Indian economy unshackling itself from Hindu growth rate is on growth expressway and GDP has exceeded eight percent every year since 2003-04 except previous two financial years.

The world economies were affected severely by recession in USA. The world GDP fell by -2.1, GDP of Euro 27 fell by -4.1, USA fell by -2.4, but Indian economy with stood it with positive growth of 7.7 percent (Global Economic Prospects, 2010, World Bank). The continued recession in the developed world, for the better part of 2009-10, meant a sluggish export recovery and a slowdown in financial flows into the economy. Yet, over the span of the year, the Indian economy posted a remarkable recovery, not only in terms of overall growth figures but, more importantly, in terms of certain fundamentals, which justify optimism for the Indian economy in the medium to long-term (*Economic Survey*, 2009-10).

The one of the reasons for the Indian economic growth is attributed to FDI. India is gradually becoming the prime destination of FDI in Asia after China. FDI in India is increasing significantly as India have skilled and cheap labor, enormous domestic market, English speaking technical skilled potential, more than 350 million middle class population, and favorable government policies.

During 1991 August to 2010 October, India has attracted FDI to the tune of US $ 1,39,536392 million which is 3 percent of its GDP and 7 percent of its Gross capital formation in the economy. Hence, the number of MNCs in India has also increased significantly. All the major MNCs have their branches in India and few of them are on verge of opening one in the India.

There is contradictions regarding the role of FDI in India in the process of growth for few, India is not only attracting FDI but also utilizing it successfully for its development. But few others points out that India is definitely attracting relatively more FDI, but it is leading to growing Inequality, increasing poverty and jobless growth. The MNCS have failed to generate the employment they have promised. Hence, the main objective of this paper is to:

Objectives of the Study

1. To analyze the growth of FDI in India.
2. To analyse the impact of Foreign Direct Investment on growth in India.
3. To analyse the Impact of FDI in India on exports, GDI, FOREX and other macro-variables

Hypothesis

The study seeks to verify the following hypotheses:
1. The impact of FDI on Indian economic development is moderate.
2. The role of FDI on GDI, Forex is positive.

Methodology

The present study makes use of secondary source of data collected from the publications of Government of India, Reserve Bank of India, Ministry of Industry and Commerce, World Bank, and IMF, UNCTAD, Centre for Monitoring Indian Economy (CMIE), Government of China, other than books, Journals and Periodicals. The reference period of this study relates from 1981 to 2008. Relevant statistical techniques, especially regression, have been used in the study along with simple ratios and averages.

Table 1: Major Investors
Share of Top Investing Countries FDI Equity Inflows *(Financial years)*

[Amount Rs. in Crores (US$ in millions) Ranks]

	Country	2008-09 (April-March)	2009-10 (April-March)	2010-11 (April-October)	Cumulative Inflows (April '00 - October '10)	%age to total Inflows (in terms of US $)
1.	Mauritius	50,899 (11,229)	49,633 (10,376)	20,523 (4,480)	231,429 (51,720)	42%
2.	Singapore	15,727 (3,454)	11,295 (2,379)	5,815 (1,282)	50,962 (11,472)	9%
3.	U.S.A.	8,002 (1,802)	9,230 (1,943)	4,168 (908)	41,357 (9,186)	7%
4.	U.K.	3,840 (864)	3,094 (657)	1,571 (342)	27,569 (6,226)	5%
5.	Netherlands	3,922 (883)	4,283 (899)	3,488 (768)	23,614 (5,255)	4%
6.	Cyprus	5,983 (1,287)	7,728 (1,627)	1,956 (423)	19,734 (4,322)	4%
7.	Japan	1,889 (405)	5,670 (1,183)	2,652 (586)	19,547 (4,300)	4%
8.	Germany	2,750 (629)	2,980 (626)	380 (83)	12,848 (2,882)	2%
9	France	2,098 (467)	1,437 (303)	1,485 (322)	8,404 (1,851)	2%
10.	U.A.E.	1,133 (257)	3,017 (629)	1,233 (266)	8,256 (1,815)	1%
	Total FDI Inflows	123,025 (27,331)	123,120 (25,834)	56,755 (12,397)	549,491 (122,808)	—

Source: SIA Newsletter.

Post-2000 AD, Mauritius was in first place with Investment to the tune of 47,240$ million which is 43 per cent of total investment in India from 2000 to March 2010, whereas the Singapore was in second place with investment of 10190$ million which is 9 per cent of total investment in India, closely followed by the USA with 8278$ million which is 8 per cent of total investment in India is in third place. It was followed by UK 5 per cent, Netherlands and Cyprus 4 per cent, Japan and Germany 3 per cent, UAE and France 1 per cent.

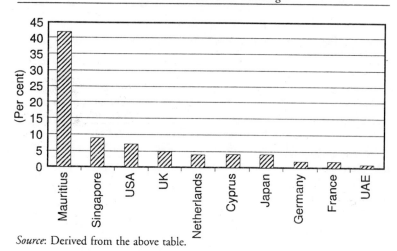

Source: Derived from the above table.

Sectors Attracting Highest FDI Equity Inflows

Table 2: Cumulative Sector-wise FDI equity inflows (from April 2000 to October 2010)

[Amount ' in crores (US$ in million)]

Ranks	Sector	2008-09 (April-March)	2009-10 (April-March)	2010-11 (April-October)	Cumulative Inflows (April 2000 to October 2010)	%age to total Inflows (In terms of US$)
1	2	3	4	5	6	7
1	Services Sector (financial & non-financial)	28,516 (6,138)	20,776 (4,353)	9,933 (2,163)	115,162 (25,764)	21%
2	Computer Software & Hardware	7,329 (1,677)	4,351 (919)	2,524 (553)	46,371 (10,426)	9%
3	Telecommunications (radio paging, cellular mobile, basic telephone services)	11,727 (2,558)	12,338 (2,554)	4,824 (1,062)	45,530 (9,993)	8%
4.	Housing & Real Estate	12,621 (2,801)	13,586 (2,844)	3,294 (716)	40,664 (9,072)	7%
5.	Construction Activities (including roads & highways)	8,792 (2,028)	13,516 (2,862)	3,239 (718)	38,932 (8,771)	7%
6.	Power	4,382 (985)	6,908 (1,437)	4,482 (729)	25,402 (5,609)	5%
7.	Automobile Industry	5,212 (1,152)	5,754 (1,208)	1,964 (436)	22,786 (5,033)	4%

1	2	3	4	5	6	7
8.	Metallurgical Industries	4,157 (961)	1,935 (407)	4,220 (920)	17,660 (4,050)	3%
9.	Petroleum & Natural Gas	1,931 (412)	1,328 (272)	2,421 (529)	13,925 (3,195)	3%
10.	Chemicals (other than fertilizers)	3,427 (749)	1,707 (362)	949 (207)	12,223 (2,703)	2%

The service sectors, both financial and non-financial was most sought after for investment, where 21 per cent of total inflows during April 2000 to October 2010 was attracted by it. it was followed by the computer Software and Hardware with 9 per cent, Telecommunications with 8 per cent, Housing and real estate and Real estate with 7 per cent, power with 5 per cent, Automobile Industry with 4 per cent, Metallurgical Industry and Petroleum and Natural Gas with 3 per cent and Chemicals with 2 per cent were other sectors which attracted more FDI during April 2000 to October 2010. the following pie chart gives the pictorial description of the same.

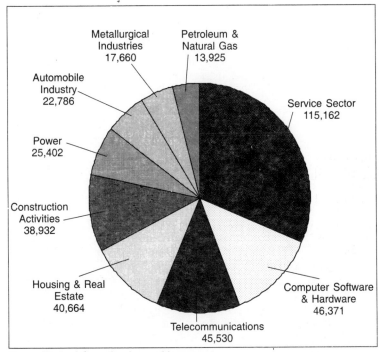

Source: Derived from the above table.

The Effect of FDI on Growth of Indian Economy

In this section an attempt is made to analyse certain variables that determines FDI, so that we can estimate the effect of FDI on economic growth. To assess the effect of four major variables namely Gross Domestic Investment (GDI), Foreign Direct Investment (FDI), Human Capital (HC), Labour Force (LF) on Gross Domestic Product (GDP). The data for the variables have been collected from the publications of Government of India, Central Statistical Organization, Reserve Bank of India and EPW Research Foundation.

The familiar Coub-douglas Production Function has been used for such an analysis, that is

$$Y = A + X_1 \alpha + X_2 \beta + X_3 \gamma + X_4 \lambda \qquad (1)$$

Where
  Y = Gross Domestic Product in year 't'
  X_1 = Gross Domestic Investment in year 't–1'
  X_2 = Foreign Direct Investment in year 't–1'
  X_3 = Human Capital in the year 't–1'
  X_4 = Labour Force in the year 't–1'

Further A is the total factor productivity that explains output growth, i.e. not accounted by all the four factors listed, α, β, γ, λ are the respective elasticity coefficient of the concerned variables as usual. This equation is transformed into linear one to facilitate to use of ordinary least square method by taking logarithmic transformation,

That is:

$$\text{Log } Y = \text{Log } A + \alpha \log X_1 + \beta \text{ Log } X_2 + \gamma \text{ Log } X_3 + \lambda \text{ Log } X_4 \qquad (2)$$

After making such a transformation the final equation is expressed as follows by the corresponding lower case letters.

$$\text{Log } y = \text{Log } a + \alpha \log x_1 + \beta \text{ Log } x_2 + \gamma \log x_3 + \lambda \text{ Log } x_4 \qquad (3)$$

The ordinary least square method yielded the following regression equation:

$$y = 2.349^* + 0.497^* + 0.121^{***} + 0.346^* + 0.069^{**}$$
$$\quad (5.916) \quad (3.928) \quad (1.655) \quad (3.710) \quad (2.339)$$

$R^2 = 0.996 \quad R^{-2} = 0.993 \quad F = 532.30 \quad \text{Durbin-Watson} = 1.825$
*—Significant at 10% level
**—Significant at 5% level
***—Significant at 1% level.

The 't' ratio for the constant (a), GDI (x_1), HC (x_3), LF (x_4) all are greater than two implying the strong significance of these variables on the GDP, but FDI is showing positive, but not relatively significant effect on GDP.

The R^2 for the model as a whole is 0.93, the F value is significantly high revealing the significance of the fitness of the model. The D-W Statistics for the model is 1.825 revealing, the problem of auto-correlation has been fairly solved.

The model shows that 1 percent increase in GDI leads to increase in GDP by all most 0.5 percent. The 1 per cent increase in FDI brings about an increase in GDP by 0.12 percent. The coefficient for human capital is 0.34 percent and that of the labour force is 0.7 percent. Thus, GDI and HC significantly affect the GDP. However, the coefficient of FDI though not significant as other variables in the study, is positive.

The Impact of FDI on Various Macro Economic Variables

In this section an attempt has been to assess the impact of FDI separately on various macro economic variables. As we all by now known, FDI involves the transfer managerial resources to the host country. There have been disagreements about the costs borne and the benefits enjoy by host and recipient country between pro-liberalization and anti-liberalization/anti-market views. One country losses need not necessarily be another country gains. Kindelberger (1969) argues that the relationship arising from the FDI process is not a zero sum game. Ex-ante, both countries must believe that the expected benefits to them must be greater than the costs to be borne by them, because an agreement would not otherwise be reached and the under lying project would not be initiated. However, believing in something ex-ante is not guarantee that it materializes ex-post. The impact of FDI on host country can be classified into economic, political, and social effects. The main intention at heart of every MNC is profitability and hence they invest where the returns are high, buy raw materials including cheap labour where it is relatively cheap. MNCs succeed because of market imperfections and cast doubts on it as claim on welfare of host country.

The conventional wisdom that FDI is always improving is no longer a conventional wisdom (Leahy and Montangna, 2000). The economic effect of FDI can be classified into micro and macro effects.

Micro Effects: The micro-effects of FDI reflect on structural changes in the economic and industrial organization. An important issue is whether FDI is conducive to the creations of competitive environment in the host country. Markusen and Venables (1997) put forward two

simple analysis channels to find the micro effect of FDI. They are:
1. Product Market Competition.
2. Linkage Effect.

Product Market Competition (PMC)

Through PMC the MNCs will be substituting the products of domestic firms in host country.

Linkage Effect

MNCs may work as complimentary firms to domestic firms in host country where it is possible for FDI to act as a catalyst leading to the development of local industry. FDI may have benefits, but it will not come without costs. The decade of liberalization and the impact of the FDI on macro-economic factors in India have to be found in this study.

To assess the impact of FDI on various relevant macro-economic variables namely exports, private final consumption expenditure, Forex, Gross Domestic Investment, gross domestic savings, trade balance, balance of payments.

23 years data from 1980-81 to 2007-08 has been taken to analyse the impact of FDI, the independent variable here is FDI which has been lagged (t–1) to assess the impact on said macro-economic variables.

Partial Coefficients with Respect to FDI

	Constant	β-coefficients	R^2	F
Exports	19084.47	7.899*	0.933	264.113
	(4.434)	(16.252)		
GDS	74930.04	19.472*	0.925	233.354
	(6.638)	(15.276)		
PFCE	444033.259	18.044*	0.855	111.859
	(29.389)	(10.576)		
GDI	3.910	0.378*	0.829	86.997
	(31.359)	(9.327)		
BOT	-8275.833	-3.0988*	0.962	483.442
	(-6.632)	(-21.987)		
Forex	8518.077	7.957**	0.934	286.329
	(1.980)	(16.381)		
BOP	578.479	1.278*	0.632	32.67
	(0.292)	(5.716)		

Notes: * Significant at 1% level;   ** Significant at 5% level.

The table furnishes the estimates of relationship of the selected individual variables with FDI. The R^2 has been significantly high excepting for the BOP variable. The signs are also as expected and the coefficient is statistically significant. Therefore, when looked at from individual variable angle, FDI is significantly affected by different by different Macro-economic variables. However, FDI being affected by several factors, the results should be cautiously read. The results do not indicate the exact 'contribution' of each variable to FDI. But at this stage it would be revealing to quote some of the studies that have arrived at similar conclusions.

Lall (1985) found a positive relationship between FDI and exports in India whereas Subramanyam and Pillai (1979) Panth (1993) and Kumar (1994) did not find any empirical evidence supporting the thesis of better export performance by foreign enterprises. Fry (1993) indicated that increase in FDI reduced national savings in the cross section data for 16 developing countries. But that does not seem to have occurred in India (Kumar and Pradhan, 2002). There is also a vibrant discussion regarding whether FDI crowds out or crown in domestic investment, but in many cases, FDI is found to complement GDI which is also the case in India.

Conclusion

India, when compared to China in becoming the attractive FDI destination, for the obvious reason such as power shortage, poor infrastructure, security consideration, absence of an exit policy etc. If India has to reach its target of attractive more FDI for its development, The Indian Policy-makers should understand that the good intentions and mere plan layouts alone are not sufficient condition, but a bold aggressive third generation reforms is the need of the hour.

Apart from it India should also channelize the FDI to the development channels and monitor the exact implementation, so that the fruits of it reach the masses.

References

Books

Bimal Jalan (1996): *Indian Economic Policy Preparing for Twenty-first Century*, Viking, New Delhi.

Blomstom, Magnus, Arikokko and Mario Zejan (2002): *FDI—Firm and Host Country Strategies*, MacMillan Press Ltd., London.

Chai, Joseph H. (1998): *China Transition to a Market Economy*, Carendon Press, Oxford.

Chopra, Chanchal (2003): *Foreign Investment in India: The Emerging Scenario*, Deep & Deep Publications, New Delhi.
Coyne, Edward J. (1995): *Targeting the Foreign Direct Investor—Strategic Motivation, Investment Size and Developing Country Investment Attraction Packages*, Kluwer Academic Publishers, Boston.
Daniels, J.P. and Vanhouse, D. (2002): *International Monetary and Financial Economics*, South Western Publishers, UK.
Easson, A.J. (1999): *Taxation of FDI: An Introduction*, Kluwer Law International, The Hague-London-Boston.
Fengli and Jing li (1999): *Foreign Direct Investment in China*, Macmilan Press, London.
Gedam, Rathnakar (1996): *Economic Reforms in India: Experiences and Lessons*, Deep & Deep Publications, New Delhi.
Kojima Kiyoshi (1986): *Foreign Direct Investment*, Croom Helm, London
Lal, S. (1985): *Multinationals, Technology and Exports*, Allied, London.
Mahajan, V.S. (1994): *Manmohan's India and other Current Writings*, Deep & Deep Publications, New Delhi.
Moosa, Imad A. (2002): *FDI: Theory, Evidence and Practice*, Palgrave, New York.
Moran, Theodore H. (2001): *Parental Supervision: The New Paradigm For FDI and Development*, Institute For International Economics, Washington.
Nagesh Kumar (2002): *Globalisation and the Quality of FDI*, Oxford University Press.
Negandhi, Anant R. (1966): *The Foreign Private Investment Climate in India*, Vora and Co., Publishers Pvt. Ltd., Bombay.
Nguyen, D.T. and Roy, K.C. (1994): *Economic Reforms, Liberalisation and Trade in Asia-Pacific Region*, Willey Eastern Ltd., New Delhi.

Reports

Relevant issues of Centre for Monitoring Indian Economy (CMIE), *New Economic Policy Measures*, Bombay.
CSO (2001: 2002): *Selected Socio-Economic Statistics of India*, Government of India, New Delhi.
EPW Research Foundation, 2002: *National Accounts Statistics of India, 1950-51 to 2000-01*, EPW Research Foundation, Mumbai.
Government of India, *Economic Survey*, Various years.
India Investment Centre: *News Letters, Monthly Reports*; Relevant Issues.
Ministry of Commerce and Industry: *SIA Newsletters*, Secretariat of Industrial Approvals, Government of India, Relevant Issues.
Relevant issues of *World Investment Report*, United Nations Conference and Trade and Development, Geneva.

Foreign Direct Investment and Economic Growth: Issues in Attracting FDI into India

S. PREETHI AND K.T. GEETHA

Introduction

Investment in capital is an important ingredient in the growth process. Countries lacking capital accumulation and technological progress usually grow much slower than countries with high investment rate and huge research and development (R&D) expenditures. Through foreign direct investment (FDI), Multinational Corporations (MNCs) can provide countries with both capital and new technology. Indeed, some recent studies conclude that FDI has been one of the most effective means of transferring technology and knowledge (Addison *et al.*, 2004; UNCTAD, 2003; Dunning and Hamdani, 1997).

Compared to most industrializing economies, India followed a fairly restrictive foreign private investment policy until 1991—relying more on bilateral and multilateral loans with long maturities. Inward foreign direct investment (FDI, or foreign investment) was perceived essentially as a means of acquiring industrial technology that was unavailable through licensing agreements and capital goods import. Technology imports were preferred to financial and technical collaborations. Even for technology licensing agreements, there were restrictions on the rates of royalty payment and technical fees. Development banks largely met the external financial needs for importing capital equipment. However, foreign investment was permitted in designated industries, subject to varying conditions on setting up joint ventures with domestic partners, local content clauses, export obligations, promotion of local R&D and so on—broadly similar to those followed in many rapidly industrializing Asian economies. Such a restrictive policy is believed to have retarded domestic technical capability (as reflected in the poor quality of Indian goods); it also meant a loss of export opportunity of labor-intensive manufactures—in contrast to many successful East Asian economies.

All this changed since 1991. Foreign investment is now seen as a source of scarce capital, technology and managerial skills that were considered necessary in an open, competitive, world economy. Over the decade, India not only permitted foreign investment in almost all sectors of the economy (barring agriculture, and, until recently, real estate), but also allowed foreign portfolio investment—thus practically diverging foreign investment from the erstwhile technology acquisition effort. Further, laws were changed to provide foreign firms the same standing as the domestic ones.

Foreign Direct Investment in India

Foreign direct investment (FDI) has played an important role in the development of the Indian economy by enabling India to achieve a certain degree of financial stability, growth and development. This money has allowed India to focus on the areas that needed economic attention, and address the various problems that continue to challenge the country. In 1998 and 1999, the Indian national government announced a number of reforms designed to encourage FDI and present a favorable scenario for investors. The Indian national government also provided permission to FDIs to provide up to 100 per cent of the financing required for the construction of bridges and tunnels, but with a limit on foreign equity of INR 1,500 crores, approximately \$352.5 m; in financial services, including the growing credit card business; buy up to 40 per cent of the equity in private banks, although there is condition that stipulates that these banks must be multilateral financial organizations; and buy up to 45 per cent of the shares of companies in the global mobile personal communication by satellite services (GMPCSS) sector. The stock of foreign direct investment (FDI) in India soared from less than US\$ 2 billion in 1991, when the country undertook major reforms to open up the economy to world markets, to almost US\$ 39 billion in 2004 (UNCTAD online database). Currently, it is being discussed to deregulate FDI restrictions further, e.g., by allowing FDI in retail trade.

Policymakers in India as well as external observers attach high expectations to FDI. According to the Minister of Finance, P. Chidambaram, "FDI worked wonders in China and can do so in India" (Indian Express, November 11, 2005). The Deputy Secretary General of the OECD reckoned at the OECD India Investment Roundtable in 2004 that the improved investment climate has not only resulted in more FDI inflows but also in higher GDP growth (OECD India Investment Roundtable 2004). The implicit assumption seems to be that higher FDI has caused higher growth. Kamalakanthan and Laurenceson (2005) however argue that FDI cannot reasonably be considered an important driver of economic growth in India because its contribution to gross fixed capital formation has remained small. Moreover, some observers doubt that economic reforms went far enough to change the character of FDI in India and, thus, result in types of FDI that may have more favorable growth effects. For example, Balasubramanyam and Mahambare (2003) as well as Fischer (2002) argue that the reforms implemented so far have not eliminated the distinct anti-export bias of India's trade policy. This may explain why, according to Arabi (2005) and Agarwal (2001), FDI in India has remained domestic market seeking. Agrawal and Shahani (2005) reckon that it is the quality of FDI that matters for a country like India rather than its quantity. FDI is often supposed to be of higher quality if it is export oriented, transfers foreign technologies to the host country, and induces economic spillovers benefiting local enterprises and workers (Enderwick, 2005).

Chakraborty and Nunnenkamp (2006), put forth that foreign direct investment (FDI) has boomed in post-reform India. Further, the composition and type of FDI has changed considerably since India has opened up to world markets. This has fuelled high expectations that FDI may serve as a catalyst to higher economic growth. They assess the growth implications of FDI in India by subjecting industry-specific FDI and output data to Granger causality tests within a panel co-integration framework. It turns out that the growth effects of FDI vary widely across sectors. FDI stocks and output are mutually reinforcing in the manufacturing sector. In sharp contrast, any causal relationship is absent in the primary sector. Most strikingly, they find only transitory effects of FDI on output in the services sector, which attracted the bulk of FDI in the post-reform era. These differences in the FDI-growth relationship suggest that FDI is unlikely to work wonders in India if only remaining regulations were relaxed and still more industries opened up to FDI.

Economic Growth and FDI Nexus

According to the standard neoclassical theories, economic growth and development is based on the utilization of land, labor and capital in production. Since developing countries in general, have underutilized land and labor and exhibit low savings rate, the marginal productivity of capital is likely to be greater in these countries. Thus, the neo-liberal theories of development assume that interdependence between the developed and the developing countries can benefit the latter. This is because capital will flow from rich to poor areas where the returns on capital investments will be highest, helping to bring about a transformation of 'backward' economies. Furthermore, the standard neo-classical theory predicts that poorer countries grow faster on average than richer countries because of diminishing returns on capital. Poor countries were expected to converge with the rich over time because of their higher capacity for absorbing capital. The reality, however, is that over the years divergence has been the case, the gap between the rich and poor economies has continued to increase. The volume of capital flow to the poor economies relative the rich has been low.

At present the consensus seems to be that there is a positive association between FDI inflow and economic growth, provided the enabling environment is created. Given the fact that economic growth is strongly associated with increased productivity, FDI inflow is particularly well suited to affect economic growth positively. The main channels through which FDI affect economic growth have been uncovered by the new growth theorists (Markusen, 1995;; Barro and Sala-I-Martin, 1995; and Borensztein, *et al*, 1998 Lemi and Asefa, 2001). Barro and Sala-I-Martin (1995) and Borensztein, *et al* (1998) in particular, developed a simple endogenous growth model which demonstrates the importance of FDI in engendering growth through technological diffusion. Typically, technological diffusion via knowledge transfer and adoption of best practice across borders is arguably a key ingredient in rapid economic growth. And this can take different forms. Imported capital goods may embody improved technology. Technology licensing may allow countries to acquire innovations and expatriates may transmit knowledge. Yet, it can be argued that FDI has greatest potential as an effective means of transferring technical skills because it tends to package and integrate elements from all of the above mechanisms. First, FDI can encourage the adoption of new and improved technology in the production process through capital spillovers. Second, FDI may stimulate knowledge transfers, both in terms of manpower training and skill acquisition and by introduction of alternative management practices and better organizational arrangements.

There have been extensive studies on the effects of foreign direct investment (FDI) on economic growth, either at the firm level or at national level. The researches in this area have been intensified during this last decade due to the increased role of FDI in total capital flows. In 1999, FDI accounted for more than half of all private capital flows to developing countries. The main argument in favor of FDI is the belief that FDI has several positive effects which include productivity gains, technology transfers, the introduction of new processes, managerial skills, and know-how in the domestic market, employee training, international production networks, and access to markets. For developing countries, FDI is also viewed as an attractive alternative to long-term bank loans as a form of capital inflow. The opposing arguments, by Singer (1950), state that FDI has a detrimental effect on the process of development of developing countries and leads to uneven global development.

Early studies on FDI, such as Singer (1950) and Prebisch (1968) claimed that the target countries of FDI receive very few benefits, because most benefits are transferred to the multinational company's country. One view about the negative effect of FDI on the host country's economic growth is that although FDI raises the level of investment and perhaps the productivity of investments, as well as the consumption in the host country, it lowers the rate of growth due to factor price distortions or misallocations of resources. Bos, Sanders and Secchi (1974) identified another factor that caused the negative effects of FDI on growth, the price distortions due to protectionism and monopolization and, finally, natural resources depletion. Saltz (1992) agree with those of Bos, Sanders and Secchi (1974), that the level of output of a host country will stagnate in cases of FDI where there might occur monopolization and pricing transfers, which will cause underutilization of labor, that will cause a lag in the level of domestic consumption demand and eventually will lead growth to stagnate.

Borensztein, De Gregorio and Lee (1998) showed that FDI allowed for transferring technology and for higher growth when the host country had a minimum threshold stock of human capital. Their results indicated also that the main way that FDI increases economic growth is by increasing technological progress, instead of increasing total capital accumulation in the host country. Their results indicated that for host countries with very low levels of human capital the direct effect of FDI on growth is negative, otherwise it is positive. Barrell and Pain (1999) explored the benefits of FDI by U.S. multinationals in four European Union countries and found that FDI may affect the host country's performance positively in cases where there are transfers of technology and knowledge though the FDI to the host economy. According to the United Nations (2001) the countries that usually attract large amounts of FDI are those with good economic conditions, a certain high level of education, a high level of macroeconomic and political stability, favourable growth prospects and favourable investment environments. It was found that although there were significant technology transfers through FDI there were no positive productivity spillovers and actually in some cases there were negative intra-industry spillovers (Czech Republic, Slovenia, Estonia).

Campos and Kinoshita (2002) examining the effects of FDI on growth for the period 1990-98, for 25 Central and Eastern European and former Soviet Union transition economies observed that FDI had a significant positive effect on the economic growth of each selected country. These results were consistent with the theory that equates FDI with technology transfers that benefit the host country. Alfaro, et al. (2002) argued that the lack of development of the domestic financial markets can reduce the domestic economy's ability to benefit from potential FDI spillovers. Carkovic and Levine (2002) indicated that for both developed and developing economies FDI inflows did not exert an independent influence on economic growth. Specifically the exogenous component of FDI did not exert a reliable positive impact on economic growth, even allowing for the level of education, the level of economic development, the level of financial development and trade openness of the recipient country.

Effendi and Femmy (2003) found that FDI has positive and significant effect on regional economic growth in the short-run but not in the long-run. They also found that export is a more important determinant of regional economic growth than import. In general, at micro-firm level-data, FDI is significant in supporting growth but at macro, national level, it is not. Balamurali and Bogahawatte (2004) indicated that foreign direct investments exert an independent influence on economic growth and there is bidirectional causality between foreign direct investment and economic growth. The finding suggests that better trade policy reforms, implementation aimed at promoting foreign direct investment and domestic investment, and restoring international competitiveness to expand and diversify the country's exports have the potential for accelerating economic growth in the future.

Kornecki et al., (2008) probing the impact of the FDI on economic growth in the Central and Eastern Europe (CEE) reiterated tremendous influence of the FDI stock on GDP growth in these countries. Jayachandran and Seilan (2010) investigating the relationship between Trade, Foreign Direct Investment (FDI) and economic growth for India over the period 1970-2007 showed that economic growth, trade and FDI appear to be mutually reinforcing under the open-door policy. In short, the undisputable world wide trend is that countries compete to win FDI capital and that global FDI stock has risen substantially over the years.

Factors Inhibiting FDI in India

As the largest democracy with the second largest population in the world and with rule of law and a highly educated, English speaking work force, India must have been considered as a safe haven for foreign investors. Yet, India seems to be suffering from a host of self-imposed restrictions and problems regarding opening its markets completely to global investors by implementing full scale economic reforms. Some of the major impediments for India's poor performance in the area of FDI are: political instability, poor infrastructure, confusing tax and tariff policies, Draconian labor laws, well entrenched corruption and governmental regulations.

1. *Political instability:* Indian politics is cacophonous and fractious, playing itself out in one of the most socially heterogeneous societies in the world with sharp social inequities, a corrupt and inefficient bureaucracy, and poor accountability of politicians (Kapur and Ramamurti, 2001). Adding to these problems is the political instability. In such an environment, the much needed economic reforms have been slow and inadequate.
2. *Infrastructure:* It is generally recognized that the state-controlled physical infrastructure is the weakest link in the economy (Sheel, 2001). The Indian government has vowed to bring its infrastructure up to date, but power cuts remain daily events, and transporting goods from place to place takes weeks (Lane, 1998). This bottleneck in the form of poor infrastructure may discourage foreign investors from investing their money in India. However, this in itself can be an opportunity for investment with the government's willingness to open the infrastructure sector to foreign investors. Even state governments are welcoming projects like roads, rural

electrification, and power generation and transmission (Pathak, Venugopal and Chandra, 2000)

3. ***Commercial Law and Government Regulations:*** Indian company law has undergone a number of significant changes in 1999, supposedly paving for smoother inflow of FDI. The Companies (Amendment) Act of 1999 allowed Indian companies for the first time to buy back their shares and substantially relaxed the restrictions on inter-corporate loans and investments. However, an indirect amendment of the law by the new guidelines of the Ministry of Industry has effectively rendered investments by international investors subject to veto by their local partners (Viswanathan, 2000). Several joint ventures between foreign and Indian companies have unraveled, forcing the investors to waste a lot of time negotiating with their Indian partners over the premium demanded for a buy-out.

4. ***Tax and Tariff:*** India has been sending mixed signals to investors by changing it tax and tariff policies without notice Sales taxes are levied by individual states and these taxes vary from state to state. This complex sales tax structure can sometimes be a deterrent to foreign investors. Coca Cola Company found that carbonated soft drinks face an excise tax of 40 per cent. These are also subjected to 17 different sales tax rates ranging from 12 to 25 per cent. Such complex tax structure can make it difficult for potential investors to project their returns accurately. In some cases, Indian government can tax companies not physically present in India but doing business there (Klein and Hirji, 2001).

5. ***Labor Laws:*** One of the biggest impediments to privatization in India is the lack of an exit policy, that is, a policy to govern the dismissal of redundant workers (Ramamurthi, 2000). The present Indian labor laws forbid layoffs of workers for any reason (Kripalani, 1998). To retrench unnecessary workers, firms require approval from both employees and state governments-approval that is rarely given (Kripalani, 2000). The pharmaceutical company Parke-Davis, India was recently reported to have paid $6.6 million to retire just 300 workers, about four times the usual rate (Treadgold, 1998).

6. ***Corruption:*** India is afflicted with what some refer to as a crisis in governance, with corruption in nearly every public service, from defense to distribution of subsidized food to the poor

people, to the generation and transmission of electric power. The complex approval procedures confronting the foreign investors are also very often intimidating. Kumar (2000) observes that a combination of legal hurdles, lack of institutional reforms, bureaucratic decision-making and the allegations of corruption at the top have turned foreign investors away from India. According to the United Nations Development Project report for South Asia in 1999, if corruption levels in India come down to those of Scandinavian countries, India's GDP growth would increase by 1.5 per cent and FDI will grow by 12 per cent (Vittal, 2001).

Conclusion

To conclude, the theoretical examination of the nexus between foreign direct investment and economic growth suggests that, by and large, foreign direct investment leads to economic growth. Still, few studies also suggest that foreign direct investment has negative influence on economic growth. But growing demand for FDI among the developing countries points to positive impact of FDI on economic growth. But for many reasons cited India lags behind and is less attractive than its neighbouring country China. If appropriate policies are adopted by the government, if the environment is conducive for FDI and if India is more absorptive then no doubt in few years India would be far ahead of many Asian countries.

REFERENCES

Addison, T. and G. Mavrotas (2004), *"Development Financing through ODA: Trends, Financing, Gaps, Key-issues and Challenges"*, UNU-WIDER, paper prepared for Track II of the Helsinki Process.

Agarwal, D.R. (2001), *Foreign Direct Investment and Economic Development: A Comparative Case Study of China, Mexico and India*. In: R.K. Sen (ed.), *Socio-Economic Development in the 21st Century*. New Delhi (Deep & Deep): 257-88.

Agrawal, R., and R. Shahani (2005), *Foreign Investment in India: Issues and Implications for Globalisation*. In: C. Tisdell (ed.), *Globalisation and World Economic Policies: Effects and Policy Responses of Nations and their Groupings*. New Delhi (Serials Publ.): 644-658.

Alfaro, L., Chanda, A., Kalemli-Ozcan, S., and Sayek, S. (2002), *FDI and Economic Growth: The role of Local Financial Markets*, paper presented at a joint Conference of the IDB and the World Bank: The FDI race : Who Gets the prize ? Is it Worth the effort?* Paper also available at: http://www.iadb.org/res/index.cfm

Arabi, U. (2005), *Foreign Direct Investment Flows and Sustained Growth: A Case Study of India and China*. Paper for DEGIT conference in Mexico-City, mimeo.

Balamurali, N., and C. Bogahawatte (2004), "Foreign Direct Investment and Economic Growth in Sri Lanka", *Sri Lankan Journal of Agricultural Economics*, Vol. 6, No. 1, pp. 37-50.

Balasubramanyam, V.N., and V. Mahambare (2003), *FDI in India. Transnational Corporations*, 12 (2): 45-72.

Barrell, R. and Pain, N. (1999), "Domestic Institutions, Agglomerations and Foreign Direct Investment in Europe," *European Economic Review*, 43, 925-34.

Barro, R. and X. Sala-I-Martin (1995), *Economic Growth*, New York: McGraw-Hill.

Borenzstein, E., J. de Gregorio and J. Lee (1998). "How does Foreign Direct Investment affect Economic Growth", *Journal of International Economics*, Vol. 45, pp. 115-35.

Campos, N.F. and Kinoshita, Y. (2002), *"Foreign Direct Investment as Technology Transferred: Some Panel Evidence from the Transition Economies"*, Centre for Economic Policy Research. Discussion Paper No. 3417. Paper also available at www.cepr.org/pubs/dps/DP3417.asp

Carcovic, M. and Levine, R. (2002), *Does Foreign Direct Investment Accelerate Economic Growth?*, Department of Business Finance, University of Minessota, Working Paper Series. Paper also available at www.worldbank.org/research/conferences/financial_globalization/fdi.pdf

Chakraborty, Chandana and Peter Nunnenkamp (2006), *"Economic Reforms, Foreign Direct Investment and its Economic Effects in India"*, Kiel Working Paper No. 1272 (March), pp.1-42.

Dunning, J.H. and K.A. Hamdani (1997), *The New Globalism and Developing Countries*, Tokyo and New York: United Nations University Press.

Effendi, Nury and Femmy M. Soemantri (2003), *"Foreign Direct Investment and Regional Economic Growth in Indonesia: A Panel Data Study"*, Working Paper in Economics and Development Studies (July), pp. 1-13.

Enderwick, P. (2005), 'Attracting "Desirable" FDI: Theory and Evidence', *Transnational Corporations* 14 (2): 93-119.

Fischer, S. (2002), *Breaking Out of the Third World: India's Economic Imperative.* (http://www.imf.org/external/np/speeches/2002/012202.htm).

Jayachandran G., and A. Seilan (2010), "A Causal Relationship between Trade, Foreign Direct Investment and Economic Growth for India", *International Research Journal of Finance and Economics*, No. 42, pp. 74-88.

Kamalakanthan, A., and J. Laurenceson (2005), *How Important Is Foreign Capital to Income Growth in China and India?* (http://www.buseco.monash.edu.au/units/aberu/papers/1405Abby.pdf).

Kapur and Ramamurthy (2001). *"India's Emerging Competitive Advantage in Services,"* *The Academy of Management Executive*, Vol. 15, No. 2, May 2001, 20-33.

Klien and Hirji (2001), *"Tax Issues When Starting a Business in India".* Vol. 27, No. 4, Fall 2001, 1-13.

Kornecki, Lucyna, Vedapuri, Raghavan and Dianne, H.B. Welsh (2008), *"Foreign Direct Investment Stimulates Economic Growth: An Empirical Evidence from Central and Eastern Europe"*, USASBE Proceedings, pp.1-10.

Kripalani (1998), "Why Indian Reforms Keep Biting Dust?" *Business Week*, May 1999, 30.

Kripalani (2000), *"India: Luring Investors Will Take Real Change"*. *Business Week*, June 4, 2001, 21-23.

Kumar (2000), *"India Rubber." Management Accounting*, Vol. 28, No. 6, June 2000, 24-27.

Lane (1998), *"World Trade Survey: India's Hesitation." The Economist*, Vol. 349, No. 8088, October 1998, 536-37.

Lemi, A. and S. Asefa (2001), *"Foreign Direct Investment and Uncertainty: Empirical Evidence from Africa,"* Paper prepared for the Allied Social Association Annual meeting held at Atlanta, GA, January 4-6, 2002.

Markusen, J.R. (1995), "The Boundaries of Multinational Enterprises and the Theory of International Trade," *Journal of Economic Perspectives*, Vol. 9, 169-89.

Pathak, Venugopal and Chandra (2000), "Destination India: What the Foreign Investors Must Know". *International Journal of Commerce and Management*, Vol. 10, No. 2, 2000, 20-31.

Prebisch, R. (1968), *Development Problems of the Peripheral Countries and the Terms of Trade*, in: James D. Theberge, ed. *Economics of Trade and Development*. New York: John Wiley and Sons Inc.

Saltz, S. (1992), *The Negative Correlation Between Foreign Direct Investment and Economic Growth in the Third World: Theory and Evidence*, Rivista Internazionale di Scienze Economiche e Commerciali, 39, 617-33.

Sheel (2001), *"Political Economy of India 1800-2001"*. *International Journal of Commerce and Management*, Vol. 11, No. 2, 2001, 1-17.

Singer, H. (1950), "The Distribution of Gains Between Investing and Borrowing Countries," *American Economic Review*, 2, pp. 473-85.

Treadgold (1998), *"India: The Good, The Bad, and The Ugly." Corporate Location*, November/December 1998, 42.

UNCTAD (2003), Trade and Development Report, 2003: *Capital Accumulation, Growth and Structural Change*, New York: United Nations.

United Nations, Secretariat of the Economic Commission for Europe (2001), *Economic Growth and Foreign Direct Investment in the Transition Economies*, Chapter 5 in Economic Survey of Europe 2001, No 1, United Nations Publications, Geneva and New York, Paper also available at www.mece.org/ead/pub/011/011_c5.pdf

Viswanathan (2000), *"Is India Being Fair to Foreign Investment?" International Financial Law Review*, Volume Nineteen, Number One, January 2000, 21- 23.

Vittal (2001), *"Corruption and the State"*. *Harvard International Review*, Volume Twenty-Three, Number Three, Cambridge, Fall 2001, 20-25.

Foreign Direct Investment, Non-Oil Export and Economic Growth in India: An Empirical Investigation

J. SRINIVASAN AND M. SHANMUGAM

I. Introduction

In India there has been large number of opportunities opened to foreign investors in early 1990s by connecting domestic economy into the global economy. As a consequence, India has achieved considerable economic growth in recent years. Accordingly export sectors shows expanation path and its annual growth rate was 32.43 percent in 2008-09 as against 21.59 percent in 1991-92. The contribution of export sector to GDP also increased from 3.56 percent in 1991-92 to 16.4 percent in 2008-09. Several factors appear to have contributed to this phenomenon including a rapid improvement in trade liberalization, concerted efforts to diversify the productive base of the economy, and a substantial increase in foreign direct investment (FDI) inflows into the country. Conversely, FDI is one of the most important strategies for the promotion of economic growth and development in poor developing countries. FDI can serve as an engine of growth and development for developing countries by increasing the opportunity for their integration into global financial and capital flows, expand employment and exports base, generate technological capability-building and efficiency spillovers to local firms, as well as establish investment arrangements that increase the potential of host countries for economic growth.

FDI may allow a country to bring in technologies and knowledge that are not readily available to domestic investors, and in this way increases productivity growth throughout the economy. Goldberg and Klein (1998) asserted that FDI may encourage export promotion, import substitution, or greater trade in intermediate inputs which often exist between parent and affiliate producers. The orientation of most investments by multinational firms is towards exports and this may most likely serve as a catalyst for the integration of the FDI host economy to a global production network in sectors in which it may formerly have had no industrial experience (OECD, 1998).

It is generally believed that growth rate of export in the developing country as an indicator of internal and external equilibrium. Now days concentration on high Foreign Direct Investment in export oriented sectors can be generate more employment and high percapita productivity and thus promote economic growth. The purpose of the study is to empirically examine casual relationship between FDI and export growth and economic growth in India that whether. In India major part of the FDI directed towards non-oil production industries. Accordingly the study seeks to answer certain questions, does FDI play any role in the ELG relationships? Are they casual relationship among the GDI, export growth and economic growth?

The rest of the paper divided into three sections. Section II comprises brief review of related literature and methodology and data source and econometric methods are given in third section. Followed by empirical findings and discussion are presented in fourth section and conclusion made in fifth section.

II. Literature Review

The role of exports in economic performance of developing countries has become one of the more intensively studied topics in recent years. The major impetus for most studies on this relationship is the export-led growth (ELG) hypothesis which interestingly represents a dominant explanation in this context. The ELG hypothesis states that the growth of exports has a favorable impact on economic growth. However, the empirical evidence on the causal relationship between exports and growth is mixed. In particular, available time series studies fail to provide uniform support for the ELG hypothesis while most cross-sectional studies provide empirical evidence in support of the hypothesis.

There have been some researcher contributed their study on FDI and economic growth and they found evidence that FDI has led to significant positive spillover effects on the labour productivity of domestic firms and on the rate of growth of domestic productivity in Mexico [Blömstrom and Persson (1983), Blömstrom (1986), Blomström and Wolf, (1994)]. Conversely, studies carried out in Mexico and Uruguay by Kokko, Tansini and Zejan (1996) cautioned that spillovers are difficult to identify in industries where foreign affiliates have much higher productivity levels than local firms.

Goldberg and Klein (1998) their attempt fails to support the significant link between FDI and aggregate exports in Latin America. According to them, the trade-promoting effects of FDI appear to be weak or insignificant with regard to Latin American trade with the United States and Japan. Their results also failed to find a systematic linkage between sectoral trade and FDI in Latin America. The generation of productivity spillovers is one possible channel through which FDI can affect growth.

Dolan and Tomlin (1980) found that FDI flows were positively associated with growth of per capita income but that the stock of FDI had a negative effect on growth. This result is supported by Saltz (1992) who confirms a negative stock effect for a sample of 75 developing countries for the period 1970-80.

Using cross-sectional data Balasubramanyam, Salisu, and Sapsford (1996) analyses how FDI affects economic growth in developing economies. OLS regression result reveals that FDI has a positive effect on economic growth in host countries with an export promoting strategy but not in countries using an import substitution strategy.

Sudhakar S. Raju (2005) found that export performance was an important cause of growth does not by itself explain how exports could have contributed to economic growth in India. In addition to their study found the existence of strong forward and backward linkages in Indian industries. The dynamic spillover effects from the export sector may have lead to an overall increase in productivity

III. Methodology

The present study was undertaken to examine the role of FDI to export growth and economic growth in Indian economy. Required data were collected from hand book on statistics of Indian economy 2009-10 and the study cover the period from 1991-92 to 2008-09. As per the literature, the variables are identified, such as real GDP (at market price) taken as a measure of economic growth. The inflow of foreign direct investment (direct investment and foreign institutional investment) and non-oil export are measured in real GDP term. The present study applied the Augmented Dickey Fuller (ADF) and Phillips Perron (PP) tests and Johensen cointegration test and Vector Error-Correction Modeling (VECM) and Impulse response functions (IRFs).

The Empirical Model

We proceed to specify the baseline empirical model which captures the hypothesized relationship among the core variables under investigation. In doing this, the endogenous growth theory is considered a very useful guide. This theory of course emphasizes the role of exports on long-run growth via a higher rate of technological innovation and dynamic learning from abroad (Lucas, 1988; Romer, 1986). The specified model is provided in equation (1) below.

$$Growth = f\, FDI\, NOX\, (1) \quad (1)$$

where,

GDP represents annual growth rate of real Gross Domestic Product at market price

FDI represents inflows of foreign direct investment as percentage to GDP, and

NOX represents non-oil export, which is measured as the ratio of as the ratio of non-oil export to GDP.

Equation (1) may only be estimated in its econometric form which is stated as follows:

$$Growth = \alpha + \beta_1\, FDI + \beta_2\, NOX + \mu_t \quad (2)$$
$$\alpha, \beta_1\, and\, \beta_2 > 0$$

where

α denotes the intercept term,

β_1, β_2 are slope coefficients representing parameters to be estimated, t,

μ_t is the disturbance term assumed to be purely random.

Testing for Co-integration

The co-integration test is meant to know the existence of long run equilibrium relationship between foreign direct investment non-oil export and economic growth. The long-run equilibrium relationship, as a statistical point of view, means the variables move together over time so that short-term disturbances from the long-term trend will be corrected. A lack of co integration suggests that such variable have no long run equilibrium relationship and in principle, they can wander arbitrarily far away from each other (Dickey *et al.*, 1991). Note that regression among integrated series is meaningful, if they involve co integrated variables. The Johansen (1988) maximum likelihood (ML) test is applied to examine the co-integration between financial deepening, foreign direct investment and economic growth. The econometric procedure of this technique is as follows: Let Xt be a (n × 1) vector of variables with a sample of t. Assuming Xt follows I (1) process, identifying the number of:

$$\Delta x_t = A_o \Pi X_{t-1} + \sum_{i=1}^{p-1} A_i \Delta X_{t-1} + \varepsilon_t \qquad (3)$$

where, vector Δx_t and ΔX_{t-1} are I (1) representation. The long run equilibrium relationship among Xt is determined by the rank of P (say r) is zero. If 0 < r < n, then there are n X r matrices of a and b such that

$$\Pi = \alpha \beta$$

Where both α and β are (n×r) matrices. The cointegrating vector have the property that $\beta' X_t$ is stationary [I (0)] even though X_t is nonstationary [I (1)] . In addition to johensen likelihood ratio test looks for two statistics such as trace and maximum eigenvalue.

The likelihood ratio tests statistics for the null hypothesis that thare are at most r cointegrating vectors is the trace test is computed as:

$$\text{Trace} = -T \sum_{i=r+1}^{n} Log\,(1 - \hat{\lambda} i) \qquad (4)$$

where $\hat{\lambda}_{r+1} - \hat{\lambda}_n$ are (*n*–1) smallest estimated Eigen values.

Likelihood ratio tests statistics for null hypothesis of r cointegrating vectors against the alternative of r + 1 cointegrating vector is the maximum eigen value test and given by

$$\text{Eigen value} = -T\,Log\,(\hat{\lambda} r + 1) \qquad (5)$$

Here, the null hypothesis of *r* cointegrating vectors is tested against the alternative hypothesis of *r* + 1 cointegrating vectors. Hence, the null hypothesis *r* = 0 is tested against the alternative *r* = 1, *r* =1 against the alternative *r* = 2, and so forth. It is well known that the cointegartion tests are very sensitive to the choice of lag length. The AIC statistics has been applied for the same.

Granger Causality Test Based on ECM

The Granger causality test (Granger, 1988) is applied to examine the causality between foreign direct investment, non-oil export and economic growth in India. The model is used for the same is as follows:

$$GDP_t = \theta_t \sum_{i=1}^{p} \alpha_1 GDP_{t-1} + \sum_{i=1}^{p} \beta_1 FDI_{t-j} + \sum_{i=1}^{p} \gamma_1 NOX_{t-k} + \lambda EC_{t-1} + e_t \quad (6)$$

$$FDI_t = \theta_t \sum_{i=1}^{p} \alpha_1 FDI_{t-1} + \sum_{i=1}^{p} \beta_1 GDP_{t-j} + \sum_{i=1}^{p} \gamma_1 NOX_{t-k} + \lambda EC_{t-1} + e_t \quad (7)$$

$$NOX_t = \theta_t \sum_{i=1}^{p} \alpha_1 NOX_{t-1} + \sum_{i=1}^{p} \beta_1 FDI_{t-j} + \sum_{i=1}^{p} \gamma_1 GDP_{t-k} + \lambda EC_{t-1} + e_t \quad (8)$$

IV. Result and Discussion

It is important in the empirical analysis to test the order of integration and co integration among the model variables. To begin with the Augmented Dickey Fuller (ADF) and Philips Perron (PP) test was performed to clarify whether the model variables level stationary or differentiated stationary.

Table 1: Unit Root Test for Stationarity

Variables	ADF Unit Root Test			
	Level (constant)	First differenced	Level (constant with trend)	First differenced
Growth	-3.515 (0)	-6.172*(0)	-3.561(0)	-6.046* (0)
FDI	1.387 (3)	-0.817 (3)	-3.994 (0)	-5.228*(0)
NOX	0.0189 (1)	-2.053 (1)	-5.157*(2)	-4.366***(2)

Philips Perron (PP) Unit Root Test

	Level (constant)	First differenced	Level (constant with trend)	First differenced
Growth	-3.499**[2]	-6.172* [0]	-3.582***[2]	-6.046*[0]
FDI	-2.095[1]	-8.437*[15]	-3.994** [0]	-8.301*[15]
NOX	0.453[1]	-6.553* [4]	-.-3.620**[3]	-6.068*[4]

Note: * indicates significant at 1 percent or rejection of the null hypothesis of no unit root at one percent Significant level, (** represents 5 percent level, and *** denotes significant at 10 percent level), ( ) parenthesis is represents optimal lag based on the Schwartz information criteria and optimal Newey-West bandwidths are in square brackets [ ].

The results of the unit root tests for stationarity of individual time series are reported in Table 1 above. The PP tests are non-parametric unit root tests that are modified so that serial correlation does not affect their asymptotic distribution. PP tests reveal that all variables are integrated of order one with and without linear trends. An inspection of the figures reveals that each series is first difference stationary at the one percent level using the PP test. What this means is that we cannot reject the presence of a unit root for any of the variables under the PP tests. However, the ADF test result is not as impressive, as only the growth variable passed the differenced stionarity test at the one percent level. We therefore rely on the PP test result as a basis for a cointegration test among all stationary series of the same order.

Testing for Co-integration (the Johansen Approach)

We investigate for the existence of any unique equilibrium relationship(s) among the stationary variables of the same order of integration. The Johansen methodology is a VAR based approach. The results based on VARs are generally found to be sensitive to the lag length used and this compelled us to devote a considerable time to the selection of the lag structure. Variables lag lengths were chosen by minimizing the Akaike information criterion. The selected lag length(s) are thus those that reduce autocorrelation in the model. The results are presented in Table 2 below.

Table 2: Results of the Co-integration

Trace Tests				
Hypothesized number of CEs	Alternative hypothesis	Eigen value	Trace statistic	5 percent level of significance
r=0*	r=1	0.806001	39.324	35.011
r<=1	r=2	0.541794	13.086	18.397
r<=2	r=3	0.036728	0.599	3.841

Maximum Eigen value Test

Hypothesized number of CEs	Alternative hypothesis	Eigen value	Trace statistic	5 percent level of significance
r=0*	r=1	0.806001	26.238	24.252
r<=1	r=2	0.541794	12.487	17.148
r<=2	r=3	0.036728	0.599	3.841

*denotes first order rank co-indegration at 5 percent significant level.

Both the trace and maximum eigenvalue test results reveal the existence of two unique cointegrating vectors between test variables. These assumptions are in any case consistent with the level that minimizes the Akaike information criterion for the selection of the optimal lag interval of (1, 1). Using co-integration tests we found the presence of one co-integrating vector between foreign direct investments, non-oil export and economic growth. The result indicates that there is long-run equilibrium relationship between the model variables.

Causality Results Based on Vector Error Correction Model

The existence of cointegration relationship implies that there is long run equilibrium relationship between them. The existence of cointegration indicates that an Error Correction Model is appropriate. All variables in the cointegrating equation are assumed endogenous in a VAR structure. The VECM extends this by making use of differenced data and lagged differenced data of the chosen variables in a VAR structure. An essential element of the VECM is the error correction term or factor. The coefficient of the error correction term is theoretically expected to be negatively signed and have a value between zero and one. This is to ensure that equilibrium error correction within the system over time is at least meaningful. Besides, the VECM contains vital information on causal relationships and the dynamic interactions among the cointegrating variables.

Table 3: Estimated Co-efficient of the Vector Error Correction Model Result

	Growth	FDI	*****NOX
Growth	—	0.117	0.272***
FDI	1.963**	—	0.259
NOX	0.665	0.423	—
EC_{t-1}	-0.442	0.271	-0.476*

except lagged error correction term (ECT_{t-1})
*denotes significant at 1 percent level.

Table 3 clearly show that the presence of a unidirectional short-run causality running from non-oil export to economic growth. The above results found evidence to the export led growth hypothesis in India. In addition to uni-directional causality runs from economic growth to foreign direct investment and FDI to economic growth. The empirical evidence fails to explain the causality between FDI to non-oil export growth. The error correction term for changes in non-oil export is highly significant even at the one percent level indicating the evidence in support of long-run casual relationship from non-oil export to economic growth in India. The following impulse response are clearly indicating the relationship between the foreign direct investment, non-oil export and economic growth.

V. Conclussion

The export led hypotheses were investigated by using econometric tools. The study results provide evidence to support the ELG hypothesis. Moreover the study fails to demonstrate evidence of causal relationship between FDI and non-oil export.

REFERENCES

Balasubramanyam, Salisu and Sapsford (1996), Foreign Direct Investment and Growth in EP and IS Countries, *The Economic Journal*, Vol. 106, pp. 92-105.

Blomström and Wolf (1994), Multinational Corporations and Productivity Convergence in Mexico. In W. Baumol, R. Nelson and E. Wolf (Eds.) *Convergence of Productivity: Cross-National Studies and Historical Evidence*. Oxford: Oxford University Press.

Dolan, Michael and Brian Tomlin (1980), First World-Third World Linkages: External Relations and Economic Development, *International Organization*, Vol. 34, No. 1. (Winter, 1980), pp. 41-63.

Goldberg and Klein (1998), Foreign Direct Investment, Trade, and Real Exchange Rate Linkages in Developing Countries. In Reuven Glick (ed.) *Managing Capital Flows and Exchange Rates: Lessons from the Pacific Basin*. Cambridge University Press.

Kokko, Tansini and Zejan (1996), Local Technological Capability and Spillovers from FDI in the Uruguayan Manufacturing Sector, *Journal of Development Studies*, 34, 602-11.

OECD (1998), *Foreign Direct Investment and Economic Development: Lessons from Six Emerging Economies*. Paris.

Saltz (1992), The Negative Correlation between Foreign Direct Investment and Economic Growth in the Third World: Theory and Evidence. *Rivista Internazionale di Scienze Economiche e Commerciali*. 39(7), pp. 617-33.

Sudhakar S. Raju (2005), Export and economic growth in India: Co-integration, causality and Error Correction Modeling: A note, *Indian Journal of Economics and Business*, FindArticles.com. 29 Dec, 2010.

Foreign Direct Investment and Economic Growth

M. THAHIRA BANU AND R. VAHEEDHA BANU

Introduction

FDI is the process whereby residents of one country (the home country) acquire ownership of assets for the purpose of controlling the production, distribution and other activities of a firm in another country (the host country).

The literature on foreign direct investment (FDI) and economic growth generally points to a positive FDI-growth relationship. However, very few studies offer direct tests of causality between the two variables. In theory, economic growth may induce FDI inflow, and FDI may also stimulate economic growth. India's recently liberalized FDI policy (2005) allows-up to a 100 per cent FDI stake in ventures. Industrial policy reforms have substantially reduced industrial licensing requirements, removed restrictions on expansion and facilitated easy access to foreign technology and foreign direct investment FDI. The upward moving growth curve of the real-estate sector owes some credit to a booming economy and liberalized FDI regime. In March 2005, the government amended the rules to allow 100 per cent FDI in the construction business. This automatic route has been permitted in townships, housing, built-up infrastructure and construction development projects including housing, commercial premises, hotels, resorts, hospitals, educational institutions, recreational facilities, and city- and regional-level infrastructure. A number of changes were approved on the FDI policy to remove the caps in most sectors. Fields which require relaxation in FDI restrictions include civil aviation, construction development, industrial parks, petroleum and natural gas, commodity exchanges, credit-information services and mining.

India is widely recognized as an emerging global economic power. Indian economy recorded rate of economic growth 8.4 per cent in the current fiscal year 2005-06. This is evidence enough for an economy to be called as high performing economy. The sustained high rate of economic growth in the first half of the first decade of the 21st century has allowed India to join the club of high growth performing economies of East Asia and China. Indian policy-makers have been encouraged to pursue more vigorously the ongoing reform program because of the fact that it is their firm belief that high growth is the result of liberal economic policy. Therefore, Indian policy-makers are preparing through their painstaking endeavors to achieve double digit rate of growth in the coming years.

Foreign direct investment has been seen as a dominant determinant to achieve high rate of economic growth because it brings in scarce capital resource, raise technological capability and increase efficiency through enhancing domestic competition. Chinese experience of achieving high growth through foreign direct investment has been sited as worth emulating policy lesson for the Indian economy.

However, the skeptics have argued that the high growth rate of the Indian economy is path dependent and have had the long experience of institution building which ultimately resulted into high rate of economic growth. Furthermore, the structure of the Indian economy is such that it is highly rural-oriented and large section of population is still very poor and lacking essential capabilities to participate in the modern process of economic growth. There is growing evidence of marginalization of the large section of the rural population and increasing unemployment in the rural areas. The economic advisory council of Prime Minister of India has recently cautioned for adverse consequences of such a grave situation in the face of high performing Indian economy. The market-oriented policies normally have exclusionary impact which needs to be prevented through articulate response of the policy-makers.

Accelerated Economic Growth

With a GDP of US$ 803 billion in 2005, India is the third largest economy in Asia, after Japan and China. Worldwide, the Indian economy ranks 10th on a nominal basis, according to a July 2005 World Bank report (it is the fourth largest economy on a purchasing power parity basis), generating about 2 per cent of global GDP. Between 1947 (when India gained independence) and 1990, a system of elaborate regulations known as the "License Raj," which was dismantled in the early '90s, stifled private-sector growth. During the early '90s, the government also decided to shift toward greater integration with the world economy. Since then, India has gradually opened its market by reducing government controls on foreign trade and investment.

Economic liberalization and structural reforms provided the foundation for strong economic growth, averaging 5.9 per cent per year. As reforms progressed, the GDP growth rate rose from 3.5 per cent in the 1950s and 1960s to about 6 per cent in the 1990s. Social indicators also reflect a matching improvement. According to World Bank reports, the percentage of India's population living below the poverty line fell from more than 50 per cent in the 1950s to about one-quarter of the population today. Despite ongoing reforms and progress in liberalizing foreign direct investment (FDI), India remains a relatively closed economy. On the IMF's trade restrictiveness index, India scores seven out of 10, suggesting that the country is still not as open to foreign goods and services and, more importantly, knowledge as it could be. This is partly reflected by a relatively low historic GDP correlation with the major economies

Trends of Foreign Direct Investment in India

The sources of FDI usually affect the nature of economic outcomes. Therefore, it is important to analyze the most important source countries from where FDI is pouring in India. It is amazing to note that Mauritius has emerged as the top most investor countries in India (Table 1).

Table 1: Top 10 Investor Countries in India, 1991-2004

Country	FDI Inflows Millions $	Percent Share
Mauritius	9000.8	27.53
USA	4440.68	13.58
Japan	1891.32	05.78
Netherland	1867.83	05.71
UK	1692.45	05.18
Germany	1255.57	03.84
France	743.69	02.27
South Korea	682.98	02.09
Singapore	641.02	01.96
Switzerland	530.60	01.62
Total	32690.99	100.00

Total stock of investment from Mauritius was 9000.8 million dollars with 27.53 per cent share. It is important to note here that India has tax avoidance treaty with Mauritius since 1982.

Therefore, multinational companies preferred to invest in India via Mauritius. Second largest investor country is USA and accounts for 13.58 per cent of the total FDI. Japan is not only an important investor in India but has been regarded as most beneficial in terms of brining in new technology and having higher spillover effects on Indian firms. Apart from traditional investors (UK, Germany and France), South Korea and Singapore have emerged other important Asian countries which have substantially increased their stakes in India.

Table 2: Top Ten Sectors Attracting FDI Inflows, 1991-2004

Country	FDI inflows (Millions $)	Percent share
Electrical Equipments	4862	16.62
Transport industry	3124	10.39
Service sector (financial and non-financial)	2908	09.94
Telecommunication	2863	09.60
Fuels	2514	08.49
Chemicals	1887	05.92
Food processing industries	1173	03.72
Drugs and pharmaceuticals	946	03.21
Cement and gypsum product	746	02.57
Metallurgical industries	624	02.13

The sectors/activities-wise FDI inflows and respective relative shares are presented in Table 2. The most attractive sector for FDI is the electrical equipment. The relative share of FDI in this industry was 16.62 per cent. Transport industry accounts for 10.39 per cent of FDI. These two industries alone cover more than one-fourth of the total FDI which clearly shows the high degree of concentration FDI in a few activities. Financial and nonfinancial services were also quite important where foreign investment has poured in. This share is nearly10 per cent. Fourth and fifth place goes to telecommunication and fuels where foreign investors have shown substantial interest and their respective shares are 9.6 per cent and 8.49 per cent respectively. Rest of the economic activities has relative shares which lie between less than six per cent to more than two per cent of the FDI.

Table 3: Top Seven States According to FDI Approvals Between August 1991 to December 2004

State	Amount Approved (Millions $)	Percent share
Maharashtra	9640.37	14.82
Delhi	8445.36	12.19
Tamil Nadu	5895.99	09.05
Karnataka	4837.22	07.63
Gujarat	3278.24	04.98
Andhra Pradesh	3055.12	04.65
Madhya Pradesh	252093	03.70

State-wise FDI approved amount and their relative shares are presented in Table 3 to examine the preference for destination of foreign companies. National capital city, that is, Delhi and surrounding areas of Utter Pradesh and Haryana, Maharashtra-Dadra and Nagar Haveli, and Daman and Diu constituted for almost 50 per cent of the total inflows during the period 1991 to 2004 (*Economic Survey*, 2005-06). However, when we examine the amount approved Maharashtra state topped in terms of preferred destination for foreign investors. Tamil Nadu, Karnataka and Gujarat attracted substantial amount approved and their respective shares were 9.05 per cent, 7.63 per cent and 4.98 per cent. The top seven states received investment proposal and amount approved more than 55 per cent which show high degree of concentration of FDI. Therefore, there is a strong need to make some changes in FDI policy so that equitable distribution of such flows can be ensured.

In recent years, India's share in the global FDI inflows has increased from 0.5 per cent in 2002 to 0.8 per cent in 2004. In terms of FDI inward stock, the global share of India is 0.44 per cent in the year 2004. However, China has received 9.4 per cent of global FDI inflows and 2.75 per cent of the global FDI inward stock in the year 2004 (UNCTAD, 2005). India has received one-twelfth of FDI inflows in the year 2004 compared with China. India's effort have not yet realized in comparison to the changes which has been made in the FDI policy. Global ranking of India in terms of FDI preferred destination has improved but realization is very low. Even the FDI approvals are largely in the infrastructure, but the actual inflows are more in the consumer durable goods and automotive industries. Capital goods sector has more or less been bypassed by the FDI.

This clearly points out the tendency of foreign investment to exploit the pent up domestic demand for consumer durable goods. Furthermore, there is a gradual increase in the mergers and acquisitions during the 1990s which show a tendency of FDI inflows to acquire existing industrial assets and managerial control without actually engaging in new productive activities. India's large size of domestic market seems to have been the major attraction for foreign firms. Economic reform program in general and FDI reforms in particular has been regarded as pro-economic development. The suggested mechanism through which it can work is the increase in competition that compels domestic agents of production to improve their efficiency and productivity as well as introduce new variety and high quality products. The presence of FDI has also been considered as a rich source of indirect effects on the domestic firms to learn to improve numerous business practices. Foreign investment inflows are expected to bring in widely publicized technology and productivity spillovers which will make domestic firms more efficient and competitive.

These positive effects as contemplated in theory if are realized in actual practice, then economic agents of production brings in self-sustained economic growth in an economy. These kinds of arguments have been put forward by Indian policy-makers while making economic policy more FDI friendly. One and half decade of liberalization program has passed and therefore, there are enough evidence which have accumulated to test especially the impact of the presence of MNEs on the improvement in efficiency and productivity of the Indian firms.

In a comprehensive study, Das (2004) has shown that total factor productivity of Indian industries increased at a slower pace during the 1990s compared with the pre-reform period. Further evidence, while dividing the 1990s period into the early and late nineties, has been provided to shows that total factor productivity growth was lower in the second half (1996-2000) compared with the first half (1991-95). Economic Survey, 2005-06 of the Government of India has also recognized this fact on the basis of several other studies conducted by various institutions and well acclaimed economists. These 14 results have been obtained with homogeneity assumption (that is, all firms are alike) might not be valid. Firms operating in an industry may differ in terms of their access to technology and other intangible assets, therefore, reforms might result in gainers and losers. Thus, there is a possibility of widening productivity gap—a phenomenon called convergence and divergence in economic literature.

Indian Economy: Current Status and Future Prospects

Per capita income of India was US $ 620 in the year 2004. However, per capita income when measured in terms of purchasing power parity (PPP) was US $ 3120 in the year 2004. Thus, both the figures of per capita income of India provide her the status of a low income country. It is little on the higher side of average per capita income of the low income countries. India's low per capita income is mainly because she supports huge size of population which was 1.08 billion- approximately 17 per cent of the world population in the year 2004. In absolute terms, India is now recognized as one amongst the large sized economies of the world. When we judge Indian economy in terms of gross national product, it was US$ 673.2 billion. Accordingly, her global rank was 11th in the year 2004.

This is quite a respectable global rank and the expectation is that in the next quarter century or so she will be occupying third position just next to USA and China. Furthermore, this is being justified by both international institutions and the leading economists on the basis of recent growth momentum shown by the Indian economy have designated her as a running tiger. India has been placed at a better pedestal in terms of achieving global position compared even with China because of the strong institutional system developed by democratic India over the years. However, the matter of fact is that India is now widely acclaimed and recognized as an emerging global economic power. This recognition granted by the credible experts and institutions is a ground enough to look back and analyze how has India emerged as a faster growing country and how will India sustain growth momentum in terms of constraints of huge size of population which is poor and looking for gainful economic opportunities.

India began her development program with the First Five Year Plan in the year 1950-51. The policy process adopted during the early planning era fundamentally strived to achieve self reliant growth under the import substitution regime like many other Asian countries. This process has allowed Indian economy to initiate modern economic growth and as was expected to face numerous problems. Therefore, policies have to match to encounter the problems as and when aroused. This evolution of policy process and economic growth has ultimately resulted into the mature response of policy-making and high rate of economic growth. Indian economy has grown steadily at 4.36 per cent per annum during the period 1950-51 to 2004-05, that is, nearly five and half decades. During the same period, per capita income has grown at a rate of 2.02 per cent (Table 4). When we divide the whole period into two sub-periods, that is, 1950-51 to 1979-80 and 1980-81 to 2004-05, the growth rates of GDP and per capita income recorded in the first sub period and second sub-period differ substantially.

Table 4: Rates of Economics Growth of Indian Economy, 1950-51 to 2004-05 (at 1993-94 prices)

Year	Gross Domestic Product	Per Capita Income	Primary Sectors	Secondary Sectors	Tertiary Sectors
1950-51 to 2004-05	4.36	2.02	2.50	5.30	5.40
1950-51 to 1979-80	3.50	1.22	2.20	5.30	4.50
1980-81 to 2004-05	5.70	3.50	2.90	6.10	7.10
1980-81 to 1990-91	5.40	3.20	3.10	6.70	6.60
1991-92 to 2004-05	6.09	4.10	2.50	6.00	7.80

The first period rate of GDP growth was 3.5 per cent which is typically known as the Hindu rate of growth associated with the name of late Raj Krishna. Per capita income increased at a rate of growth of 1.22 per cent during the first sub period. This growth of GDP and per capita income has been regarded as meager when viewed from the perspective of high performing Asian economies, but quite respectable compared with India's colonial period growth. It is important to note here that the second sub period, that is, 1980-81 to 2004-05, recorded amazingly high growth rates which can very easily regarded as a departure from the Hindu rate of growth. The rates of growth of GDP and per capita income were 5.7 and 3.50 per cent per annum respectively (Table 4). If we divide the second sub-period into two further sub-periods, that is, 1980-81 to 1990-91 and 1991-92 to 2004-05, the growth rates perceptibly higher for the period 1991-92 to 2004-05 compared with the period 1980-81 to 1990-91. The growth rate of GDP during the eighties was 5.4 per cent and for per capita income it was 3.2 per cent per annum. Whereas, the GDP and per capita income growth rates were 6.09 and 4.1 per cent per annum respectively during the period 1991-92 to 2004-05. This high growth rate of both GDP and per capita income compared with the previous period has been essentially attributed to the success of the pro-market oriented policies adopted by the Union government of Indian since July 1991. An important fact need to be noted here with regard to long-run growth rate in the second half of the twentieth century is that the structural break in the growth has occurred at the year 1980-81 and not at 1991-

92. The stepping up of the rate of growth in the 1980s has been essentially attributed to the expansionary macro-economic policies of the late seventies.

Table 5: Distribution of Gross National Product Across Sectors

Year	Primary Sector	Secondary Sector	Tertiary Sector
1950-51	59.20	13.29	27.51
1960-61	54.75	16.61	28.64
1970-71	48.12	19.91	31.97
1980-81	41.82	21.59	36.59
1990-91	34.93	24.49	40.58
2000-01	26.55	23.62	49.83

And the eighties resulted into expansion of aggregate demand. These policies also stepped up the investment-GDP ratio from 18.7 per cent in the 1980-81 to 24.1 per cent in 1990- 91. Trade liberalization in the late seventies and deregulation of industrial policies in the 1980s has substantially contributed in the acceleration of rate of growth in the eighties. The liberal import of capital goods and restrictions to borrow from international institutional sources has generated strains on the balance of payments. Government's debt financing from commercial borrowings along with current account imbalance due to liberalization of imports has culminated in the crisis of 1991. The occurrence of 1991 crisis has been used by some of the prominent economists as evidence against the sustainability of growth momentum which was unleashed by the expansionary macroeconomic policies initiated in the late 1970s and during the decade of 1980s. It needs to be noted here that it has been recognized that the acceleration of economic has occurred in the 1980s which was a dramatic departure from the earlier three decades.

This acceleration of economic growth rate was maintained in the 1990s. However, there is further acceleration in the rate of economic growth in the early 21st century. The sectoral rates of economic growth also showed a similar acceleration except primary sector. An important distinction which can be noted from the sectoral growth rates is that tertiary sector recorded higher growth rate compared with secondary sector during the 1990s and beyond (Table 5). The engine of economic growth of the Indian economy is now service sector rather than industrial sector.

The sect oral distribution of the GNP during the period 1950-51 to 2000-01 presented in Table 5 clearly show structural changes which has occurred during the second half of the twentieth century. The primary sector which was predominant in the 1950-51 with GDP share 59.2 per cent has reduced to a marginal sector with a relative share of GDP 26.55 per cent in 2000-01. The secondary sector has improved its relative position from 13.3 per cent in 1950-51 to near 24 per cent in the year 2000-01. Tertiary sector has emerged as a leading sector of the Indian economy and improved its relative share in GDP from mere 27.5 per cent from 1950-51 to nearly 50 per cent in 2000-01. The structural change that has occurred during the second half of 20th century provides the credence to the view that engine of growth of the Indian economy is service sector led.

The strong macroeconomic fundamentals, growing size of the economy and improving investment climate has attracted global corporations to invest in India. A major outcome of the economic reforms process aimed at opening up the economy and embracing globalization has led to tremendous increase in Foreign Direct investment inflows into India.

According to AT Kearney, India ranks second in the world in terms of attractiveness for FDI. AT Kearney's 2007 Global Services Location Index ranks India as the most preferred destination in terms of financial attractiveness, people and skills availability and business environment. Similarly, UNCTAD's World Investment Report, 2005 considers India the 2nd most attractive investment destination among the Transnational Corporations (TNCs). The positive perception as a result of strong economic fundamentals driven by 16 years of reforms has helped FDI inflows grow at about 20 times since the opening up of the economy to foreign investment since August 1991.

The major sources of FDI in India are through both the equity route, which accounted for 82 per cent of the total FDI inflows in India. Reinvested earnings of FDI companies accounted for 15 per cent of the total Direct Investment. Acquisitions accounted for 32 per cent of total FDI.

Mauritius has been the major route for FDI inflows into India due to the Mauritius's stature with India as a tax haven and most volume of FDI inflows through Mauritius has been from the USA and the major investor (FDI) in India for the last 16 years has been USA.

Sectors that have attracted major portion of FDI are manufacturing industries and services such as Financial and Business Services. During the year 2006-07, the major recipient of FDI was Financial and business

Figure 1: Foreign Investment (In Billion $)

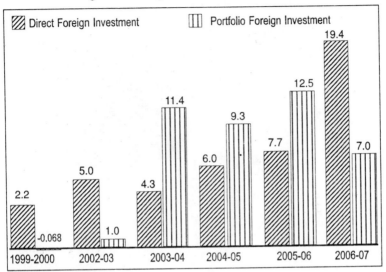

Source: Reserve Bank of India.

services (US $ 4.4 billion) during 2006-07.

Manufacturing was the next largest recipient of FDI at US $ 1.6 billion. Overall, during the period August 1991 to May 2007, Manufacturing attracted the major portion of FDI inflows in India.

Figure 2: Country-wise FDI Inflows in India (From August 1991 to May 2007)

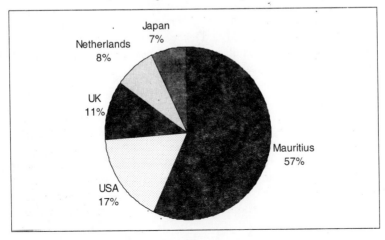

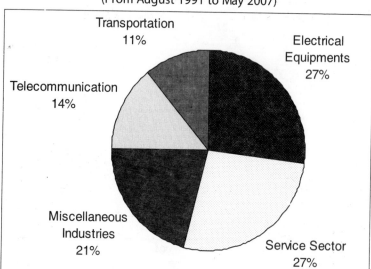

Figure 3: Shares of Major Sectors in FDI Inflows (From August 1991 to May 2007)

Overseas FDI by Indian Corporations

Increasing Competitiveness of Indian industry due to globalization of Indian Economy has led to emergence and growth of Indian multinationals. This is evident from the FDI overseas from India, which increased by 13.5 times during the last 7 years. The year 2006-07 witnessed large overseas acquisition deals by Indian corporate to gain market shares and reap economies of scale, supported by progressive liberalization of the external payments regime.

Overseas investment that started off initially with the acquisition of foreign companies in the IT and related services sector has now spread to other areas such as manufacturing including auto components and drugs and pharmaceuticals.

Conclusion

Direct investment is a category of cross-border investment made by a resident entity in one economy (the "direct investor") with the objective of establishing a "lasting interest" in an enterprise resident in an economy other than that of the investor (the "direct investment enterprise"). The lasting interest is evidenced when the direct investor owns 10 per cent of the voting power of the direct investment enterprise.

A foreign direct investor is an entity that has a direct investment

Figure 4: FDI Abroad (US $ billion)

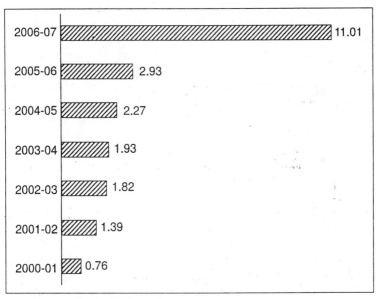

Source: Reserve Bank of India.

Figure 5: Sectoral Share of FDI Abroad (1 April 2003 to 31 March 2007)

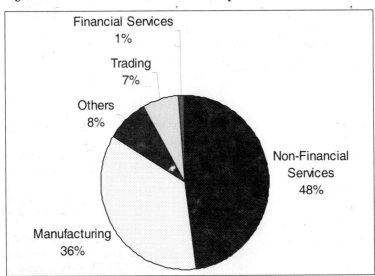

Source: Reserve Bank of India.

enterprise operating in a country other than the economy of residence of the foreign direct investor. A direct investor could be: an individual (or a group of related individuals; an incorporated or unincorporated enterprise; public or private enterprise (or a group of related enterprises); a government; estates, or trusts or other organisations that own enterprises.

A direct investment enterprise is as an incorporated or unincorporated enterprise (including a branch) in which a non-resident investor owns 10 per cent or more of the voting power of an incorporated enterprise or the equivalent of an unincorporated enterprise. Direct investment is composed of: equity capital, reinvested earning and other capital. Equity capital comprises: (i) equity in branches; (ii) all shares in subsidiaries and associates (except non-participating, preferred shares that are treated as debt securities and included under direct investment, other capital); and (iii) other capital contributions.

India is experiencing a tremendous structural transformation. Although still an emerging market, India's demographic and economic growth prospects are very favorable; the country is expected to become one of the world's five largest economies within 20 years. India's shift to a service-based society supported by its promising growth profile is generating long-term demand across all major investment sectors in its many markets. However, foreign investors trying to capitalize on growth opportunities and diversification benefits face typical merging market risks, such as low liquidity and a lack of transparency. Investors need patience and a long-term strategic approach backed by local partners to enter this key global economy and to take advantage of the increasing institutionalization of India's real estate market.

REFERENCES

Ahluwalia, M.S., 2002. "Economic Reforms in India since 1991: Has Gradualism Worked?," *Journal of Economic Perspective*, Vol. 16, No. 7, 67-88.

Banga, R., 2004. "Impact of Japanese and US FDI on Productivity Growth: A Firm-Level Analysis", *Economic and Political Weekly—Review of Industry and Management*, Vol. 34, No. 5, 441-47.

Das, D.K., 2004. "Manufacturing Productivity Under Varying Trade Regimes, 1980-2000", *Economic and Political Weekly—Review of Industry and Management*, Vol. 34, No. 5, 423-33.

Dasgupta, S. and A. Singh, 2005. "Manufacturing, Services, Jobless Growth and the Informal Economy: Will Services be the New Engine of Indian Economic Growth?" Paper presented in the conference on WIDER Thinking Ahead: The Future of Development Economics, June 17-18, 2005, WIDER, Helsinki, Finland, 17.

Gill, A., 2006. "The Punjab Peasant: He Too Dies in Debt", *Mainstream Weekly*, Vol. XlIV, No. 24, 19-25. Government of India, 2005. Handbook of Industrial Statistics, 2003-05, Department of industrial Policy and Promotion, Ministry of Commerce and Industry.

Government of India, 2005-06. Economic Survey, 2005-06, Ministry of Finance, Government of India, New Delhi: Government of Indian Press.

Nagraj, R., 2006. *Aspects of India's Economic Growth and Reforms*, New Delhi: Academic Foundation.

Nayyar, D., 2006. "Economic Growth in Independent India: Lumbering Elephant or Running Tiger?" *Economic and Political Weekly*, Vol. XLI, No. 15, April 15, 1451-58.

Panagariya, A., 2004. "Growth and Reforms during the 1980s and 1990s", *Economic and Political Weekly*, Vol. 39, No. 25, 2581-94.

Panagariya, A., 2006. "Pro-Market Reforms and Growth", *The Economic Times*, Vol. 3, No. 126, June 28, Chandigarh.

Ray, S., 2004. "MNEs, Strategic Alliances and Efficiency of Firms: Emerging Trends", *Economic and Political Weekly—Review of Industry and Management*, Vol. 34, No. 5, 434-40.

Siddharthan, N.S. and K. Lal, 2004. "Liberalisation, MNE and Productivity of Indian Enterprises", *Economic and Political Weekly—Review of Industry and Management*, Vol. 34, No. 5, 448-53.

Srinivasan, T.N. and S. Tendulkar, 2003. Reintegrating India with the World Economy, New Delhi: Oxford University Press.

UNCTAD, 2005. World Investment Report, 2005: Transnational Corporations and the Internationalization of R&D, New York: United Nations.

Foreign Direct Investment and Economic Growth in India

TRIPURA SUNDARI, C.U. AND BALAJI, B.

Introduction

Investment in a country by individuals and organisations from other countries is an important aspect of international finance. This can take the form of portfolio investment or Direct Investment. Foreign Direct Investment will continue to be an increasingly important source of development finance. It has become a key battleground for emerging markets and some developed countries. Given the appropriate host-country policies and a basic level of development, a number of research studies had shown that FDI triggers spillovers, assists in human capital formation, contributes to international integration, helps to create a more competitive environment and enhances the chances of surprise development. All these factors contribute to a higher level of economic growth.

(i) Theoretical Literature

The FDI theory and growth theory have been developed separately for several years. The theoretical foundation for empirical studies on FDI and growth is derived either from the neo-classical models of growth or the endogenous growth models. The Neo-classical model was an extension of the 1946 Harrod-Domar model that included a new term, productivity growth. The most important contribution was by Robert Solow in 1956 where Solow and T.W. Swan developed a relatively simple growth model. In neo-classical model of growth, FDI increases the volume of investment or its efficiency and leads to long-term and medium-term level effects and a transitional increase in growth. The endogenous growth theory or new growth theory was developed in 1980s as a response to criticism of the neo-classical growth model. This model considers long-run growth as a function of technological progress and provides a framework in which FDI can permanently increase the rate of growth in the host economy through technology transfer, diffusion, and spillover effects.

Foreign direct investment is viewed as a major stimulus to economic growth. Despite FDI's potential to boost technology, productivity, investment and savings, economists have somewhat surprisingly struggled to find a strong causal link to economic growth. Economic growth also leads to foreign direct investment due to the fact that higher levels of economic growth will be attained through efficient use of resources, which reduces cost per unit of output, and creates market for the output produced. This will attract higher levels of Foreign Direct Investment. The above arguments create the phenomenon of economic growth and Foreign Direct Investment as complex in nature. The question of the causality between investment and growth is not a new one. Even Kuznets, who was a foremost proponent of the crucial role of investment in fixed capital, noted that there were cases where the acceleration in economic growth had preceded the rise in capital formation (Kuznets, 1973, p. 129). If FDI has a positive impact on economic growth, then a host country should encourage FDI flows by offering tax incentives, infrastructure subsidies, import duty exemptions and other measures to attract FDI. If FDI has a negative impact on economic growth, then a host country should take precautionary measures to discourage and restrict such capital inflows.

(ii) Empirical Literature

Studies on FDI are enormous and ranges from simple case studies to cross country comparisons. It is an indisputable fact that a good number of studies have been conducted in the field of FDI. Various theoretical studies have shown that FDI can serve as a channel for transferring technology to a host country. De Gregorio (1992) argues that a positive role for FDI generates economic growth mainly in a particular environment. A positive effect on economic growth from the interaction between secondary school enrolment and imports of machinery was found by Romer (1993). Balasubramanyam, *et al.* (1996) stress that trade openness is vital for obtaining the growth effects of

FDI. Borensztein, et al. (1998) argues that FDI has a positive growth effect when the country has a highly educated workforce that allows it to exploit FDI spillovers. Dua and Rashid (1999) attempts to identify the causality between FDI and growth in India using monthly data, Alfaro, et al. (2000) find that FDI promotes economic growth in economies with sufficiently developed financial markets. Chakraborty and Basu (2002) found that real GDP in India is not Granger caused by foreign direct investment. The impact of foreign direct investment and imports on the economic growth in Indonesia, Malaysia, Philippines and Thailand was analysed by Marwaha and Tavakoli (2004) by employing separate production function for each country. A strong and positive effect was revealed when Yao (2006) tried to find the effect of exports and foreign direct investments (FDI) on economic performance in china. The FDI-led growth hypothesis was re-examine by Herzer, et al. (2008) and finds no positive unidirectional long-term effect from FDI to GDP.

If a positive link between FDI and growth is accepted, investigation of the determinants of FDI becomes crucial. To explain the choice of FDI, it is necessary therefore to take into consideration the location specific factors either in home or host countries. These include variables such as trade barriers and other government policies, market characteristics, costs and productivity. Wang and Swain (1995), Lansbury, et al. (1996), Woodward, et al. (1997) and Holland and Pain (1998), conclude that the main factors, which have driven FDI in transition countries, have been a need to secure market access, opportunity to participate in large scale privatization process and the degree of political and economic stability. A number of survey studies by Andrews (1972), Reuber, et al. (1973) Wang and Swain (1995) confirmed that size or growth of market is one of the most important determinants of FDI. Riedel (1975), Young (1978), Majumdar (1980) and Tsai (1991) concluded that relative low wage is one of the most important factors of absorbing FDI in the case of South-East Asian economies. Moore (1993) and O'Sullivan (1993) find that exchange rate changes/risks are strongly correlated with FDI. Ahmed (1975), Root (1978) and Petrochilos (1989) supported a negative correlation between the inflow of FDI and political instability. Edwards (1992), Singh and Jun (1995), and Bathattacharya, et al (1997) have found that openness has a positive influence on FDI. Hermes and Lensink (2003), Alfaro, et al. (2004) and Durham (2004) provide evidence that only countries with well-developed financial markets gain significantly from FDI in terms of their growth rates.

The main limitations in most of the studies is that, the analysis is conducted based on yearly data series, while economic growth process may be influenced either in the short-run or in the long-run. However, short-run impacts of relationship between economic growth and Foreign Direct Investment and country specific studies pertaining to developing countries are limited in the literature. Also, the study is based on limited theoretical foundation and is also limited by data considerations.

According to the United Nations (2001) the countries that usually attract large amounts of FDI are those with good economic conditions, with a high level of education, a high level of macroeconomic and political stability, favourable growth prospects and favourable investment environments. They are considered to be fast growing economies. During the first three decades after independence, foreign investment in India was highly regulated. In the 1980's there was some easing in the foreign investment policy in line with the industrial policy regime of the time. The major policy thrust towards attracting FDI wad outlined in new industrial policy statement of 1991. Since then, continuous efforts have been made to liberalise and simplify the norms and procedures pertaining to FDI. India's FDI inflow registered a rapid growth as shown in the Table 1. From US $ 45.86 million in 1970, the FDI flows rose to $ 79.16 million in 1980 and further to $ 236.69 million in 1990. It reached $ 3587.99 million in 2000, and further increased to $ 34,613 million in 2009.Also, the share of India when compared with developing economy rose from 1.18 percent in 1970 to 7.24 percent in 2009.

Table 1: Trends in FDI Inflow (in US$ Million)

Year	1970	1980	1990	2000	2009
Developing Economy	3,854.359	7,477.013	35,095.65	256,465.2	478,349
India	45.46 (1.18)	79.16 (1.06)	236.69 (0.67)	3,587.99 (1.40)	34,613.15 (7.24)

Figures within parenthesis indicate the percentage to the Developing Economy.
Source: UNCTAD, World Investment Report, 2009.

On the above background, the present article investigates (i) the causal nexus between Foreign Direct Investment and economic growth, and (ii) the main factor that contribute to this FDI flow, with special reference to India. The rest of the paper is organized as follows: Section 2 presents the methodology of the study. Empirical results and discussion are presented in Section 3. Finally, the concluding remarks are presented in Section 4.

II. Methodology

Simple ratio and percentage method were employed to examine the trend and pattern of Foreign Direct Investment. The causal nexus between FDI and economic growth, in India is analysed using Granger causality test (Grangers, 1969). Granger causality test assumes that data series are stationary, to verify the stationary properties of FDI and GDP, the standard unit roots test like augmented Dickey-Fuller (ADF) test and Phillips-Perron (PP) test is used. Quarterly data for FDI and GDP (proxy for economic growth) from January-April 1996 to January-April 2010 is used to check the causality. The necessary information is collected from various issues of the Handbook of Indian economy, Reserve bank of India bulletin.

(i) Granger Causality

. The Granger (1969) test for causality between two variables is employed for this study. The test indicates that, for two time-series variables X_t and Y_t, if X improves the prediction of Y, then X (Granger) causes Y. The estimating equations can be written simply as follows:

$$GDP_t = \sum_{i=1}^{n} \alpha_i GDP_{t-i} + \sum_{p=1}^{n} \beta_i FDI_{t-i} + \mu_t$$

$$FDI_t = \sum_{i=1}^{n} \lambda_i GDP_{t-i} + \sum_{p=1}^{n} \delta_i FDI_{t-i} + \eta_t$$

Where GDP_t and FDI_t are stationary time series, μ_t and η_t are white noise error term and *i* and *j* are the maximum lag length used in each time series. The optimum lag length is identified using Akaike information criterion (AIC) and Schwarz information (SC) criterion. Granger Causality test states that Y is not only influenced by lagged value of Y but also lagged values of X, then X causes Y. On the other hand if X is influenced by lagged values of Y in addition to lagged values of X then Y causes X. If X causes Y and Y also causes X then it is known as bi-directional relationship between X and Y. Further, if X doesn't cause Y and Y doesn't cause X then it is known as an independent relation between X and Y. A simple F-test can convey whether the lagged values of X contribute significantly to the explanatory power of Y equation.

(ii) Determinants of FDI

The Multiple Linear regression method which is employed to examine the determinants of FDI is presented below:

FDI = f {GDP, Openness, Exchange rate, Inflation, Labour, Govt. expenditure, Infrastructure, Attractiveness}

As it is standard in the literature, the dependent variable is the net inflow of FDI at time t. The number of independent variables examined in many theoretical and empirical studies is very large. Based on the earlier literature the major factors that are identified to influence the FDI inflow in the present study is discussed below:

Market size: GDP or GDP per capita is widely used in the literature as a proxy for market size.

Openness of the Economy: Trade intensity in terms of either share of imports or exports (or both) to GDP (in percent) is used as a proxy for openness.

Market structure: exchange rate depreciation induces foreign investors' wealth to rise, enabling them to outbid their competitors abroad for information intensive assets having monitoring costs.

Macroeconomic stability: A history of low inflation and prudent fiscal activity signals to investors how committed and credible the government is. To measure stability, the annual average inflation rate is used.

Cheap labor: Low labor costs or availability of cheap labor will be an important factor affecting FDI. Here labor force availability is proxied by ratio of economically active labor force, those with ages between 15 and 64 to total population (POP).

Size of the government: This variable is measured as the ratio of government expenditure to GDP in percent (serves as a policy variable). Therefore, aggregate FDI flows will increase in proportion to a depreciation of the domestic currency.

Infrastructure: Good infrastructure is a necessary condition for foreign investors to operate successfully, regardless of the type of FDI. It allows faster transport and communication and is therefore likely to foster FDI. Here, the number of main telephone lines per 1000 population is used as a proxy to measure infrastructure development.

Attractiveness: Growth rate per capita GDP influences the foreign capital inflow. It is used as a measure of attractiveness of the host country's market. The FDI determinant is analyzed by employing annual data from 1990 to 2009 for the variables defined.

III. Empirical Results and Discussions

To verify the stationary properties of FDI and GDP, the standard unit roots test like augmented Dickey-Fuller (ADF) test and Phillips-Perron (PP) test, is used. The optimum lag length for ADF is determined by the Schwartz Bayesian Criterion, while for PP test, the optimal bandwidth is determined by Newey-West. The test results are reported in Table 2. The ADF and PP test accepts the null hypothesis of a unit root in its level whereas it rejects it in the first order.

Table 2: Unit Root Test Statistics for FDI and GDP, 1996:01–2010:01

Variable	ADF		PP	
	Level	First difference	Level	First difference
FDI	-1.049	-6.479*	-1.080	-9.945*
	(0.72)	(0.00)	(0.71)	(0.00)
GDP	1.824	-7.174*	1.824	-6.247*
	(0.99)	(0.00)	(0.99)	(0.00)

*indicates significance at the 95 per cent level. Values in parentheses are p-values. All equations includes intercept and trend.

Table 3 reveals the results of Granger causality test between Foreign Direct Investment and Gross Domestic product. The test was experimented upto lag 3,3. The computed F value is insignificant throughout the experiment. Hence, it can be concluded that Foreign Direct Investment and Economic growth are independent. The possible reasons could be (a) Lack of full integration of capital and financial markets, (b) In India, Foreign Investment is only 2.81 per cent of Gross Domestic Product (in 2009) and its high transaction cost in the form of corruption and unnecessary regulatory requirements fails to attract Foreign Direct Investment, and (c) Higher levels of economic growth may not attract foreign investment due to lack of stability of Indian rupee in international market.

Table 4 presents the regression result of the determinants of FDI, the estimated equation is able to explain the variability of dependent variable to the extent of 96 percent and the F value is significant at 1 percent level. From the table it can be viewed that the important factor

Table 3: Granger-Causality Test Results between Foreign Direct Investment and Gross Domestic Product

Lag Length	FDI does not Granger Cause GDP	GDP does not Granger Cause FDI	Inference
1 lag	0.20387	0.02701	Independent
2 lags	0.25601	1.17935	Independent
3 lags	0.33241	0.56416	Independent

Table 4 : OLS Result for the Determinants of FDI

Variable	Coefficient	t-statistic
Constant	24.698	0.303
GDP	-11.994	2.708***
Openness	3.033	1.833**
Exchange rate	-2.987	1.00
Inflation	29.932	3.726***
Government expenditure	-6.873	2.143**
Labour	-12.709	0.255
Infrastructure	-2.860	2.354**
Growth of per capita GDP	7.977	0.903
R^2	0.9589	
F	29.198*	

*** indicates 1% level of significance, ** indicates 5% level of significance.

that determines FDI flow is the size of the market, inflation rate, openness, government expenditure and infrastructure.

IV. Concluding Remarks

The analysis revealed an independent relationship between Foreign Investment and Economic Growth in India. The possible reasons are: (a) In India, Foreign Investment is only 2.81 per cent of Gross Domestic Product and its high transaction cost in the form of corruption and unnecessary regulatory requirements fails to attract Foreign Direct Investment, (b) Lack of full integration of capital and financial markets, and (c) Higher levels of economic growth may not attract foreign investment due to lack of stability of Indian rupee in international market.

The present result calls for the following policy options to enhance economic growth through Foreign Direct Investment and *vice versa*: (i) A stable exchange rate policy is a must in maintaining good economic performance, as movements in the exchange rate may produce negative impacts on economic prosperity, (ii) Our democratic framework attracts large foreign investors. The countries should not only focus on attracting more FDI but also look into the policies that will allow maximization of benefits through appropriate composition of the flows by attracting new investment, and (iii) Maintenance of stability of Indian rupee in terms of foreign currency.

REFERENCES

1. Alfaro, L., Chanda, A., Kalemli-Ozcan, S. and Sayek, S., "FDI and Economic Growth: The Role of Local Financial Markets", *Journal of International Economics*, Vol. 64, No. 1, 2000, pp. 89-112.
2. Alfaro, L., Chanda, A., Kalemli-Ozcan, S. and Sayek, S., "FDI and Economic Growth: The Role of Local Financial Markets", *Journal of International Economics*, Vol. 64, No. 1, 2000, pp. 89-112.
3. Aneesa I. Rashid, Pami Dua & Aneesa I. Rashid, "Foreign Direct Investment and Economic Activity in India," Working papers 62, Centre for Development Economics, Delhi School of Economics. 1999.
4. Balasubramanyam, V.N., Salisu, M. and Sapsford, D., "Foreign Direct Investment and Growth in EP and IS Countries", *Economic Journal*, Vol. 106, 1996, pp. 92-105.
5. Bathattachaary, A., Montiel, P and S. Sharma, "Private Capital Flows to Sub-Saharan Africa: An Overview of Trends and Determinants" in Z. Iqbal and R. Kanbur eds, External Finance for Low-Income Countries. IMF, 1997.
6. Benson, Durham J., "Absorptive capacity and the effects of foreign direct investment and equity foreign portfolio investment on economic growth", *European Economic Review*, Vol. 48, No. 2, 2004, pp. 285-306.
7. Borensztein, E., De Gregorio, J. and Lee, J., "How Does Foreign Direct Investment Affect Economic Growth?" *Journal of International Economics*, Vol. 45, 1998, pp. 115-35.
8. Chakraborty, C. and Basu, P., "Foreign Direct Investment and Growth in India: A Cointegration Approach", *Applied Economics*, Vol. 34, 2002, pp. 1061-73.
9. Dawn Holland & Nigel Pain, "The Diffusion of Innovations in Central and Eastern Europe: A Study of the Determinants and Impact of Foreign Direct Investment," NIESR Discussion Papers 137, National Institute of Economic and Social Research, 1998.
10. Dierk Herzer, Stephan Klasen and Felicitas Nowak-Lehmann D., "In Search of FDI-Led Growth In Developing Countries: The Way Forward", *Economic Modelling*, Vol. 25, No. 5, 2008, pp. 793-810.
11. Edwards, S., "Capital Flows, Foreign Direct Investment, and Debt-Equity Swaps in Developing Countries" In H. Seibert Ed. *Capital Flows in the World Economy*, Institute Fur Weltwirtschaft an Der Univeritat Kiel. 1992.

12. Granger, C.W.J., "Investigating causal relations by econometric models and cross-spectral methods", *Econometrica*, 37 (1969), pp. 424-38.
13. Grant L. Reuber, with H. Crookell, M. Emerson, G. Gallais-Hamonno, "Private Foreign Investment in Development", Oxford: Clarendon Press, 1973.
14. Hermes, N., Lensink, R., "Foreign Direct Investment, Financial Development and Economic Growth", *Journal of Development Studies*, Vol. 40, No. 1, 2003, pp. 142-63.
15. James Riedel, "The nature and determinants of export-oriented direct foreign investment in a developing country: A case study of Taiwan," *Review of World Economics* (Weltwirtschaftliches Archiv), *Springer*, Vol. 111, No. 3, 1975, pp. 505-28.
16. Kanta Marwaha and Akbar Tavakoli, "The effect of foreign capital and imports on economic growth: further evidence from four Asian countries (1970-98)," *Journal of Asian Economics*, Vol. 15, 2004, pp. 399-413.
17. Kuznet, Simon, "Population, Capital and Growth. Selected Essays," Norton, New York, 1973.
18. Majumdar, B., "A case study of industrial organisation theory of direct foreign investment," *Weltwirtschaftliches Archiv*, Vol. 116, 1980, p. 353.
19. Moore, M.O., 'Determinants of German manufacturing direct investment: 1980-1988', *Weltwirtschaftliches Archiv*, 129, 1993, pp. 120-37.
20. Petrochilos, G.A., *Foreign Direct Investment and the Development Process: The Case of Greece*, Avebury: Gower Publishing Company Ltd., 1989.
21. Romer, P., "Idea Gaps and Object Gaps in Economic Development", *Journal of Monetary Economics*, 32, 1993, pp. 543-73.
22. Shujie Yao, "On Economic Growth, FDI and Exports in China", *Applied Economics*, Vol. 38, 2006, pp. 339-51.
23. Singh, H. and K. Jun, "Some New Evidence on Determinants of Foreign Direct Investment in Developing Countries", Research Working Paper No. 1531, 1995 World Bank Policy, Washington, D.C.
24. Tsai, Pan-Long, "Determinants of foreign direct investment in Taiwan: An alternative approach with time-series data", *Journal of World Development*, Vol. 19, Nos. 2-3, 1991, pp. 275-85.
25. United Nations, Secretariat of the Economic Commission for Europe, 2001, Economic Growth and Foreign Direct Investment in the Transition Economies, Chapter 5 in *Economic Survey of Europe*, 2001, No. 1, United Nations Publications, Geneva and New York, Paper also available at: www.mece.org/ead/pub/011/011_c5.pdf
26. Young, A.S., "Factors affecting flows of direct foreign investment in Southeast Asian economies", *Journal of Philippine Development*, Vol. 96, 1978.
27. Zhen Quan Wang and Nigel Swain, "Determinants of Inflow of Foreign Direct Investment in Hungary and China: Time-Series Approach", *Journal of Internal Development*, Vol. 9, No. 5, 1997, pp. 695-726.

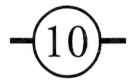

FDI in Multi-Brand Retail Business—Opportunities and Challenges

P.G. ARUL

With the acceptance of new economic policies in the 1990's, India became a free market nation. This paved way for huge amounts of Foreign Direct Investment (FDI) through NRI's International Companies and various other Foreign Investors in the different sectors of business. The growth story of India inc. and other economy has been robust since then, with occasional ups and downs. FDI has come as a shot in the arm, in terms of increased capital flow, improved technology, management expertise and access to international markets.

Over the last few years, many international retailers have entered the Indian market on the strength of rising affluence levels of the young Indian population along with the heightened awareness of global brands, international shopping experience and the increased availability of retail real estate. Development of India as a sourcing hub further makes India an attractive retail opportunity for the global retailers.

Retail Trends in India

- The total retail trade in India is estimated at US$ 330 billion. Organized retail at 6 per cent (Rs. 86400 crore 864 billion).
- According to the Credit Rating and Information Services of India, the industry ranked in US$ 25.44 billion turnover in 2007-08 as against US$ 16.99 billion in 2006-07, a whopping growth rate of 49.73 per cent.
- 97 per cent of this is accounted for by the 12 million

traditional outlets (the unorganized sector).
- According to NCAER (National Council of Applied Economic Research), the Indian middle class (household income between US$ 4,500-23,000) currently stand at 92 million, is expected to cross 153 million by 2010.
- Retail industry accounts for 35 percent of India's GDP.

Government Policy on FDI in Retail Business

"There is no proposal to change the current FDI policy on retail trade" said the Minister of State for Commerce and Industry Mr. Jyothiraditya Scindia, in the Lok Saba in a written reply in the parliament. The minister said that retail is a labour intensive sector and is the second largest employer after agriculture. The government is fully committed to securing the legitimate interests of all stakeholders engaged in the retail business. The government also fully recognizes the need to ensure that small retailers are not adversely affected by the growing organized retail and that there is no adverse effect on employment. Currently, FDI is not permitted in the retail business, except in single brand retailing where FDI upto 51 per cent is permitted with prior approval from the government. There is also a condition that products should be sold under the same brand internationally and single brand product retailing would cover only products which are branded during manufacturing.

The new regulation has kept most foreign retailers at bay. Current Government policy prohibits foreign direct investment in retail business except for single brand retail that fulfils the following conditions:

- Foreign equity does not go beyond 51 percent.
- Foreign Investment Promotion Board (FIPB)/Department of Industrial Policy & Promotion (DIPP) approval has been issued.
- Products to be sold are of a Single Brand only.
- Products are sold under the same brand internationally.
- Single Brand Products covers products that are branded during manufacturing.
- Additions to the product categories to be sold under 'single brand' require fresh Government approval.

The government of India however allows FDI only in the cash and carry formats and to the extent of 51 per cent in single brand retail. This brings an opportunity for Indian enterprise to collaborate with global majors and bring in global best practices in the business of retailing. The Current norms of government allow foreign retailers to set-up in India via the franchisee route, as has been done by the Wal-Mart, Marks & Spencer and Mango. Foreign retailers are allowed outlets if they manufacture products in India (Benetton) or source their goods domestically. The government has allowed 51 per cent FDI in single-brand retail in 2005. Single-brand retail implies that a retail store with foreign investment can sell multiple products only under one brand. Present policy allows having a presence of international brands through different routes like franchise, joint ventures, manufacturing, distribution, and cash and carry forward. 100 per cent FDI is allowed in "cash and carry" outlets, where goods are sold only to those who intend using them for commercial purposes (Metro, Shoprite) (ET, 2nd Nov., 2008). Foreign retailers therefore, have access to the Indian retail market, while India loses out on the investment. FDI is not allowed in multi-brand retail.

Foreign companies are not permitted to source goods locally and then retail them in India by using their brand names. Also, permission is granted to only those brands that are regular product lines of foreign companies and sold internationally, in effect meaning that foreign retailers cannot experiment with new brands just for the Indian consumer. The companies have to tie-up with a local partner.

Currently, the Foreign Investment and Promotion Board (FIPB) allows foreign companies to test products for a two year period, at the end of which they are required to roll out their manufacturing schedule.

Foreign Investment Entry Strategies

India's retail trade is largely in the hands of the unorganized sector. Only recently, large supermarkets, departmental stores and luxury shopping malls have started making their entry in some cities. These are owned and managed by Indian promoters, though some foreign retailers have made backdoor entry through franchises and export-oriented wholesale activity.

Since foreign retailers can enter India through some routes, the existing bans or caps on FDI have not acted as outright entry restrictions. The fallout has been two-fold; India is losing some foreign investment while policies remain unclear, and for foreigners wanting a foothold, the entry process has become opaque and complicated. To date, franchising has been the preferred route through which foreign retailers have entered India. For example, brands like Pizza Hut, Lacoste, Mango, Chanel, Louis Vuitton, Nike and Marks & Spencer have all entered via franchise agreements.

The big multinational supermarket chains have been chopping at the bit to enter India, and the only ones to have done so are Metro Cash & Carry GmbH, Shoprite Checkers of South Africa and most recently Wal-Mart, which has signed a joint venture agreements but not opened its first wholesale outlet.

Metro was the first company to bring in 100 per cent FDI through this route and has taken tentative steps so far. It started out with two outlets in the suburbs of Bangalore in 2003 and now has a third outlet in Hyderabad, but has battled regulations such as a ban on trade in agricultural products under Agricultural Produce Marketing Cooperatives Act since. Metro announced in Dec. 2007 that it plans to open another 15-18 stores by 2010.

Wal-Mart's plans are similarly cautious. Despite the perception that once in, Wal-Mart will rapidly expand, its plan so far is to open just 15 wholesale outlets with Bharati Enterprises by 2015. Given that it is the first time Wal-Mart has entered a country via the Wholesale sector, the aim appears to be investing and developing a supply chain to prepare the company for the day that all remaining barriers to investment are removed.

Another arm of the venture is an agreement to supply Bharti Retail with its products, which is setting up front end retail stores. Bharti Retail has also entered a franchise agreement with Wal-Mart, which will see Wal-Mart provide technical support to Bharti Retail.

Why India is Worried about FDI in Retailing?

- Global retailers will kill the local 'kirana' industry.
- FDI in retail could lead to millions of job losses.
- Global retailers will put pressure on farmers and suppliers.
- Predatory pricing policies will lead to monopolies and harm the consumer.
- Global retailers will trigger growth in cities, causing skewed urban development.

FDI—Opportunities for Organized Retail Business

An intense debate has been raging in the country on the policy towards FDI in the organized retail sector. At the macro-level, FDI in retail will enable Indian economy to integrate with the global economy. Entry of foreign players in Thailand and China gave a big boost to retail and the exports. It will help to overcome both the lack of experience in organized retailing as well as lack of trained manpower. If retailing is opened up to FDI, recruitment is expected to gather momentum-employment in the sector to go up to as high as 20 per cent of the workforce. In the next few years to come, retailing will be unmatched in terms of its potential for employment generation, both in numbers and quality of professionalism.

India has a particular need for FDI in distribution on a large scale. Approximately 20-40 percent of perishable produce is wasted due to multiple intermediaries, wastage during transportation and storage, high cycle times and an absence of cold storage systems. The supply chain would be made more efficient through economies of scale in procurement and transportation, bulk storage, trend forecasting and improvements in sales analysis patterns to minimize inventory

Some Experts from retail industry predicts FDI will bring technology to develop logistics and supply chains, helping food processing industry to grow, provide employment to millions, easier availability of quality products and enhance competition in the retail space. Organized retailing brings more efficiency into the supply chain, benefiting both producers as well as consumers.

The large and medium retailers have advantage over the small retailers in achieving the desired cost reduction and can offer better price to customers than the traditional retail outlets. With the emergence of large and new forms of retailing after liberalization, Indian consumers started gaining from the market. They not only offer competitive price but also force the competitors to reposition their strategies to remain in the business.

A proposal to allow FDI in food retail is being considered. This will boost our agriculture sector and our farmers will be able to reap benefits of economic liberalization. It could transform the rural economy by generating economic activity and large scale employment in rural areas. FDI would help in putting in place an efficient retail network, which in turn would benefit millions of small farmers and artisans. The logic is that since 30 per cent of agricultural produce goes waste, opening up of the retail sector will trigger higher investments in supply chain and back-end infrastructure such as cold chains and enable better market access to farmers. The development of back-end linkages and structured distribution network will reduce agricultural wastage and thereby lower food grain prices. There is a great disparity between the price which the producer gets and price the consumer pays. The need of the hour is an efficient supply chain backed by improved infrastructure, cold storage, packaging and transportation facilities.

Greater competition amongst players will further keep prices under control. Foreign food retailers could help in the transmission and adoption of better practices throughout the supply chain and could also facilitate access to export markets. FDI in food retail is the need of the hour. It would mean use of latest technology in the sector, more yield per hectare and optimum usage of arable land. Allowing FDI will create demand across all levels from raw materials to finished products, and, at the same time, maintaining every level of quality and standards. Economic growth cannot ignore farm sector. FDI would mean inclusive growth in the sector, contrary to the prevailing fear of price war between big retail and local kirana stores (*ET*, 22 April, 2008).

India need a rational approach toward FDI in retail trade. The government should not miss the opportunity to create millions of jobs throughout India. It will also give a boost to its overall GDP. A well-calibrated approach to the opening up of retail sector for FDI will ensure balanced regional development without cannibalizing the business of domestic retailers (Rao, 2006).

Some of the benefits that follow from FDI in Retail Business:

- Faster take up of modern retail formats.
- Improved productivity and efficiency on the retail sector.
- Enhanced sourcing.
- Improved quality of employment.
- Investment in supply chain.
- Reduced number of intermediaries because of closer integration of suppliers, logistic service and retailers.
- Linked local suppliers, farmers, manufacturers to global markets.
- Low prices for consumers.
- Improved product quality and service for consumers.

Issues in Allowing FDI in Retail Business

The critics highlight the deleterious effect of retail FDI on the unorganized sector comprising about 12 million, the so called "pop and mom stores". People believe that foreign retailers will squeeze suppliers and engage in predatory pricing to wipe out competition, only to raise prices again once they gain monopoly over the market. Also that lifting the floodgates of retail sector to FDI means dislocating millions from their occupations and pushing a lot of families beneath the poverty line.

Introduction of very large retail chains would push gigantic brands, mostly MNC brands much deeper into the domestic economy since large retail chains find it much easier to negotiate, with a few brands, which are then carried by its branches, the rich diversity of products and produce that exist in an economy like India would be destroyed. The big branded producers achieve a larger market presence less due to lower cost or better product and more due to their ability to sell.

While the government dithers as the debate rages, organized retail operations of large local business houses are expanding, and MNCs are finding backdoor entries to the country by forming cash and carry JVs with local business houses. Organized retail would obviously affect unorganized players adversely. But the question is: do we expect a foreign-owned organized retailer to displace more unorganized retailers compared to a locally-owned organized player? If not, the potential damage to the unorganized sector is already being done by the locally-owned retail chains that are rapidly expanding throughout the length and the breadth of the country in grocery, apparel, jewellery, pharmacy, consumer durables, among other segments.

In most respects the favorable and downside effects of locally and foreign-owned organized retail are quite similar except for one. That is, captive access of foreign multinational retailers to their global procurement chains. This privileged access can lead to foreign-owned retail chains relying on a greater proportion of their procurement outside India as compared to their locally-owned counterparts. But, even, locally-owned organized retailers stock quite a variety of imported goods largely procured from China or Thailand, although the proportion of imports could be higher in the case of foreign-owned ones. Seen against the background of deteriorating balance of trade situation, it could be a matter of concern. However, we can use it to our advantage by pushing Indian products abroad especially those produced by SMEs through a balanced policy regime. We can maximize the gains and minimize the threats by insisting on certain performance requirements like through JV and Exports. The JV requirement will assist in absorption of technology brought by them by their local partners. The export performance ones will encourage foreign retailers to procure from India for their other markets through their global procurement chains. The experience from several developing countries suggests the same. In India, the growth of auto component exports virtually from the scratch to nearly $4 billion over the past few years owes largely to the foreign exchange neutrality condition that used to be imposed on foreign auto producers among other consumer goods industries during the 1990s. The export performance requirement imposed on retail FDI in the form of say 25-50% of sales depending upon the extent of foreign ownership could push the foreign retailers to procure a growing quantity from the country as their domestic sales expand. There is a huge potential of foreign retailers working with Indian SMEs. Such requirements are fully consistent with our obligations under WTO's General Agreement in Trade in Services and Trade-Related Investment Measures Agreement. Such requirements will also help offset their imports and other remittances that their operations in India may entail.

Government may employ additional requirements such as on minimum floor space per outlet to confine them outside thickly populated areas to minimize the competition with unorganized retail. It could also provide access to cheaper credit and assist them in creating self-help groups to develop and mange supply chains for them. Hence, India has an opportunity to leverage access to her expanding consumer market for developing a vibrant SME sector catering to the global market. We should do it before it is too late and foreign players losing interest in taking obligations in return for entry having exploited the back-door opportunities.

State like West Bengal needs to overcome issues like bandhs and strikes which send a negative message to prospective investors. One example is the storm against Metro Cash & Carry's agro-wholesale business in Bengal (*HT*, 27 Sept., 2008).

FDI in Global Context of Organized Retailing

The governments in the developing countries are anxious to meet consumers' expectations by strengthening the network of organized retailers and bringing in FDI. But most countries are aware of the dislocation that such a policy could cause to the traditional supply chain in different sectors. They have accordingly adopted a somewhat cautious approach by attaching several caveats to the entry of foreign investors.

China has played a successful role in attracting FDI for the benefit of its economy, whereas India is lagging far behind. Major determinants, China attracted high FDI flows are: (a) China has more business-oriented policies; (b) Its FDI procedures are easier; (c) It has more flexible labor laws, a better labor climate and better entry-exit procedures for business entities. The main reasons why India has low FDI flows are: (a) Bureaucratic tangle; (b) Infrastructural drawback; (c) Labour inefficiency and unrest; (d) Tax incentives; (e) Procedural disputes; (f) non-implementation of approved projects; (g) Political instability; and (h) Corruption, etc. (Chary and Gangadhar, 2006).

Thailand has been cited as one of the countries in which the expansion of organized retailing caused dislocation to the traditional supply chains during the 1997-98 during Asian financial crisis. The report points out that once these economies started reviving after the crisis came to an end, the presence of large-scale foreign retailers benefited the unorganized retailers by offering them greater market opportunities. Thereafter, the unorganized retail sector recovered gradually by upgrading their business and reaping the benefits of growth in the sector. The report seems to gloss over the problems of adjustment faced by the suppliers and traders who form part of the traditional supply chain in some of these countries.

Malaysia requires that FDI should be routed through JVs, with minimum of 30 percent of the equity held by the bhumiputras.

There are minimum capital requirements for foreign retailers in Sri Lanka and Malaysia. Philippines has imposed "'sourcing"' and reciprocity requirements on foreign retailers. Thailand has zoning restriction for large retailers.

It has to be remembered that countries like China, Thailand and Malaysia which opened their retail sector to FDI were forced to reverse this policy and enact new laws to control the entry of giant retail players in the retail sector. According to All China Federation of Trade Unions, as a result of the entry of multinational companies, the domestic retail trade is shrinking. The Chinese Newspapers have been stressing this point that indigenous retail market is facing extinction. Moreover, a good number of Chinese producers had to stop their production because of competition from Wal-Mart reduced their margins to such a low level that the domestic producers found it impossible to sustain themselves.

Even in advanced countries, opposition to the entry of US Retail Giants has started. In France, as against level of 30 years ago, the numbers of retail shops has declined to 17 percent. In Denmark, during a period of 10 years (1982-92), about 30 percent of small retail shops were closed as a result of competition of US retail giants. It is estimated that in the subsequent 10 years, only 3,000 retail shops will be left in Denmark.

Even within US, Wal-Mart has to face strong criticism. The Municipal Corporation of California and Chicago have imposed a ban on opening of Wal-Mart stores. Even in the big cities of France and Germany, Wal-Mart is required to obtain permission from local authorities to open a new store. Even in Japan, South Korea and France, the foreign retail traders are banned to enter the trade in petroleum products, rice, tobacco, salt, fresh vegetables, meat and intoxicants.

Suggestions

- Before allowing foreign direct investment focus should be on direct and indirect employment potential of each of these sectors in relation to the magnitudes of investments required. The employment and investment implications may vary from sector to sector, region to region and rural to urban. Such a study should necessarily cover all segments of the supply chain, so that the government may have a better appreciation of the total benefits and costs, in the short-term as well as long-term.
- Before opening up the retail sector, the regulatory structures in the related sectors need to be strengthened; as otherwise, foreign players as well as the larger domestic retailers could exploit the traditional retailers. It may not be desirable to open up retailing to FDI until reforms in the related sectors are undertaken and the competitiveness of domestic retailers is enhanced.
- The government should examine the constraints faced by traditional retailers and other players in the supply chain and institute safety nets as has been done in Thailand and other countries in Asia. Most Asian countries have put in place restrictions in terms of sourcing, capital requirement, zoning, etc., in order to regulate the expansion of organized retailing. India should draw lessons from this.
- The retail sector is a highly sensitive one because of its immense contribution to the economy. Decisions regarding FDI in this sector should not therefore be taken in haste.
- FDI is welcome in sectors like lifestyle goods, home sectors, fashion and electronics. But there should be chance given an easy entry into any country. Everywhere, the top retailer of the country is local retailer. There is no reason for us to give away our business and our customers so early in life. It should be made difficult and not so easy.
- The other issue we agree on is that private equity and FII investments should be allowed. In 2-3 year's time, we should be competitive enough to take on international players. A roadmap should be given by the government on the manner in which it plans to open up. If we are aware of the way things are going to happen, we are more than willing to compete.
- As far as the role of the government is concerned, we are still coming under too many ministries like commerce; agriculture

finance, etc., there should be a single body to look at modern retaining in this country.
- Foreign investments have two components—FII and FDI, in retailing, unfortunately, there has been an anomaly that, while FII investments are permitted in retail companies that are listed, and they are not allowed in primary market issues or in unlisted companies. There is no rationale for not permitting primary market investments when you are allowing secondary market deals to take place. So, in the whole process, you are only allowing the manipulators and the speculators in the market place to make money.
- Indian retail industry has no dearth of retail experience, entrepreneurship, technology and the mindset of thinking big. But there is lack of capital. In terms of retail formats, food and groceries is one segment where some large Indian players have demonstrated that they can deliver value to the customer. They can bring in the concepts, which have been prevailing abroad and Indianise the model and even make it better.
- Even with the capital constraints, a lot of progress has been made by us. Indian retailers are investing in infrastructure and technology. Each one of us is talking of investing Rs.10 crore in technology, despite constraints on profitability. If you give us access to cheap funds, other investments also in terms of cold chains or warehousing facilities will come up. Retailers need to be supported, encouraged and given access to cheaper capital.
- If we allow foreign retailers to come in, there will be incremental growth. In fact, we need more brands in the lifestyle retail segment. So one must choose the categories carefully and, therefore, not open up completely. Another factor causing a lot of bullishness among the foreign players is the much talked about Global Retail Development Index (GRDI) of A.T. Kearney, where India is right on top.
- Indian Consumers are showing a trend, which is different and you cannot stop it. Just take what is happening to consumer spending. Last year 3 million Indians traveled abroad spending $25,000. Then, look at the grey market, which is as big as the organized sector. The questions here is can you stop the consumers from doing what he or she wants to do? But if consumers want Tommy Hilfiger, Marks & Spencer's or Espirit, they will go out and buy it. Secondly, the consumers

are clearly saying I want this. The government is giving them access outside and are saying do not give them access inside. All the lifestyle sectors should be opened up to allow the consumers to make the choice.
- In a country where banking, insurance and telecom have opened up, can a case be made that FDI in retail should not be allowed? What is so special about retail? Unless we are saying we cannot compete with the foreigners and, hence, they should not be allowed. The logic of profits being exorbitant is also not true. The profit in the retail business with its single digit margin, is small. In sector after sector, we have seen that when competition intensifies, prices actually fall sharply. So, the clear logic is that, if you look at it from the consumer point of view, competition is going to result in cost reduction. As long as you are protected against unfair competition, there is no case for restricting FDI in retail. Retail is not a special industry or different from any other industry.
- It is not fair to compare the retail industry with the telecom or banking sectors, simply because we are talking of only a 3 per cent organized retail. There is another 97 per cent it which is informal. So, any comprehensive opening up will have enormous social implications across the country, where 75 per cent of our population is staying in rural India. So, a phased and transparent policy would be welcomed by every one.
- Infrastructure is one of the impediments that the government needs to address. Today, we have malls but no roads or public transport for people to access them. This is where government can invest and drive up consumption.
- FDI can help us in many ways. Entry of foreign players can definitely improve the competitions here. It will also improve practices and processes. It can benefit the industry as a whole, but if it is allowed unrestricted it can create issues in the short-term.

Conclusion

Organized retail is sure to fulfill its potential in the Indian sub continent and to provide more and more opportunities to the Indian investors. The unfulfilled opportunities to the Indian consumers for quality products at the right price and environment with the perfect service and ambience will fuel the growth of the Indian retail industry. The different service providers would also get a level playing field in such an environment. Change in the Governmental stance would be of course required for realizing the full potential of this vibrant sector. Organized retailing in India is yet to get an industry status. The consequence is quite obvious. 100 per cent FDI is not permitted in retailing in India. The fear that the small-scale retailers will be displaced is delaying the FDI approvals. On the other hand, without the FDI, the sector is deprived of access to foreign technologies that is imperative for faster growth. The government of India has allowed FDI in direct marketing, but the reservations about extending it to the retail sector. Retailing is a technology-intensive industry. Under the liberalized regime of WTO the 'protected nature' of an industry may do more harm than good. In the short-run the government may succeed in protecting the domestic industry, but in the long run we would be loosing too many opportunities and technological innovations. This, in addition would also block any attempt by the domestic industry to become competitive internationally.

REFERENCES

Anand, M. and Aarti Kothari (2005), Who's Afraid of FDI? *Business World*, 24th Oct. 2005.

Arpita Mukherjee and Nitisha Patel (2005), FDI in Retail Sector: India by Academic Foundation in association with ICRIER and Department of Consumer Affairs, New Delhi.

Brain Carvalho, Small Town, Big Business, *Business Today*, July 18, 2004.

Buareau (2006), "51 per cent FDI in Single Brand Retail Cleared, Business Line, Financial Daily from *The Hindu*, Internet Edition Jan. 25th, 2006.

Chary, S. Narasimha & Gangadhar, V. (2006), "Foreign Direct Investment: A Study of India and China", *The Indian Journal of Commerce*, Vol. 59, No. 4, Oct.-Dec.

Kumar, Nagesh (2008), " FDI in Retail for Development", *Economic Times*, 3rd Oct.

Gupta, S.L. (2006), "Trends in Retailing Industry in India: Shopping Malls—the Need of the Hour", *The Indian Journal of Commerce*, Vol. 59, No. 4, Oct.-Dec.

Indian Retail Forum 2008: The Renaissance, Mumbai, India, 16-18 Sep. 2008.

Images Retail: The 10 Talking Points, October 2008.

Lucas, George H, Jr., Robert P. Bush, and Larry G. Gresham, "Retailing" All India Publishers and Distributors, Chennai, 1997.

Malini, Phupta, "Mall Mania," *India Today*, Nov. 21st 2005.

Madavan, Kutty G. (2005), "FDI in Boon or Bane," ICFAI Reader, November, pp. 19-28.

Mukherjee, Writankar (2008), "In the Firing Line", *Economic Times*, 17th Oct.

Naik, S.D. (2005), "Retail Boom: FDY can give extra thrust, Business Line, Financial Daily from *The Hindu*, Internet Edition, Friday, May 27th, 2005.

Pancholi, Radhika (2008), "Middle-Class Save the Day for Retailers", *Hindustan Times*, 18th Sept.
Qureshi, Nasir Zameer and Amin, Mir M. (2007), "FDI in India's Retail Sector: Prospects and Hurdles", *The Indian Journal of Commerce*, Vol. 60. No. 4, Oct.-Dec.
Rao, M.V.S. Srinivasa (2006), "Foreign Direct Investment in Indian Retail Business", *The Indian Journal of Commerce*, Vol. 59, No. 2, April-June.
Rao, Subba, S.R. Dr. (2005-06), "FDI and the Retail Sector in India: A Study of Opportunities and Threats," *The Alternative*, Vol. V, No. I (Oct.-Nov.), pp. 23-36.
Sabharwal, Shruti (2008), "Some Excalibur Outlets to Dress Up as Megamart", *Economic Times*, 18th Sept.
Turakhia, Saurabh (2008), "Falling Property Rentals Keep Retail Boom Going", *Hindustan Times*, 4th July.
Vishal Krishna (2009), In the News Retail, Culture Connection, *Business World*, 19th Jan. 2009.

Foreign Direct Investment in Telecom Sector

FAYAZ AHAMED

1.1 Introduction

India has witnessed a gradual change in the Government's attitude to Foreign Direct Investment since 1948. As India had severe scarcity of capital resources at the time of independence; it welcomed foreign investment in a restricted manner. Since the second five year plan period (1956-61) greater emphases was given to Industrialization which led to development of the local industries. To protect the domestic industry from foreign competition, Government adopted a more restrictive attitude towards FDI in the late 1960s. In the 1980s, as a part of the industrial policy resolutions, the attitude towards FDI was liberalized. "The year 1991 was marked with severe balance of payments deficits. Foreign exchange reserves went down to US$ 1.1 billion in June 1991—less than sufficient for two weeks of import requirements" (Misra, S.K., 2000). India was on the verge of default and it got financial assistance from IMF on certain terms and conditions. This involved "Structural Adjustment Programme (SAP)" by India. These "SAP" apart from bringing about changes in fiscal policy, industrial policy and changes in other important economic policies involved a major change in FDI policy of India. Under this scenario it was not possible for India to continue with its past policy of restrictions and it became essential to liberalize the economy. Liberalization involves free operation of international market forces. This led to removal of most of the restrictions in FDI. As a result, India is now among the top five most attractive destinations for FDI.

1.2 Review of Literature

FDI in Telecom sector of India was Rs. 9,950.94. It is expected that Rs.700 to 900 million FDI is expected in Telecom sector in coming five years. Europe, Korea and Japan are showing their active participation in investment in Telecom sector of India (A. Goel, 2006). India started its liberalization process in Telecommunication by allowing private competition in value added services in 1992 followed by the opening of cellular and basic services for local area to private competition. National Telecom policy, 1994 stated that license bidding process should be initiated to end the monopoly on basic telephone and mobile services. As a result India was divided into 21 Telecom circles. One fixed operator other than department of Telecom was allowed in each circle for the period of 10 years after which the situation was to be reviewed. In 1996 licenses were issued to 34 private companies to operate in 18 of the 20 circles opened for bidding. Foreign firms were allowed to hold up to 49 percent of shares in private consortium. Investment of foreign firms in Telecom sector of India enhanced gradually (K. Venugopal, 2003). A brief review of literature on FDI and related aspects is provided below Hymer (1960), Caves (1996), Dunning (1993) found that MNEs have both tangible and intangible resources, or explicit and tacit knowledge, in the form of technologies, managerial skill, international networks, capital, and brand names and goodwill (Hymer, 1960; Caves, 1996; Dunning, 1993).

1.3 Statement of the Problem

The Telecom services have been recognized the world-over as an important tool for socio-economic development for a nation. It is one of the prime support services needed for rapid growth and modernization of various sectors of the economy. The process of liberalization in the country began in the right earnest with the announcement of the New Economic Policy in July 1991. This opened the way to the private sector and value added services were declared open in 1992 and Telecom equipment manufacturing was delicensed in 1991, following which radio paging, cellular mobile and other value added services were opened gradually to the private sector. This has resulted in large number of manufacturing units been set-up in the country. As a result most of the equipment used in Telecom area is being manufactured within the country. A major breakthrough was the clear enunciation of the government's intention of liberalizing the Telecom sector in the National Telecom Policy resolution of 13th May 1994. In the field of international telephony, India had agreed under the GATS to review its opening up in 2004. However, open competition in this sector was allowed with effect from April 2002 itself. There is now no limit on the number of service providers in this sector. India offers an unprecedented opportunity for Telecom service operators, infrastructure vendors, manufacturers and associated services companies. A host of factors are contributing to enlarged opportunities for growth and investment in Telecom sector:

- An expanding Indian economy with increased focus on the services sector.
- Population mix moving favourably towards a younger age profile.
- Urbanization with increasing incomes.

Investors can look to capture the gains of the Indian Telecom boom and diversify their operations outside developed economies that are marked by saturated Telecom markets and lower GDP growth rates. Inflow of FDI into India's Telecom sector during April 2000 to Feb. 2010 was about Rs. 405,460 million. Also, more than 8 per cent of the approved FDI in the country is related to the Telecom sector. India has proven its dominance as a technology solution provider. Efforts are being continuously made to develop affordable technology for masses, as also comprehensive security infrastructure for Telecom network. Foreign Direct Investment (FDI) appears to be bypassing the Telecom sector, despite India being one of the most attractive and fastest growing Telecom markets. An analysis of the ownership details reveals that the average FDI holding is just below 40 percent. This changes the common perception that FDI levels in the Telecom sector are very high. Hence, there is a need to assess the FDI in Telecom Sector in order to offer suggestions to the government and others to build Brand India in the globe.

1.4 Methodology

As the study is exploratory and qualitative in nature an extensive use of secondary data is made. In the present article, at the outset the theoretical background of the term FDI has been elaborated. The sources of data are websites of the sectors under study, different periodicals, journals in the relevant fields, magazines, different reports, etc., the details of which have been duly incorporated in the reference section which implies that the date base of the article is secondary in nature. The period of data includes last eight years. Further the secondary data pertaining to the study is fathered from Department of Telecommunications, and Telecom Regulatory Authority of India (TRAI) reports, leading journals and a number of news items. In order to compare the FDI inflow over the period under study, the percentage method is used.

1.5 Objectives of the Study

This article brings about the current scenario of the Indian Telecom sector. The article intends to bring out the benefits and usefulness of having FDI in this sector and it will help the readers to understand the strengths, weaknesses, opportunities and threats of Indian Telecom sector.

The study is directed towards the following objectives:

(1) To evaluate FDI inflow in India and to analyze the challenges and opportunities faced by FDI inflows in Telecom Sector.
(2) To explore the role of FDI in Telecom Sector and to study the future outcome towards the phase of FDI initiated at Telecom Sector.
(3) To offer suggestions in FDI policy about FDI inflow in Telecom Sector.

1.6 Scope of the Study

The study will highlight the current scenario of the FDI inflows in India. It is concerned with FDI in Telecom Sector and discusses the relevant measures to formulate and force regulatory and legal reforms in this sector and achieve its aim of National Growth and quality services through the investor's dynamic relationship to attract India as their FDI destination. The study is confined to a period from 1991 to 2010.

1.7 Limitations of the Study

The study suffers from the following limitation:
1. The study is limited to India. Hence, the result arrived from the study may or may not be applied to other countries. This study covers only the limited caps of the FDI flow.
2. The result cannot be generalized for the FDI flow in other challenging sectors.
3. The generalization of the finding of the study is subject to limitations.

2.1 Indian Telecom Sector

The Indian Telecom Industry is one of the fastest growing in the world. The Telecom sector is one of the highly regulated sectors in the country. The Telecom Regulatory Authority of India (TRAI) regulates the sector including fixation/revision of tariffs for various Telecom services. Experts in the Telecom space estimate that India holds the promise of becoming the second largest Telecom market of the world. The various reforms introduced by successive Indian governments over the last decade have dramatically changed the nature of Telecommunications in the country. The rapidly evolving challenges and opportunities facing Telecom companies domestically as well as globally are driving ongoing change in the industry's risk universe. The Telecommunication sector, one of the major components of the economy, has undergone a sea change and is poised for further growth. This will culminate in the economic prosperity of every country. The communication which was initially between short distance places subsequently spread among towns and cities of long distances as well as between countries with improvement in those devices. Such a development led not only to progress of co-operation between countries, but also in trade and commerce, etc. (M. Ibrahim, 2010).

The Indian Telecom sector continues to attain robust growth, adding 191.55 mn new connections during the financial year 2009-10. At the end of March 2010 the number of Telecom subscribers in the country was 621.28 mn and the overall teledensity was at 52.74 percent.

2.2 Foreign Direct Investment: Current Scenario

Presently FDI is allowed in India in almost all the sectors; except a few which are of strategic concerns. It is prohibited in Activities not opened to private sector investment including Atomic Energy and Railway Transport (other than Mass Rapid Transport Systems), Multi-Brand Retail Trading, Lottery Business including Government and private lottery, online lottery, Real Estate Business or Construction of Farm Houses, Gambling and Betting including casinos, Manufacturing of Cigars, cheroots, cigarillos and cigarettes, of tobacco or of tobacco substitutes, Business of chit fund, Nidhi company and Trading in Transferable Development Rights (TDRs).

In all the other sectors it is permitted with different equity limits ranging from 26 percent to 100 percent subject to certain terms and conditions wherever applicable.

FDI is permitted in India through two routes; the Automatic Route and the Government Route. Under the Automatic Route, the non-resident investor or the Indian company does not require any approval from the RBI or Government of India for the investment. Under the Government Route, prior approval of the Government of India through Foreign Investment Promotion Board (FIPB) is required. Proposals for foreign investment under Government route as laid down in the FDI policy from time to time are considered by the Foreign Investment Promotion Board (FIPB) in Department of Economic Affairs (DEA), Ministry of Finance (DIPP). Table 1 depicts entry route and FDI caps in Telecom sector.

Table 1: Route-wise FDI Inflows in Telecom Sector with Equity/CAP

S. No.	Sector/Activity	Percent of FDI Cap/Equity	Entry Route
1.1	Telecommunication: Telecom services	74%	Automatic up to 49%
1.2	(a) ISP with gateways (b) ISP not providing gateways	74%	Automatic up to 49% Government route beyond 49% and up to 74%
1.3	(a) Infrastructure (b) E-mail and Voice mail	100%	Automatic up to 49% Government route beyond 49%

Source: Compiled from Consolidated FDI Policy-Circular 2 of 2010, Department of Industrial Policy & Promotion, Ministry of Commerce and Industry, Govt. of India

Services sector has attracted the highest FDI equity inflows of 20.93 percent for the period April 2000 to June 2010. It is followed by Computer Software & Hardware, Telecommunications, Housing & Real Estate, Construction Activities and Power having 8.78, 8.49, 7.50, 7.13, and 4.37 percentage shares respectively in total FDI inflows for the same period.

Figure 1 shows that there is a gradual growth in the FDI flows starting from 2003-04 to 2009-10. During the year 2003-04 there was a down in FDI flows due to the western trade policies and it recovered in the subsequent years.

3.1 Foreign Direct Investment in Telecom Sector

Since the Indian Telecom industry has the certainty policy it is growing the fastest in the world and it affects investment and thus growth. On December 3rd 2010, Government of India has approved 8 Proposals of Foreign Direct Investment amounting to Rs. 883.166 crore approximately, of which only one is from the Telecom and Media

Figure 1: Foreign Direct Investment in India
(As per DIPP's FDI data base—Equity capital components only)
[in rupees crores]

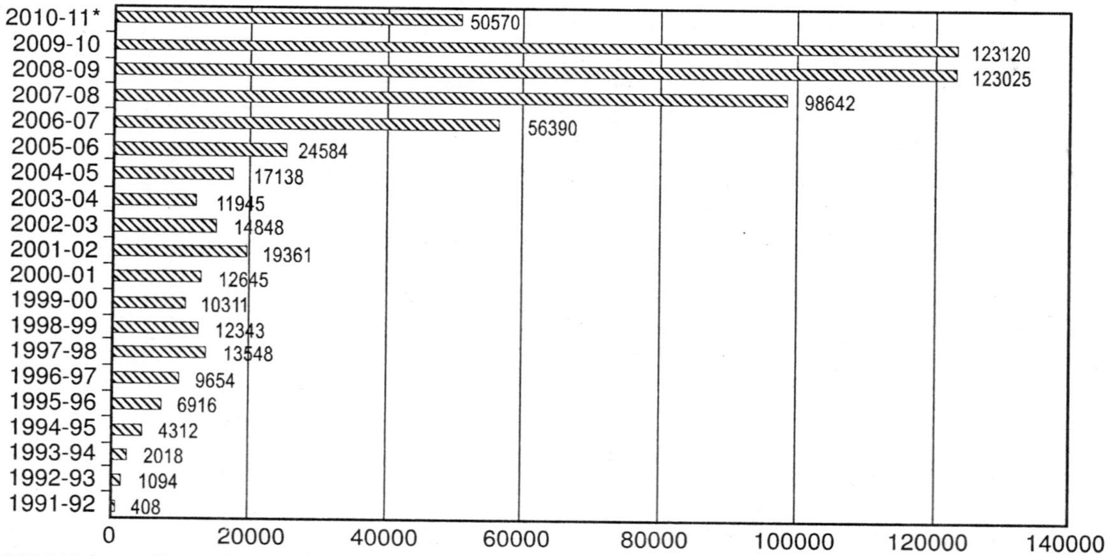

2010-11*	50570
2009-10	123120
2008-09	123025
2007-08	98642
2006-07	56390
2005-06	24584
2004-05	17138
2003-04	11945
2002-03	14848
2001-02	19361
2000-01	12645
1999-00	10311
1998-99	12343
1997-98	13548
1996-97	9654
1995-96	6916
1994-95	4312
1993-94	2018
1992-93	1094
1991-92	408

2010-11* (up to September 2010).
Source: Compiled from FDI facts sheet, Department of Industrial Policy & Promotion, Ministry of Commerce and Industry, Govt. of India.

domain. Several proposals, including those from Qualcomm for the induction of foreign investment in the group companies which won Broadband Wireless Access spectrum in four circles across India, have been deferred.

Table 2: Facts on Telecom Sector Foreign Direct Investment in India
(As per DIPP's FDI data base—Equity capital components only)
[U.S. $ million]

Financial Year (April-March)	Total FDI Flows (US$ Million)	FDI in Telecom Sector (US$ Million)	FDI Telecom Share Percentage with Total FDI	Telecom FDI Growth percentage
Aug. 1991 to April 2002	23,831	2,262	9.49	—
2002-03	3,116	223	7.15	—
2003-04	2,597	116	4.46	-52
2004-05	3,759	129	3.43	+11
2005-06	5,540	624	11.26	+283
2006-07	12,492	478	3.86	-47.5
2007-08	24,575	1,261	5.13	+163
2008-09	27,330	2,558	9.35	+102
2009-10	25,834	2,554	9.88	-9.9
2010-11 (up to Sep. 2010)	11,005	1,057	9.60	8
Cumulative Total	1,40,079	11,262	8.03	—

Source: Compiled from FDI in India Statistics, Department of Industrial Policy & Promotion, Ministry of Commerce and Industry, Govt. of India.

Table 3: Indian Telecommunications at a Glance
(As on 31 March 2010)

Rank in world in network size	3rd
Tele-density (per hundred populations)	52.74
Telephone connection (In millions)	
Fixed	36.95
Mobile	548.32
Total	621.28
Village Public Telephones inhabited (Out of 5,93,601 uncovered villages)	5,69,385
Foreign Direct Investment (in millions) (from April 2000 till March 2010)	4070

(Contd.)

	Licenses issued
Basic	2
CMTS	38
UAS	241
Infrastructure Provider I	219
ISP (Internet)	371
National Long Distance	29
International Long Distance	24

Source: Compiled from, Department of Telecommunications (DOT), Ministry of Communications & IT, Govt. of India.

Foreign Direct Investment (FDI) was permitted in the Telecom sector beginning with the Telecom manufacturing segment in 1991—when India embarked on economic liberalisation. According to the Department of Industrial Policy and Promotion (DIPP), the Telecommunications sector which includes radio paging, mobile services and basic telephone services attracted foreign direct investment (FDI) worth US$ 2,554 million during 2009-10. The cumulative flow of FDI in the sector during August 1991 to September 2010 is US$ 11,262 million.

In Basic, Cellular Mobile, Paging and Value Added Service, and Global Mobile Personal Communications by Satellite, Composite FDI permitted is 74 percent (49 percent under automatic route) subject to grant of license from DOT subject to security and license conditions. The Reserve Bank has liberalised the outlay norms for Indian Telecom companies by allowing them to invest in international submarine cable consortia through the automatic route.

3.2 FDI in Telecom Sector: Challenges and Opportunities

Since the introduction of the New Telecom Policy (NTP), 1999, by the government, the growth in the Telecom sector has been only gaining steam. India's telecom density has risen to 51.05 per cent after 18.76 million new phone connections were added in February 2010. The number of telephone subscribers in India is more than 600.69 million in February 2010. The country already has a 15.35 per cent rural teledensity as of June 2010. However, the growth path is not as rosy as it appears to be. The sector is faced with several challenges such as (a) Organization of strategic partnerships, (b) Resources for expansion, (c) Attracting and managing talent and intellectual capital, (d) Processes and systems to support exponential industry growth, (e) Concentration of equipment manufacturers, (f) Corporate social responsibility and sustainability, (g) Lack of protection for digital intellectual property, (g) Move for rural clientele employment creation and attrition, and (h) Rising subscribers falling turnover.

4.1 Suggestions and Conclusion

The Concerned Ministry should issue necessary and clear cut guidelines as to what activities constitute the Corporate Social Responsibility (CSR) activities to bring uniformity in the CSR activities undertaken by different sectors of the Indian Economy which will, *inter alia*, ensure real implementation of CSR.

The Indian Telecom industry has a lot of potential for growth and it needs the precise policy to prolong growth. But of late, in Telecom industry, the greater need for competitive support has risen due to improved competition, larger customer focus, globalization, and the significance of quality. A competitive price environment is hammering down call charges, giving pressure on earnings and share prices and threatening bruising stake-out in a sector crowded with new players. Competition was already fierce but has become even more aggressive as new players unleash deeper price cuts with innovative per-second billing plans that have pushed call costs down to reach rock bottom. Thus, the sector is affected by illogical pricing. Urban mobile markets are already saturated but there are still hundreds of millions of customers to be signed up in rural areas—a tantalising prospect for new entrants that see India as one of the few global growth areas. The days ahead throw a challenge of survival before the competing players. Telecommunications infrastructure is the key to the rapid economic and social development of the country.

Telecom sector has the potential to emerge as a major contributor of GDP of the country. A large population and rise in consumers' income and spending owing to strong economic growth enabled India to achieve the fastest growing Telecom market in the world.

REFERENCES

Assaf Razin & Efraim Sadka (2007), Foreign Direct Investment, Analysis of Aggregate Flows, Princeton University Press, U.S.A.

A. Goel (2006), "Foreign Direct Investment in Telecom Sector", MIB (2005-07), IMT, Ghaziabad, Available at http:// www.indianmba.com.

Kenneth Froot (1993), Foreign Direct Investment, University of Chicago Press, U.S.A.

K. Venugopal (2003), "Telecommunication Sector Negotiation at the WTO: Case Studies of India, Sri Lanka and Malaysia", ITU/ESCAP/WTO Regional Seminars on Telecommunications and Trade Issues, Bangkok, Thailand.

Misra, S.K. (2000), *Indian Economy*, Himalaya Publishing House, 18th Edition, p. 739, New Delhi.

M. Ibrahim (2010), *The Management Accountant*, December 2010, ICWA, Kolkata, India.

Reports

Central Statistical Organization (2008-09), Economic Survey (2009), Quick Estimates of National Income, Delhi, India.

Department of Industrial Policy & Promotion (DIPP), Government of India, Revised Data on FDI Reports (2010), New Delhi.

Foreign Direct Investment and Indian Manufacturing Industry Output Growth

PESALA BUSENNA

Introduction

This paper is divided into two sections. Section one explains briefly introduction about the Foreign Direct Investment (FDI), FDI policy, Definitions, FDI phases and structure of the Manufacturing Industries in India. Section two explains the Share of global FDI in distribute countries and sectoral distribution of India's FDI. It also deals causality relationship between FDI and economic growth, conclusion and findings. Foreign investment may either come in direct or indirect form. It is called foreign direct investment (FDI). The later (other) kind of investment is called foreign portfolio investment. FDI has been defined by various institutions in different ways.

IMF Definition

According to the BPM5 (Balance of payments manual 5th edition) Foreign Direct Investment is the category of international investment that reflects the objective of obtaining a lasting interest by a resident entity is one economy in an enterprise resident in another economy. The lasting interest implies the existences of long-term relationship between the direct investor on the management of the enterprise.[1]

Methodology

For the purpose of analysis Granger causality test has been used between FDI and manufacturing output. For this purpose data has been collected on FDI and total output in selected manufacturing industries. The data has been collected from CMIE Proves, during 1990-91 to 2005-06 and RBI Hand Book of Indian Economy and ASI respectively.

Review of Literature

Many economists argue that foreign direct investment creating economic growth. The economic growth also comes through adopting new technology, adopting managerial skills, human resources development. And also few economists argue that FDI is not direct cause to economic growth particularly developing countries and underdeveloped countries.

Charkraborty Chandra & Peter Nunnenkhamp (2006)[2] examined Economic Reforms Foreign Direct Investment and its economic effects in India. In Indian manufacturing industries sector experienced a temporary growth acceleration after reforms in 1991 when FDI stock doubled, but output growth is weakened in 1995-2000, even though FDI stock continue too diverse risk. They investigated two things namely, first, is there a long-run steady state relationship between FDI and output for all of the 15 industries included. Secondly, it has given the existence of a co-integrated relationship; accurately identify the chronology of causal effects between FDI and output by unrevealing the short run dynamics of the long-run relationship. That purpose they were taken 15 industries in the primary, secondary and tertiary sectors, the data collected from RBI and CSO during the period 1987-2000, they applied a panel co integration framework for heterogeneity across 15 industries. They also they examined causality between FDI and output. However, the aggregate levels the Granger causality test suggest an effect was there in FDI and output both in the short-run and the long-run. The impact of output growth in attracting FDI is relatively stronger than that of FDI in inducing economic growth. Authors also support according to their result, the growth implications depend on various factors, including supportive capacity and local skills, technological spillovers and linkages between foreign and local firms and export orientation all of which may differ across industries and sectors in the host country.

Prakash[3] argue that FDI can directly and indirectly contribute to economic growth. The main objective of this study is that the direct contribution of FDI to the economic growth of India by being a source of capital formation. He collected data from CSO, NAS, the data details are net fixed capital FDI stocks and output during 1970 to 1997. He found statistically significant over the period 1986-97 but it is not in the case of 1970-85. A 1 percent increase in the FDI stock in the economy an average, result is 0.04 percent increase in the output over the period 1986-87. Therefore, the contribution of FDI stock of the economy's production is significantly positive during the liberalized phased of FDI regime. Finally he said that FDI stock has largely beneficial impact on the economy.

Dua & Aneesa (1998)[4] investigated the relationship between economic activities and FDI in India. They says that the higher economic growth leads to large market, that can increase the attractiveness of a country for multinational the market size may investor to exploit potential economic scale. They used vector autoregressive model for the post-liberalization period and also they tested Granger causality test. They used data during January 1992 to March 1998, from RBI Bulletin. Their Granger causality test and innovation accounting analysis suggest that Index of Industrial production has yet to respond to actual inflows while FDI approvals do affect output.

Krishna Dutt Amitava (1997)[5] argue that there are good theoretical reasons to expect that the growth consequences of DFI on less developed countries depend on what kind of sector receive DFI, because of the differential effects of such DFI North-South terms of trade and on the nature of southern technological development. The main objective of the study is that there has been a change in the sectoral pattern of DFI into LDCs, which has strengthened the positive development effect of DFI inflows while it has weakened the negative effects. His concentration is on two regions namely South regions and north region, in two regions there are two classes in each region, capitalist and workers. They used cross-country data growth questions to see whether the pattern of DFI can explain rate of growth across countries. Their theoretical analysis suggest that the pattern of DFI matters for the growth effects of DFI, since they failed to find regulation using cross-country regression analysis. Their analysis implies that a promising direction for future research is to examine of led developed countries with respect to their sectoral pattern of DFI inflows.

Bhat, Sham K., Tripura Sundari, C.V. and K. Durail Raj (2004)[6] examined the causal nexus between foreign Direct Investment and economic growth in India. The study argued that the direct relationship between inward Foreign Direct Investment in relation to their size and economic development of country. Second view is pertaining to negative relation between foreign direct investment and economic growth. For that purpose he collected data from Handbook of Indian Economy Bulletin, World Investment Report and CMIE, they used quarterly economic growth is qualified in terms of Industrial productivity index and FDI, from 1990-2002. The authors tested simple ratios, percentage method, granger-causality test and Dicky-Fuller test. The study found that an independent relationship between foreign investment and economic growth main reasons are (a) foreign direct investment comes to those sectors in which the domestic firms are themselves contemplating investment and it will act against the investment contemplating investment and it will act against the investment and it will act against the investment contemplating investment and it will act against the investment opportunities of domestic firms and another possible reasons are in India, foreign investment is only 0.9 percent of Gross Domestic products and its high transaction cost in the form of corruption and unnecessary regulatory requirements fails to attract foreign direct investment, etc.

India, the largest country in the world in terms of GDP at current exchange rates is able to attract FDI equal to 0.9 percent of its GDP in 2001. India is one of the most transparent and liberal FDI regimes among the developing economies. There are a few banned sectors (like lotteries & gaming and legal service) and some sectors with limits on foreign proportion. The entry rules are clear and well defined and equity limits for foreign investment in selected sectors such as a telecom quite explicit and well known. Most of the manufacturing sectors have been on the 100 percent automatic route for many years. Foreign equity is limited only in production of defense equipment (26 percent), oil marketing (74 percent) and government owned petroleum refineries (26 percent). Most of the mining sectors are similarly on the 100 percent automatic route, with foreign equity limits only on atomic minerals (74 percent), coal & lignite (74 percent), exploration for oil (51 percent to 74 percent) and diamonds and precious stones (74 percent). 100 percent equity is also allowed in non-crop agro-allied sectors and crop agriculture under controlled conditions[7] (e.g. hot houses).

The foreign equity limits on production of drugs using recombinant DNA technology or a specific call/tissue targeted formulation was raised from 74 percent to 100 percent. In private petroleum refineries 100 percent FDI is allowed. Where as in public sector refineries, it is restricted to 26 percent. The public sector refineries are under the control of government appointed boards. Government as the owner has the right to decide how much it wants to sell to a domestic or foreign investor. Further, as long as the refineries remain in the public sector government either has management control (50.1 percent) or the right any fundamental (25.1 percent equity). FDI can therefore be control or directly supervised or any other FDI investors. When it loses 25 percent share the company becomes a private company and 100 percent FDI is allowed in this case. Therefore there is no need for any equity limit and this should be raised to 100 percent and put on the automatic route. Indian companies are currently prohibited to have more than 24 percent equity in small-scale units (SSI). The same limits are applicable to foreign direct investors (i.e. this is not strictly on FDI policy issues). These limits reduce the ability of SSI to raise the equity capital. In a situation in which every expert ever shades of political opinions supports a greater flow of funds to the SSI, the equity limits are illogical. If a small-scale enterprise wants to expend to domestic company by offering equity to FDI investors to domestic companies, it can be free to do so. This will not only ease the financing constraint but also promote backward and forward linkages with medium-large (domestic and foreign) industry. Such synergy is essential for healthy growth of both sectors and for enhancing industrial efficiency and competitive strength.

The infrastructure is acquiring more equity. For example, in airport is already allowed up to 100 percent but anything between 75 percent and 100 percent has to go through the FIPB route. Even 100 percent foreign equity should be made automatic as no specific purpose is served by FIPB security in this heavy sector. In service sector 100 percent foreign equity is already allowed in courier services and this can be transferred to the automatic route. And also 100 percent equity can be allowed in industrial, commercial and residential complexes (covering one acre or more). The power sector played a vital role in industrial development. Private investment in the power sector, both domestic and FDI depends on power sector reforms. Policy and regulatory reform, relating to user charges, reduction of theft and private entry into distribution are the pre-requisites for increasing private investment.

Foreign Investment Promotion Board (FIPB)

A special empowered body, i.e. the foreign investment promotion board has been created to invite negations and facilitates investment from international companies on the basis of commercial viability and mutually acceptable profitability. This is a high powered body having full flexibility to consider and finalise proposals even outside policy parameters. No formal application forms are prescribed, on fee payable, the FIPB is located in the Prime Minister's office. Since July, 1992 all foreign investment proposals, which are not under the parameters of automatic approval, are being considered by the foreign investment promotion board.

Capital formation plays an important role in the process of development. Developing countries at initial level are unable to generate capital formation due to lack of sufficient resources such as FDI, FII and, etc. So it is understood that external resources are needed for economic development. External resources are mainly used to improve the machinery, technology and raw materials. This resource gap can be filled by the FDI. FDI can provide some resources such as skills, training technology, capital goods and intermediate inputs in order to exploit a country's existing comparative advantages. The FDI played a prominent role in the exports of developing countries in the manufacturing sector. FDI can help a country in its efforts to raise exports in all kinds of manufacturing industries by providing the missing elements in order to improve local based skills and capabilities. Most of the economists say that two possible relationships between FDI and exports. (1) Substitutes, and (2) Complementories. The substitute relationship assumes that internal trade is driven by differences in factor endowments and factor prices for homogeneous products. Complementary relationship explains that FDI and exports move in the same direction. Empirical evidence shows that FDI has complementary relationship with exports.

FDI and Economic Development

The economic theory suggests that FDI can create positive impact on economic development. And the output influences FDI in-flows in manufacturing industries. Literature says that FDI has been expanding technology, improving the managerial skills, labour productivity and developing the economic growth. Most of the empirical studies investigate the relationship between FDI and economic growth; literatures say that FDI creates economic growth; very few economists arguing that FDI is not creating economic growth. Many studies reveal that the economic growth of a country is influenced not only by FDI but also by some other factors such as domestic policies pertaining to monetary, fiscal and external policies.

The growth of exports has been much faster than GDP over the past few decades in India, as FDI played a main role in increasing industrial exports. The east and south east countries show that FDI is a powerful instrument of exports in making multinational companies. They are producing more qualitative manufacturing goods and service, etc., through its functions.[8] The FDI methods are used in for the future the counties to activities. The economic theory suggests that FDI can have a positive effect on the economy and also plays a vital role in positive effect on growth in the host country.[9] And another study found that FDI played a critical role in expanding their process of economic development.[10] It can also be observed in Indian context. One of the studies collected 160 affiliated MNC's operating in India. This study found the spillover effect of FDI in India has been the production of better quality products, rather than in the form of improved managerial abilities. Because of FDI the productivity of local labour has improved, where as there was a decline in the labour productivity in IT sector.[11]

FDI Policy

After independence the Government of India has given importance for the development of industrialization. So, many industries were established for further development in public sector. Due to lack of large capital requirements in private sector, the government also gave priority for the development of human resources, expansion of educational technical engineering facilities, scientific technology and network. In primary stage Government took initiative to develop these issues. The government made investment development of industrial, institutional and capital market. In this process, technological skills and entrepreneurships were quite limited. FDI was the only source in India to develop the economic growth. At the same time the foreign investors have imposed restrictions on the remittances of profits and dividends. So many foreign enterprises were established in manufacturing sectors in India.[12] The industrial policy Resolution in 1948 had specific role on public sector, private sector and foreign investment. As a result of the policy resolution effect the government welcomed foreign investment in the overall national development strategy. The domestic enterprises capability influenced not only the pattern of FDI but also an investments made by Indian enterprises.[13]

The government of India has three regulations to approach FDI. They are the Industrial Development and Regulation Act (IRDA, 1951), the Monopolies and Restrictive Trade Practice Act (MRTPA, 1969) and Foreign Exchange Regulations (FERA, 1973). The IRDA provided license for the establishment of new industries and exit units. FERA has control on foreign investment and restriction in the limiting the participation of foreign companies up to 40 percent paid-up capital. In the early 1980's the restrictions were liberalized. In this process the foreign technology came into India. This effect caused to increase countries production in this period, during 1970-80 the FDI investment is very low or negative.[14]

FDI Policy in the 1980s

In 1980s the Foreign Direct Investment attitude changed as part of modernization of Industry with liberalized capital goods, new technology, etc. In this period the liberalization of industrial licensing rules and regulation were changed. The exemptions foreign equity restriction under FERA of 100 percent export-oriented units.

FDI Policy (1990-2006)

The new Industrial policy gave importance to the FDI. The main objective of the New FDI policy was to promote infrastructure development and exports promotion. New Industrial policy 1991 brought some important points. They were: (i) Abolition of Industrial licensing required for business initiation and expansion. This has promoted to free competition, and (ii) Restriction of 40 per cent equity participation of FERA companies which is raised up to 51 per cent in 35 priority sectors which was automatic approval by RBI which includes metals, electric and electronic equipment, transport equipment, industrial equipment, chemical, pharmaceutical, glass cement rubber, food processing, software, tourism and trade.

The Indian external payments crisis brought about complete change in its economic policy after 1990. In 1991 the government of India faced the macro-economic, i.e. high inflation, large fiscal current deficits, and unsustainable burden of domestic and foreign debt. The government of India introduced market oriented reforms in 1991. The FDI policy was a part of package encompassing industrial policy, trade policy, exchange policy and financial sector policy. In 1991 the industrial policy was deregulated; the Government abolished the industrial system. In 1991 the public sector industries were reduced from 17 to 6, i.e. Defense, Atomic energy, coal and lignite, minerals, mining and Railway transport. The reforms influenced foreign direct investment, portfolio investment and new institutions. The FDI has encouraged export-oriented industries and generated employment opportunities in manufacturing sector.

Foreign Direct Investment Inflows and its Main Broad Heads

1. Reserve Bank of India (RBI) automatic approval route for equity holding up to 51 percent,

2. Foreign Investment Boards discretionary approval route for larger projects with equity holding greater than 51 percent,
3. Acquisition of shares rout (since 1996),
4. RBI's non-resident Indian (NRI) schemes, and
5. External commercial borrowings (ADR/GDR route).

Type of Foreign Directs Investment

There are four categories of foreign direct investment, they are:
(i) Government approvals (SIA/FIPB),
(ii) RBI automatic approvals,
(iii) NRI investment, and
(iv) Acquisition of shares.

And also one way is FDI inward to India, i.e. if it is more than 51 percent of its holding. Permission has to be sought from secretariat for Industrial approvals (SIA) or the foreign investment promotion board (FIPB) through RBI route. The share FDI in India came through SIA/FIPB.

(i) Foreign Currency Non-Resident Bank (FCNR),
(ii) Non-Resident (External) Rupee Account (NRI) (NR RD) scheme.
(iii) Non-Resident (Non-Repayable) Rupee-deposits (BRNR).

FDI Determinant Factors

Main factors which determinants (attract) FDI, are market size (income level and population) extent of urbanization, quality of infrastructure geographical and cultural proximity with major source of capital and policy factors, viz. tax rates investment incentives and performance requirements. The disadvantages are her low-income levels, low level disadvantage of urbanization and relatively poor quality of infrastructure. The economic factors, such as, trade investment regime, the openness of the host country, the adequacy of basic infrastructure and location.[15] Also determine factors Dunning identified FDI. According to him there are three main determinant factors of FDI: Firstly, location: market force (including market size and growth, as determined by the national income of the recipient country), Secondly, Cost of factors (such as labour cost and availability and domestic inflation situation), and Thirdly, investment climate (as determined by such consideration as the extent of foreign indebtedness and the state of the balance of payments).

Problems

India's poor performance in terms of competitiveness. As per the world economic Forum's latest Growth competitiveness Report, 2002-03, India was ranked 48th in the Growth Competitiveness Index (GCI) during 2002 which is much lower than that of other Asian countries like Malaysia (27th), Thailand (31st) and China (33rd), nonetheless. India's overall position on the GCI improved by positions in 2002 from 56 in the previous year. More significantly, in terms of technology ranking, India's ranking at 57th in 2002 represents an improvement of 8 places from the earlier ranking of 65. The quality of infrastructure and skills and productivity of labour, there are several other factors that make India a far less ground foreign direct investment than the potential she has. And many reasons for not attract more FDI. The main reasons are: (a) Restrictive FDI regime, (b) Lack of clear cut and transparent sectoral policies for FDI, (c) High tariff rates by international standard, (d) Lack of decision-making authority with the state government, (e) Limited scale of export processing zones, (f) No liberalization in exit barriers, and (g) Stringent labor laws, Financial sector reforms and High corporate tax.

SECTION II

Section two explains share of countries in global FDI, sectoral distribution of India's FDI and Causality relationship between FDI and output growth.

Share of Countries in Global FDI

In the developing countries FDI percentage declined in the years 1998, 1999, 2000, but again increased in 2001. But unfortunately FDI percentage declined in 2002, due to the personal problems of the countries. In India also declined in the same period. But in 2001 and 2002 FDI share of FDI percentage increased. The share of India in the world to FDI 1997 was 0.7. After 1997 the percent share of India in the decreased from 0.4 per cent in 2001 to 0.5 per cent in 2002 (see Table 1). China's share was very high among the Asian countries. One of the reasons's for increase of FDI was China's economy liberalized in earlier than the other developing countries. And India's share in the Asian countries to 1.6 per cent it increase (in 2001) to 2.1 per cent (in 2002). (See Table 2). India's measured FDI as percentage of total GDP is quite low in comparison to other competing countries. FDI as a percent of GDP is low (see Table 3). India's GDP in the year 2002 the FDI percent is 5.1 per cent it is very low to compare to other countries.

Table 1: FDI Inflows by Host Region/Economy

(Billions of US$)

Sl No.	Sector/Industry	1991-96 (Annual average)	1997	1998	1999	2000	2001	2002
1.	World	256.32	481.91	686.02	1079.08	1392.95	823.82	651.18
2.	Developed Economies	156.64	269.65	472.26	826.64	1120.52	589.37	460.33
3.	Developing Economies	91.50	193.22	191.28	229.29	246.05	209.43	162.14
4.	South-East Asian Economies	56.14	100.06	90.09	105.31	138.69	97.60	88.61
5.	India	1.08	3.61	2.63	2.16	2.31	3.40	3.44
6.	Percent share of developing economies in the world trade	35.9	40	27.8	21.2	17.6	25.4	26.8
7.	Percent share of India in Developing economies total	1.1	1.8	1.3	0.9	0.9	1.6	2.1
8.	Percent share of India in south Asian Economies total	1.9	3.6	2.9	2.0	1.6	3.4	3.8
9.	Percent share of India in World Total	0.4	0.7	0.3	0.2	0.1	0.4	0.5

Source: World Investment Report, Various issues.

Singapore contributed 137 per cent to FDI it is significant in compared to the other countries. Second place goes to Malaysia (59.4%), Vietnam (50.2%) and India (5.1%) respectively (see Table 3). Inflow of the FDI comes from Mauritius, USA and Germany. During the period 1995-96 to 2000-01 Mauritius contributed more FDI to India. In 2000-01 Mauritius investment in India has 843 millions of US$. USA contributed 320 US$, and Japan invested only 113 millions of US$.

Table 2: FDI Inflows in Select Asian Economies
(Percent share in Developing Economies)

Sl. No.	Host Region/ Economy	1991-96 (Annual average)	1997	1998	1999	2000	2001	2002
1.	China	27.7	22.8	22.8	17.5	16.5	22.3	32.5
2.	India	1.1	1.8	1.3	0.9	0.9	1.6	2.1
3.	Indonesia	3.2	2.4	-0.2	-1.1	-1.8	-1.5	-0.9
4.	Korea	1.3	1.4	2.8	6.1	3.7	1.6	1.1
5.	Malaysia	5.9	3.2	1.4	1.6	1.5	0.2	1.9
6.	Philippines	1.3	0.6	0.8	0.7	0.5	0.4	0.6
7.	Singapore	7.4	6.9	3.9	5.7	5.0	5.2	6.7
8.	Thailand	2.0	1.9	3.8	2.6	1.3	1.8	0.6
9.	Vietnam	1.3	1.2	0.8	0.6	0.4	0.6	0.7
10.	Pakistan	0.5	0.3	0.2	0.2	0.1	0.2	0.5

Source: World Investment Report, 2003.

Table 3: Ratio of FDI Stocks to GDP

(Percent)

Sl. No.	Host Region/ Economy	1980	1985	1990	1995	2000	2001	2002
1.	China	3.1	3.4	7.0	19.6	32.3	33.2	36.2
2.	India	0.6	0.5	0.5	1.6	6.1	6.6	5.1
3.	Indonesia	13.2	28.2	34.0	25.0	40.4	39.5	32.2
4.	Korea	-	-	3.4	13.7	10.0	9.6	9.5
5.	Malaysia	20.7	23.3	23.4	32.3	58.6	60.5	59.4
6.	Philippines	3.9	8.5	7.4	8.2	12.2	16.7	15.0
7.	Singapore	52.9	73.9	83.1	78.7	124.0	132.2	137
8.	Thailand	3.0	5.1	9.6	10.4	20.3	25.3	23.9
9.	Vietnam	0.2	1.1	4.0	28.5	48.2	48.4	50.2
10.	Pakistan	2.9	3.5	6.8	9.1	11.8	9.2	9.8

Source: World Investment Report, 2003.

Table 4: Foreign Investment: Country-wise Inflows

(Millions of US$)

Country	1994-95	1995-96	1996-97	1997-98	1998-99	1999-00	2000-01	2001-02	2002-03	2003-04	2004-05	2005-06 (P)
Mauritius	196.7	507.3	846.4	900.4	590.0	501	843	1863	534	381	820	1363
U.S.A.	202.8	196.6	241.6	687.4	452.8	355	320	364	268	297	469	346
South Korea	12.0	23.9	6.3	333.1	85.3	8	N.A.	3	22	22	14	61
Japan	96.9	60.9	96.7	163.5	235.1	142	156	143	67	67	122	86
Netherlands	46.7	49.8	123.7	158.9	53.3	82	N.A	68	197	197	196	68
Germany	36.6	99.7	166.2	151.4	589.9	31	113	74	103	69	143	45
U.K.	143.5	70.9	56.2	125.8	N.A.	N.A.	N.A.	45	224	157	84	261
Hong Kong	N.A.	100.0	41.5	62.4	N.A.	N.A.	N.A.	N.A.	N.A.	N.A.	N.A.	N.A.
Italy	N.A.	11.3	27.7	42.9	115.6	125	29	N.A.	N.A.	N.A.	N.A.	N.A.
Others	100.3	299.6	452.7	330.2	356.4	337	349	280	227	218	300	901
Total	872.0	1418	2057.0	2956.0	2000.0	1581	1910	2988	1658	1462	2320	3358

P: Provisional.

Note: Data in this table exclude FDI inflows by way of acquisition of shares by non-residents under section of FEMA, 1999.

Source: RBI Bulletin, various issues.

Sectoral Distribution of India's FDI

Services, Computers Engineering, Finance and Chemicals & Allied Products were the main industries receiving FDI in India in 2002-03. Engineering, Chemicals & Allied products, Food Dairy products and Electronic & Electrical equipment, which were more attract industries in the 1996-97, now the trend has been changed (see Table 5). The inflow of FDI into computer increased from 3 percent in 1996-97 to 17.91 percent in 2002-03. During the year of 1996-97 on words the computer receiving more FDI. But engineering industry was received 35 percent in 1996-97. After this year on words the FDI inflow percent is decreasing, except 2002-03 year. In other industry FDI inflows were up and downs are their (see Table 6). Foreign Direct Investment is continuously increasing from Rs.174 crores in 1990-91 to Rs. 24870 crores in 2004-05, but 1999-2000 year FDI declined (see Table 7). Graph-1 explained clearly. But portfolio investment increased a lot in comparatively FDI. In the post globalization period, many policies were come and encouraged to investment inflows; particularly Foreign Direct Investment and Portfolio investment (see Table 8). In India, as far FDI is concerned, it share in total foreign investment inflows was 96.99 percent in 1991-92, It was declined to 43.82 per cent in 1995-96. And again it was increased 65.89 per cent in 2001-02. Table 9 shows that fluctuation is their in FDI in the observed years.

The study has used Granger causality test. For this study purpose 8 manufacturing industries have taken into consideration. Those are Chemical and allied industry, Food and beverage, Machinery industry, Textile industry, Metal industry, Non-metal industry, Transport industry and Miscellaneous Industry. The causation between the two may take place in the following four alternative ways:

(a) FDI causes manufacturing output,
(b) Output causes FDI inflow,
(c) Bi-directional relationship between FDI and manufacturing output, and
(d) Independent relationship between the two.

Causality Result

Granger causality test has been applied to know the relationship between FDI and output. Granger Causality test is applied. In this study 8 different manufacturing industries have taken, namely:

(1) Chemical and allied
(2) Food and beverages

Table 5: Foreign Investment: Industry-wise inflows

(Millions of US$)

Sl. No.	Sectoral	1992-93	1993-94	1994-95	1995-96	1996-97	1997-98	1998-99	1999-00	2000-01	2001-02	2002-03	2003-04	2004-05	2005-06 (P)
1.	Electronic & Electrical equipment	33	57	56.4	129.6	153.6	646.6	228.3	172	213	659	95	90	14	93
2.	Engineering	70	33	131.6	251.9	730.2	579.9	427.6	326	273	231	262	N.A.	N.A.	N.A.
3.	Services	2	20	93.4	100.4	15.2	321.3	368.5	116	226	1128	509	N.A.	N.A.	N.A.
4.	Chemicals & Allied products	47	72	141.2	126.7	303.8	257.3	375.5	120	137	67	53	N.A.	N.A.	N.A.
5.	Finance	4	42	97.7	270.0	217.0	147.9	186.8	20	40	22	54	N.A.	N.A.	N.A.
6.	Computers	8	8	10.2	52.1	58.7	139.2	106.2	99	306	368	297	166	372	770
7.	Food & Dairy products	28	44	60.9	85.0	237.5	112.3	18.6	121	75	49	35	64	183	148
8.	Domestic Appliances	16	2	108.3	0.5	15.1	59.9	N.A.	N.A.	N.A.	N.A.	N.A.	N.A.	N.A.	N.A.
9.	Pharmaceuticals	3	50	10.1	56.8	47.6	33.8	28.4	54	62	69	44	N.A.	N.A.	N.A.
10.	Others	69	76	162.2	347	278.3	659.8	262.1	553	578	395	309	213	100	143
	Total	280	403	872.0	1418	2057.0	2956.0	2000.0	1581	1910	2988	1658	1462	2320	3358

Note: Data in this table exclude FDI inflows under the NRI direct investment route through the Reserve Bank and inflow due to acquisition of shares under section 5 of FEMA, 1999.

Source: RBI Bulletin, Various issues.

Table 6: Sectoral Distribution of FDI

(As a percentage of totals)

Sl. No.	Sector/Industry	1992-93	1993-94	1994-95	1995-96	1996-97	1997-98	1998-99	1999-00	2000-01	2001-02	2002-03
1.	Chemicals and Allied Products	17	18	16	09	15	09	19	08	07	2.24	3.19
2.	Engineering	25	08	15	18	35	20	21	21	14	7.12	15.80
3.	Domestic Appliances	06	01	12	N.A	01	02	N.A	N.A	N.A	N.A	N.A
4.	Finance	01	10	11	19	11	05	09	01	02	0.73	3.25
5.	Services	01	05	11	07	01	11	18	07	12	37.75	2.27
6.	Electronics and Electrical equipment	12	14	06	09	07	22	11	11	11	22.05	5.72
7.	Food and Dairy Products	10	11	07	06	12	04	01	08	04	1.63	2.11
8.	Computers	03	02	01	04	03	05	05	06	16	12.31	17.91
9.	Pharmaceuticals	01	12	01	04	02	01	01	03	03	2.30	2.65
10.	Others	25	19	19	24	14	22	13	35	30	13.21	18.63
	Total	100	100	100	100	100	100	100	100	100	100	100

Source: *RBI Bulletin*, Various issues.

Table 7: Foreign Investment Inflow

Year	A. Direct Investment		B. Portfolio Investment		Total (A+B)	
	Rs. Crores	US $ million	Rs. Crores	US$ million	Rs. Crores	US$ million
1990-91	174	97	11	6	185	103
1991-92	316	129	10	4	326	133
1992-93	965	315	748	244	1713	559
1993-94	1838	586	11188	3567	13026	4153
1994-95	4126	1314	12007	3824	16133	5138
1995-96	7172	2144	9192	2748	16364	4892
1996-97	10015	2821	11758	3312	21773	6133
1997-98	13220	3557	6696	1828	19916	5385
1998-99	10358	2462	-257	-61	10101	2401
1999-00	9338	2155	13112	3026	22450	5181
2000-01	18406	4029	12609	2760	31015	6789
2001-02	29235	6130	9639	2021	38874	8151
2002-03	24367	5035	4738	979	29105	6014
2003-04	21473	4673	52279	11377	73752	16050
2004-05	24870	5535	40029	8909	64899	14444

Source: Hand Book of Statistics on the Indian Economy, 2004-05.

(3) Machinery industry
(4) Textile
(5) Metal
(6) Non-Metal
(7) Transport
(8) Miscellaneous industries.

The results of the test reported in Table 10.

The result reveals that in Chemical and allied industries, it is shown that a lag (1, 1) FDI causes output and output does not cause FDI.

In Food industries no causation is found between FDI and output or *vice-versa*. Neither FDI influences output nor output influence FDI. F-statistics are statically insignificant.

Similar results are found in machinery industries. No causation is found between FDI and output or *vice-versa*. Neither FDI influences output nor output influences FDI. F-Statistics are statically insignificant.

In Textile industry no causation is found between FDI and output

Table 8: Foreign Investment Inflows in India

(US $ Million)

Sl. No	Source	1991-92	1992-93	1993-94	1994-95	1995-96	1996-97	1997-98	1998-99	1999-00	2000-01	2001-02	2002-03	2003-04	2004-05	2005-06(P)
1	FDI	129	315	586	1314	2144	2821	3557	2467	2155	2339	3904	5035	4322	5652	7751
A	SIA/FIBA	66	212	280	701	1249	1922	2754	1821	1410	1456	2221	919	928	1062	1126
B	RBI	-	42	89	171	169	135	202	179	171	454	76	739	534	1258	2233
C	NRI	66	51	217	442	715	639	241	62	84	67	35	-	-	-	-
D	Acquisition of shares	-	-	-	-	11	125	360	400	450	362	881	916	735	930	2181
E	Equity capital unincorporated bodies	NA	NA	NA	NA	NA	NA	NA	NA	NA	NA	NA	190	32	527	280
1(A)	Re-invested earnings	NA	NA	NA	NA	NA	NA	NA	NA	NA	NA	NA	1833	1460	1508	1676
1(B)	Other capital #	NA	NA	NA	NA	NA	NA	NA	NA	NA	NA	NA	438	633	367	255
2	**Portfolio**															
	Investment (A+B+C)	4	244	3567	3824	2748	3312	1828	-61	3026	2760	2021	979	11377	9315	12492
A	GDRs/ADRs	-	240	1520	2082	683	1366	645	270	768	831	477	600	459	613	2552
B	FIIs@	-	1	1665	1503	2009	1926	679	-390	2135	1847	1505	377	10918	8686	9926
C	Of share Bonds and others	4	3	382	239	56	20	204	59	123	82	39	2	-	16	14
	Total (1+2)	133	559	4153	5138	4892	6133	5385	2401	5181	5099	2925	6014	15699	14967	20243

P: Provisional, #: Data pertain to inter-company debt transaction of FDI entities. @: Data represent net inflow of funds by FIIs.

Note: 1. Data on reinvested earnings for 2004-05 and 2005-06 are estimates. 2. Data on foreign investment presented in this table represent inflows into the country and may not tally with the data presented in other tables. They may also differ from data relating to net investment in stock exchanges by FIIs.

Source: 1991-92 to 2001-02 data collected from *Economic Survey*, 2002-03 and 2002-03 to 2005-06 data collected from RBI Annual Reports, Various Issues.

Table 9: Foreign Investment Inflows in India

(Percent of Total)

Sl. No	Source	1991-92	1992-93	1993-94	1994-95	1995-96	1996-97	1997-98	1998-99	1999-00	2000-01	2001-02	2002-03	2003-04	2004-05	2005-06(P)
1.	FDI	96.99	56.35	16.11	25.57	43.82	45.99	66.05	102.7	41.59	45.87	65.89	83.72	27.53	37.76	38.28
2.	FII	3.00	43.64	85.80	76.42	56.17	54.00	33.94	-2.54	58.40	56.12	36.10	16.27	72.46	62.23	60.48
3.	Total	100	100	100	100	100	100	100	100	100	100	100	100	100	100	100

Source: Economic Survey, 2002-03 and RBI Annual Reports, Various Issues.

Table 10: Granger Causality Test: FDI-Output Link

Sl. No.	Name of the Industries	Lags	Maintained Hypothesis	F-Statistics	Significance Level	Inference
1.	Manufacture of Basic Chemical Industry	(1,1)	FDI→Output Output→FDI	15.27 3.99	0.00 0.07	FDI→Output Output←/→FDI
2.	Manufacture of Food Products	(1,1)	FDI→Output Output→FDI	0.75 6.23	0.40 0.06	FDI←/→Output Output←/→FDI
3.	Machinery and equipment and other transport equipment	(1,1)	FDI→Output Output→FDI	1.13 2.27	0.30 0.15	FDI←/→Output Output←/→FDI
4.	Manufacture of Textile Products	(1,1)	FDI→Output Output→FDI	0.39 0.61	0.54 0.44	FDI←/→Output Output←/→FDI
5.	Manufacture of Metal Products and Parts	(1,1)	FDI→Output Output→FDI	2.08 3.29	0.17 0.09	FDI←/→Output Output←/→FDI
6.	Manufacture of Non-Metal Products	(1,1)	FDI→Output Output→FDI	3.96 0.34	0.07 0.56	FDI←/→Output Output←/→FDI
7.	Manufacture of Transport equipment	(1,1)	FDI→Output Output→FDI	0.57 0.64	0.46 0.43	FDI←/→Output Output←/→FDI
8.	Other Manufacturing Industry	(1,1)	FDI→Output Output→FDI	3.97 0.86	0.07 0.37	FDI←/→Output Output←/→FDI
9.	Total Manufacturing Industry	(1,1)	FDI→Output Output→FDI	3.01844 0.14649	0.11633 0.71080	FDI←/→Output Output←/→FDI

Note: Log 2 level also statistically insignificant.

or *vice-versa*. Neither FDI influences output nor output influences FDI. F-statistics are statically insignificant.

In Metal industry no causation is found between FDI and output or *vice-versa*. Neither FDI influences output nor output influences FDI. F-statistic is statically insignificant.

In Non-metal industry no causation is found between FDI and output or *vice-versa*. Neither FDI influences output, output influence FDI. F-statistics is statically insignificant.

In Transport Industry no causation is found between FDI and output or *vice-versa*. Neither FDI influences output nor output influences FDI; F-statistics are statistically insignificant.

In Miscellaneous Industry no causation is found between FDI and output or *vice-versa*. Neither FDI influences output or output influences FDI. F-statistics are statistically insignificant. In the total manufacturing industry FDI causes to Output growth but Output is not more inflow FDI.

Concluding Remarks

The Ganger causality test reveals that FDI inflows causes output growth in Chemical and allied industry. Foreign investment helped only one industry to increase the output and to improve its performance. But the FDI in other industries does not influence output growth and performance of those industries.

Notes and References

1. *RBI Bulletin* (2003), "Report of the Committee competition of FDI in India", October 2002, August, pp. 533-58.
2. Chakraborty Chandra and Peter Nunnekhamp (2006), "Economic Reforms, Foreign Direct Investment and its Economic effects in India", *The Kiel Institute for the World Economy Duesternbrooker weg 120, 24105 Kiel (Germany) Kiel working paper No.1272.*
3. Prakash: "Foreign Direct Investment and Economic Growth in India: A Production Function Analysis", *Indian Journal of Economics*, Vol. LXXXII, Nos. 3-4, pp. 581-86.
4. Dua, Pami and Aneesa I. Rashed (1998), "Foreign Direct Investment Economic Activity in India", *Indian Economic Review*, Vol. XXXIII, No. 2, pp. 153-68.
5. Krushna Dutt Amitava (1997), "The Pattern of Direct Foreign Investment and Economic Growth", *World Development*, Vol. 25, pp. 1925-36.
6. Bhat, Sham K., Trupura Sundari, C.U. and K. Durai Raj (2004), "Causal Nexus between Foreign Investment and Economic Growth in India", *The Indian Journal of Economics*, October, Vol. LXXXV, No. 337 pp. 171-85.

7. Government of India, Planning Commission (2002), "Report of the Steering Group on Foreign Direct Investment", Academic Foundation.
8. Sharma (2000), "Exports Growth in India: Has FDI played a Role? Center Discussion Paper No. 816.
9. Dua & et al. (2000), "Foreign Direct Investment Economic Activity in India", *Indian Economic Review*, Vol. XXXIII, No. 2, pp. 153-68.
10. Radha & et al. (2000), "Foreign Direct Investment in India Policy Trends & Determents", *Productivity*, Vol. 41, No. 3, pp. 454-62.
11. Sumon K. Bhaunik, P.L. Beena, Laveesh Bhandari and Subir Gokan (2003), "Survey of FDI in India", DRC Working Paper No. 6.
12. Kumar, Nagesh (1998), "Liberalization and changing pattern of Foreign Direct Investment Has India's Relative Attractiveness as a Host of FDI Improved"?, *EPE*, Vol. XXXIII, No. 22, May 30, pp. 1459-69.
13. Kumar, Nagesh (2005), "Industrialization, liberalization and two-way flows of Foreign Direct Investment Case study of India", *EPW*, Vol. XXX, No. 50, pp. 3228-37.
14. Morris Sebastian (1994), "Prospects for FDI and Multinational Activity in the 1990s", *EPW*, Vol. XXXIX, No. 19, No.1141-46.
15. De Mellor Jr., Luiz, R. (1997), "Foreign Direct Investment in Developing Countries and Growth: A Selective Survey", *The Journal of Development Studies*, Vol. 34, No.1, pp. 1-34.

References

Bajpai, Nirupam and Jeffry D. Sachs (2000), "Foreign Direct Investment in India: Issues and Problems," *Development Discussion Paper No. 759*, March.

Bala Subramanyam V.N. and Vidya Mahambare (2003), "Foreign Direct Investment in India", *Lancaster University Management School Working Paper 2003/1.*

Busenna Pesala (2008), "Impact of Globalisation on Indian Manufacturing Industry", an un published Ph.D. Thesis, submitted to University of Hyderabad, Hyderabad.

Chalapati Rao K.S., M.R. Murthy and K.V.K. Ranganathan: "Foreign Direct Investment in the Post-Liberalization Period: An Overview", Vol. 11, No. 3, pp. 423-54.

Goldar Bishwanath & Easurao Ishigami (1999), "Foreign Direct Investment in Asia", *Economic and Political Weekly*, pp. M-50 to M-60.

Gopinath, T. (1997), "Foreign Investment in India: Policy Issues, Trends and Prospects", *Reserve Bank of India, Occasional Papers*, Vol. 18, Nos. 2 & 3, pp. 453-70.

Kumar, Nagesh (2005), "Liberalization, Foreign Direct Investment Flows and Development: Indian Experience in the 1990's, *EPW*, Vol. XL, No. 14, pp. 1459-69, April 2.

Nagaraj, R. (2003), "Foreign Direct Investment in India in the 1990's Trends and Issues", *EPW*, Vol. No. April 26.

Prakash Pradhan Jaya (2004), "Foreign Direct Investment and Labour: The case of Indian Manufacturing", *Labour & Development*, Vol. 10, No. 1, June, pp.58-79.

Radha Krishnan, K.G. and Jaya Prakash (2000), "Foreign Direct Investment in India: Policy Trends & Determinants", *Productivity*, Vol. 41, No. 3, October-December, pp. 454-62.

Srivastava, Sadhana (2003), "What is the True Level of FDI Flows to India?" *Economic and Political Weekly*, Vol. XXXVIII, No. 7 (February), pp. 608-10.

13

Productivity Growth of Foreign and Domestic Firms in the Indian Iron and Steel Industry: A Decomposition Analysis

T. SAMPATHKUMAR

Introduction

Productivity growth has become a buzz word in recent economic research as it increases the growth of output without an additional increase in the factor input. Productivity is a major source of higher levels of production. It is a measure of the efficiency of factors or inputs in production. An increase in the levels of productivity in an economy implies that its factors of production and commodity inputs are manifesting increase in their output efficiency. The productivity improvements along with the increase in the quantities of factors will also be contributing an additional source of output increase (Brahmananda, 1982). In view of limited factor resources, efficient of utilisation has to be given an utmost importance in policy matters, since dynamic efficiencies are critical in ensuring the industrial performance of a nation.

India happens to be labour abundant and capital deficient country. To supplement the capital needs of the country, the Indian government adopted liberalization policies in all spheres of the economy in 1991. As a consequence of the economic reforms, there was a greater inflow of foreign capital in all the sectors. The inflow of capital takes places in two ways namely foreign institutional investment (FIIs) and foreign direct investment (FDI). From the point of view of development, FDI is far more important than FPI, since the FDI implies a long-term relationship and has a direct bearing on crucial development issues such as technology transfer, growth and export competitiveness. The most common means of FDI is the transnational corporation (TNCs/MNCs). In the last two decades, the TNCs have greatly expanded their role in the global economy. It may be noted that a bulk of TNCs are owned by the developed countries but their operations are mainly concentrated in less developed countries (LDCs). It is now generally recognised that FDI can considerably help the development efforts of LDCs and in recent years, several LDCs are actively competing for FDI. FDI contributes to the economic development of LDCs in several ways mainly through the supply of capital, transfer of technology and R&D activities, creates competition, provides market access and brings in better skill and management techniques.

The debate among the economists has been changing towards estimating the performance of the economy particularly after the reforms process. The government implemented various measures mainly to make the country and its different sectors to be more effective and competitive. There are controversial arguments and findings among the economists. While some argue that the economic reforms benefited the country to record higher growth rates, others argue that the benefit of higher growth was enjoyed by the foreign entrants. Significance of FDI can well be understood from the increase in the output and a growth in the levels of productivity. The macro-economic reforms and liberalization process helped the country to procure FDI to a considerable extent. And in the years to come reform measures will place the country in the list of top recipients of global FDI. In India, except defence, all sectors are opened for foreign investment. The policy measures have even allowed 100 per cent foreign ownership in manufacturing and service sectors. The discussion on the role of FDI reveals its direct and indirect impact on productivity and economic development. Earlier studies on FDI have shown conflicting results of the impact of FDI. Some studies have found that FDI has a positive or weak positive effects on the productivity levels (Grossman and Helpman, 1991; Branstetter, 2000; Kokko, 1994; Basant and Fikkert, 1996). On the other hand, some studies have found that foreign firms have a negative effect on the productivity performance of domestic firms (Fry, 1995; Aitken and Harrison, 1999). Aitken and Harrison (1999) explained that domestically owned firms might 'benefit' from the presence of foreign firms through the movement of human capital, direct and indirect spillovers to the domestic firms. On the contrary, foreign firms can also 'reduce' productivity of domestic firms. A foreign firm, with lower costs and better technology, will have an incentive to increase production relative to its domestic competitor. In this environment, entering foreign firms producing for the local market can draw demand from the domestic firms, causing them to cut production and to a fall in the domestic productivity.

It is therefore inconclusive as the gains and losses differ in different sectors of the economy. It is in this view the present study proposes to estimate the productivity growth (decline) and major sources of such growth (decline) of foreign and domestic firms in the Indian Iron and Steel Industry during 1997-98 to 2006-07.

Profile of Indian Iron and Steel Industry

The Indian Iron and Steel Industry has scaled new heights in the post independent India to become the fifth largest producer of crude steel in the world (Ministry of Steel, 2009-10). Beginning from Tata Iron & Steel Company (1907), Mysore Iron and Steel Company (1923) and Steel Corporation of Bengal (1939), it has travelled a long way to occupy fifth position in the production of crude steel in the world. At the time of Independence, the country had a small but viable iron &steel capacity of around one million tons in the private sector. The first big push to this industry came during the first three Five Year Plans. Massive investment in the public sector with a protected market environment laid the foundation of viable and competitive indigenous iron and Steel plants (Indicus Analytics, 2009).

The Indian iron and steel sector was the first core sector to be deregulated in 1991. The de-reservation of capacity was followed by decontrol of price and distribution. Lowering of tariff rates from 100 per cent to just 5 per cent, lifting of quantitative restrictions to promote exports and the automatic approval of FDI even up to 100 per cent were chief steps implemented as part of economic reforms. The post-liberalization era witnessed the largest expansion of capacity and output of steel sector due to the entry of private firms with the financial, technological and managerial support of foreign firms. These policy measures set in motion a process of rejuvenation of this core industry, which during the 80s had shown signs of pervasive stagnation. After the process of deregulation, average yearly growth in production accelerated to 8.4 per cent compared to 5.3 per cent, recorded in the 80's. Similarly, the rate of increase in consumption of finished steel increased to 7.2 per cent compared to 5.3 per cent recorded in the decade preceding de-regulation (Planning Commission, 2006).

In a liberalized market environment, the output growth of the industry depends on the effective use of factor inputs which ultimately results in productivity improvements. The present study decomposes the productivity growth of domestic and foreign firms in the Indian iron and steel industry applying relatively sophisticated methodology of frontier analysis originally suggested by Aigner and others (1977).

Estimation of productivity changes is important for the efficient allocation of factor inputs for a firm/industry and far more important is the understanding the sources of such changes. The study decomposes productivity changes due to technical progress and technical efficiency. Technical progress is the invention of new machines or new methods of production while technical efficiency is the ability or efficiency with which the known technology is applied.

Decomposition of Total Factor Productivity Growth

A stochastic frontier production function is defined by

$$y_{it} = f(x_{it}, t) \tag{1}$$

where y_{it} is the output of the ith firm ($i = 1, ..., N$) in the tth time period ($t = 1, ..., T$), $f(\cdot)$ is the production frontier, x is an input vector, t is a time trend index that serves as a proxy for technical change and $u = 0$ is the output-oriented technical inefficiency. Note that technical inefficiency in (1) varies over time.

$$y_{it} = f(x_{it}, t) \exp(-u_{it} + v_{it}),$$

where $(u_{it} + v_{it})$ is a composed error term combining output based technical inefficiency ·· and symmetric component ·· capturing random variation across production unit and random shocks that are external to its control. Totally differentiating the logarithm of y in (1) with respect to time, the change in production can be represented as

$$\dot{y} = TP + \sum_j \varepsilon_j \dot{x}_j - (du/dt), \tag{2}$$

where $\varepsilon_j = \partial \ln f / \partial \ln x_j$ is the output elasticity of factor input j, and a dot over a variable indicates its rate of change. The overall productivity change is affected not only by TP and changes in input use, but also by the change in technical inefficiency.

Functional Form

The components of productivity change can be estimated within a stochastic production frontier framework, and the time-varying production frontier, originally proposed by Aigner et al., (1977) in translog form as—

$$\ln y_{it} = \alpha_0 + \sum_j \alpha_j \ln x_{jit} + \alpha_T t + 0.5 \sum_j \sum_l \beta_{jl} \ln x_{lit} \ln x_{jit}$$

$$+ 0.5 \beta_{TT} t^2 + \sum_j \beta_{Tj} t \ln x_{jit} + v_{it} - u_{it} \, , \, j, \, l = L, \, K, \quad (4)$$

where y_{it} is the observed output (value added), t is the time variable and the x variables are inputs. Subscripts j and l indicate inputs (j, l = L, K). The efficiency error, u, represents production loss due to company-specific technical inefficiency; thus, it is always greater than or equal to zero ($u \geq 0$), and it is assumed to be independent of the statistical error, v, which is assumed to be independently and identically distributed as $N(0, \sigma_v^2)$.

Following Greene (1977) and Battese and Coelli (1992), technical inefficiency is assumed to be defined by—

$$u_{it} = u_i \, \eta_{it} = u_i \exp(-\eta \, [t - T]), \quad (5)$$

where the distribution of u_i is taken to be the non-negative truncation of the normal distribution, $N(\mu, \sigma_u^2)$ and η is a parameter that represents the rate of change in technical inefficiency. A positive value ($\eta > 0$) is associated with the improvement of the technical efficiency demonstrated by a firm over time.

The maximum-likelihood estimates for the parameters of the stochastic frontier model, defined by (4) and (5), can be obtained by using the programme FRONTIER 4.1, in which the variance parameters are expressed in terms of $\gamma = \sigma_u^2 / \sigma_s^2$ and $\sigma_s^2 = \sigma_u^2 + \sigma_v^2$ (Coelli, 1996).

Based on the estimates of equations 4 and 5, the technical efficiency level of 'i'th firm in 't'th period is (TE_{it}) is defined as the ratio between the actual output and the potential output:

$$TE_{it} = \exp(-u_{it}). \quad (6)$$

The rate of technical progress (TP) is defined by

$$TP = \partial \ln f(x,t) / \partial t = \alpha_T + \beta_{TT} t + \sum_j \beta_{Tj} \ln x_j \, , \, j = L, \, K. \quad (7)$$

The technical progress of 'i'th firm in 't'th period is (TP..) can be estimated from the parameters by evaluating the partial derivative of the production function with respect to time. This technical progress is subject to change for different input vectors if the TP is non-neutral. Therefore, geometric mean of adjacent periods was taken as proxy following Coelli, Rao and Battese (1998).

$$TP = \left[1 + \frac{\partial \ln (x_{it,t})}{\partial t} * (1 + \frac{\partial \ln f(x_{it+1, t+1})}{\partial (t+1)} \right]$$

It is remembered that both the technical efficiency (TE) and technical progress (TP) of 'i'th firm in 't'th period vary over time and across the production units.

Data and Description of Variables

Data

The study collected required data from the "Capitaline" the electronic data base which has been a major source of data for empirical research in recent times (Banga, 2004; NCAER, 2009). Data on various variables were collected for a period of ten years from 1997-98 to 2006-07. There are large number of firms, small and large, operate in the Indian iron and steel industry. The study considered those firms which are being listed both in the Bombay Stock Exchange (BSE) and National Stock Exchange (NSE) and are present continuously during the study period in order to minimize the volatility in the levels of production in the industry. The final data set thus consisted of 35 firms which alone constitute over 80 (81.6%) per cent of the total sales turnover of the industry. Since the study proposes to estimate the productivity variations in terms of ownership, the firms were grouped into domestic firms (29 firms) and foreign firms (6 firms). The classification of foreign firms was made in accordance with the 10 per cent criterion suggested by Reserve Bank of India (RBI, 2002).

Description of Variables

In order to estimate the total productivity change, the study considered basic variables like output, labour and capital.

Output: The real gross value added was included as measure of output in the model. The gross valued added of the firms were deflated by the whole price index of the industry (WPI, 1993-94 = 100) and thus real value added was considered.

Labour: The total number of persons employed in each firm was considered as a measure of labour input.

Capital: The gross fixed asset was included as a measure of capital input. The gross fixed investment was deflated by the whole price index of machine and machine tools with the base of 1993-94=100. Thus, the real gross fixed investment was included in the model.

Decomposition of TFPG

Total factor productivity growth is calculated as the sum of technical progress, as measured by the shift in the production frontier, changes in technical efficiency.

The TFP growth estimates for the Indian Iron and Steel industry has been reported in the Table 1.

It could be observed from the Table 1 that there was a productivity improvement to the extent of 3.69 per cent during the study period. Indian iron and steel industry experienced wide fluctuations in the productivity levels varying from higher productivity deterioration of 10.62 per cent in 2002-03 to a productivity improvement of 17.68 per cent in 2001-02. The decomposition of the productivity growth into technical efficiency and technical progress throws more light on the total factor productivity growth in the industry. It was observed from the Table 1 that the technical progress was positive in all the years of the study and was further found to be increasing for the entire iron and steel industry in the country. The TP was 2.18 per cent in 1997-98 which steadily increased to 6.53 per cent in 2006-07 registering a mean TP of 4.41 for the whole study period. As against this, the technical efficiency change (TEC) was negative and further found declining during the study period. The TEC for the entire iron and steel industry was estimated at -0.728 per cent in 1997-98. The negative efficiency change was noted to be aggravating as the negative TEC further increased to -10.84 per cent in 2006-07. Except for a few years, the negative trend in the efficiency was observed with a mean TEC of -0.072 per cent for the entire study period.

It could be summarized that there was a marginal improvement in the TFPG of Indian iron and steel industry as the estimated productivity growth was positive at 3.69 per cent for the whole study period. This positive growth in the productivity of the industry was primarily driven by the positive and significant growth in the technical progress rather than the technical efficiency which was found negative and in fact pulled down the productivity growth otherwise the TFPG in the industry would have been significantly higher.

The positive growth in the TP can be attributed to the recent policy changes introduced to reform the industry. This industry was the first one which was privatized after reform process which started in the year

1991. As a consequence of the policy changes there were significant improvements in the new methods of production and modernization of plants. As a result, there was an increase in the technical progress. But the technical progress experienced in the industry could not be fully realized into productivity improvements due to lower efficiency levels of labour force. The inadequate education and training could be reasons for the poor adaptability to the latest techniques of production in the industry.

Ownership and Productivity Growth

From the Table 1, it was noted that the Indian iron and steel industry recorded a marginal productivity growth of 3.69 per cent contributed mainly by the technical progress which was estimated to be 4.41 per cent during the study period. While the TP was estimated to be positive, the TE was found to be negative and further declining. These results cannot be generalized as there may be many firm specific factors like size, ownership which should also be considered while generalizing the findings. It is with this view, the study considered ownership of the firm and accordingly estimated the total factor productivity growth and the major driving force of such growth in the industry.

Table 1: Components of Total Factor Productivity Growth in Indian Iron and Steel Industry

Year	TP	TEC	TFP
1997-98	0.0218		
1998-99	0.0244	-0.0728	-0.0484
1999-00	0.0302	0.1064	0.1366
2000-01	0.0340	-0.1158	-0.0819
2001-02	0.0391	0.1378	0.1768
2002-03	0.0429	-0.1491	-0.1062
2003-04	0.0485	0.0963	0.1448
2004-05	0.0535	-0.0758	-0.0223
2005-06	0.0591	0.1163	0.1755
2006-07	0.0653	-0.1084	-0.0430
Mean	0.0441	-0.0072	0.0369

Table 2 presents estimates total factor productivity growth (TFPG), technical progress (TP) and technical efficiency (TE) of domestic firms.

During the period of study, the all the domestic firms were found to have a positive productivity growth of 1.54 per cent. The productivity

Table 2: Components of TFPG of Domestic Firms

Year	TP	TEC	TFP
1997-98	0.0489		
1998-99	0.0475	-0.0096	0.0379
1999-00	0.0483	-0.0131	0.0352
2000-01	0.0481	-0.0170	0.0310
2001-02	0.0521	-0.0224	0.0296
2002-03	0.0529	-0.0292	0.0237
2003-04	0.0536	-0.0381	0.0155
2004-05	0.0526	-0.0498	0.0028
2005-06	0.0552	-0.0655	-0.0104
2006-07	0.0574	-0.0844	-0.0270
Mean	0.0519	-0.0366	0.0154

growth of domestic firms was found declining from 3.79 per cent in 1998-99 to a negative level of 2.7 per cent in 2006-07. Till 2004-05, the TFPG was positive but declining and the remaining two years of the study period, productivity deterioration was observed as the positive sign changed to be negative to one cent (1.04%) in 2005-06 and 2.7 per cent in 2006-07.

While considered the components of productivity growth namely technical progress and technical efficiency, the TP was noticed to be positive and marginally increasing whereas the efficiency change was negative and was further aggravating. The TP was estimated at 4.89 per cent in 1997-98 which increased marginally to 5.74 per cent by the end of the study period. As against this, the efficiency change was negative and on the decline from 0.096 per cent to 0.844 per cent in the same period. Due to higher negative efficiency change the domestic firms in the industry recorded a modest rate of productivity growth which was estimated at 1.54 per cent for the study period. It could therefore be concluded that as results of various policy changes in the industry, the domestic firms could achieve higher levels of technical progress by introducing new methods of production and modern machineries but the lack of efficiency failed to take advantages out of these improvements. The negative efficiency change estimated for the domestic firms should be changed in accordance with the technical progress for a higher productivity growth.

Table 3 reports estimates of total factor productivity growth and its components, technical progress and technical efficiency of foreign firms in the Indian iron and steel industry. From the table, it could be noted that the productivity growth was positive and found increasing steadily and significantly throughout the study period. From a meager productivity growth of 1.52 per cent in 1998-99, it recorded a significant growth of 6.86 per cent in 2006-07 with a mean productivity level of 4.17 per cent for the entire period of study. This robust growth in the productivity level was collectively driven by both technical progress and technical efficiency. The technical progress (TP) was observed to have increased comparatively at higher rates than the efficiency change. It was 0.83 per cent in 1997-98 which increased significantly to 6.69 in 2006-07 with a mean TP of 4.01 per cent during the study period. In the same reference periods, the efficiency change increased marginally from 0.15 per cent to 0.17 per cent with a mean of 0.16 per cent for the whole period of study. It is a known fact that the foreign firms will normally have higher capital base with superior know-how and sophisticated techniques of production, inquisitiveness for new methods and invention through R&D. The net result of these measures will be a higher technological progress of the foreign firms compared the domestic firms. In the same way, these firms will have better organization and managerial practices which will lead them to have higher efficiency levels also. The positive and increasing TP and TEC together pulled up the total factor productivity growth of foreign firms in the Indian iron and steel industry to higher level.

Table 3: Components of TFPG of Foreign Firms

Year	TP	TEC	TFP
1997-98	0.0083		
1998-99	0.0137	0.0015	0.0152
1999-00	0.0208	0.0020	0.0228
2000-01	0.0270	0.0016	0.0285
2001-02	0.0334	0.0015	0.0349
2002-03	0.0396	0.0017	0.0413
2003-04	0.0464	0.0015	0.0479
2004-05	0.0535	0.0015	0.0550
2005-06	0.0599	0.0015	0.0614
2006-07	0.0669	0.0017	0.0686
Mean	0.0401	0.0016	0.0417

Conclusion

The study applying the stochastic frontier production function estimated the productivity growth of domestic and foreign firms in the Indian iron and steel industry. It was observed from the results that the Indian iron and steel industry as a whole witnessed a modest productivity growth of 3.69 per cent contributed mainly by the technical progress which recorded a mean growth of 4.41 per cent during the period of 1997-98 to 2006-07. When the firms were grouped according to their ownership, the foreign firms were found to have greater productivity levels than the domestically owned firms. It is evident from the estimated higher productivity growth of foreign firms at 4.17 per cent than the domestic firms which was found to have a negligible positive growth rate of 1.54 per cent during period under study. In order to throw more light on the source of productivity growth, the study decomposed the productivity growth into technical progress and technical efficiency. The foreign firms were found to have positive growth rates of TP and TEC whereas the TP was positive and TEC was negative for the domestic firms in the Indian iron and steel industry. It was further noticed that TP was positive for both domestic and foreign firms and the foreign firms were found to have greater levels of TP than that of domestic firms. The economic reforms, which are in force since 1991, benefited the Indian iron and steel industry to mark positive productivity growth of 3.69 per cent during the study period. But the benefit of reform process is more for the foreign firms as their growth level was higher than that of domestic firms. While the foreign firms have continuously increasing productivity growth, the domestic firms experience declining productivity growth. The reform process facilitated for the greater inflow of foreign capital, technology and technical know-how, managerial and organizational practices. As a result of these measures, both domestic and foreign firms could witness positive technical progress in the industry. But there was not corresponding change the efficiency levels. The technical efficiency was negligibly positive for the foreign firms and significantly negative for the domestic firms. Though the domestic firms witnessed a positive technical progress which was the chief factor for the productivity growth, it failed to increase the efficiency levels. Unless the domestic firms frame suitable policies to promote the efficiency to make use of the advancements in the technology, it would be very difficult for the domestic firms to compete with the foreign firms which operate in the Indian iron and steel industry.

References

Aigner,, D.J, C.A. Knox Lovell and Peter Schmidt (1977), "Formulation and Estimation of Stochastic Frontier Production Function Models", *Journal of Econometrics*, Vol. 6, pp. 21-37.

Aitken, Brian J. and Ann E. Harrison (1999), "Do Domestic Firms Benefit from Direct Foreign Investment? Evidence from Venezuela", *American Economic Review*, Vol. 89, pp. 605-18.

Banga, Reshmi (2004), "Impact of Japanese and US FDI on Productivity Growth: A Firm Level Analysis", *Economic and Political Weekly*, Vol. 39, January 31, pp. 448-51.

Basant, R. and B. Fikkert (1996), "The Effects of R&D, Foreign Technology Purchase and Domestic and International Spillovers on Productivity in Indian Firms", *The Review of Economics and Statistics*, Vol. 78, pp. 187-99.

Battese and Coelli (1992), "Frontier Production Functions, Technical Efficiency and Panel Data with application to Paddy Farmers in India", *Journal of Productivity Analysis*, Vol. 3, pp. 153-69.

Brahmananda (1982), "Productivity in the Indian Economy: Rising Inputs for Falling Outputs", Himalaya Publishing House, Bombay.

Branstetter, L.G. (2000), "Is Foreign Direct Investment a Channel of Knowledge Spillovers? Evidence from Japan's FDI in the United States", *NBER Working Paper No. 8015*, National Bureau of Economic Research, Cambridge. M.A., November.

Coelli, T.J. (1996), "A Guide to FRONTIER Version 4.1: A Computer Programme for Stochastic Frontier Production and Cost Function Estimation", *CEPA Working Papers, No. 7/96*, Centre for Efficiency and Productivity Analysis, University of New England, Australia.

Coelli, T.J., Prasada Rao, D.S., and Battese, G.E. (1998), "An Introduction to Efficiency and Productivity Analysis", Kluwer Academic Publishers, Boston.

Fry, Maxwell (1995), "Money, Interest and Banking in Economic Development", Second Edition, Johns Hopkins University Press.

Greene (1980), "Maximum Likelihood Estimation of Econometric Frontier Functions", *Journal of Econometrics*, Vol. 13, pp. 27-56.

Grossman, G. and E. Helpman (1991), "Innovation and Growth in the Global Economy", The MIT Press, Cambridge.

Indicus Analytics (2009), "Public Enterprises, Government Policy and Impact on Competition: Indian Steel Industry," Final Report Prepared for the Competition Commission of India, New Delhi, January.

Kokko, A. (1994), "Technology, Market Characteristics, and Spillover", *Journal of Development Studies*, Vol. 43, pp. 279-93.

Ministry of Steel, GOI, Annual Report, 2009-10.

NCAER (2009), FDI in India and its Growth Linkages, National Council of Applied Economic Research, New Delhi, August.

Planning Commission, GOI (2006), "Report of the Working Group on Steel Industry for the Eleventh Five-Year Plan (2007-12), December.

Reserve Bank of India (2002), "Report of the Committee on Compilation of Foreign Direct Investment in India", October.

Foreign Direct Investment and Export Performance

K. KALAICHELVI

Introduction

With an average real GDP growth rate of 7 percent over the last decade and the second largest population, India is becoming an attractive destination for foreign direct investment. Since the liberalization of the 1990s, FDI in India has increased from $237 million in 1990 to $5,335 million in 2004 and exports rose form $33,470 million in 1997 to $103,090.54 million in 2006. Indian policy makers have been encouraged to pursue more vigorously the ongoing reform program because it is evident that the high growth achieved is the result of liberalized economic policy. Indian policy-makers are aiming for double digit GDP growth in the coming years.

Export has been in the focus of economic literature and policy-making for years due to its multi-fold contribution to achieving and maintaining macroeconomic stability, resolving of macroeconomic problems like unemployment and trade deficit, accelerating economic growth and increasing the international competitiveness of economies.

The supply-increasing effects arise when FDI inflows induce increases in the host country's production capacity, which, in turn, increases export supply capacity. The FDI-specific effects arise because foreign capital inflows may incorporate different competitive advantages, such as superior knowledge and technology and thus, higher productivity, or better information about export markets as compared to local firms. We believe that differentiating between these two effects of FDI on exports is especially important in terms of policy implications. It is often argued that successful FDI-promoting policies should lead to, among other things, a significant increase in the host country's exports. However, if evidence indicates that FDI increases exports only through increasing export supply capacity, then FDI inflows are not special in that policymakers could increase exports through alternative means as well, such as promoting domestic investment, rather than FDI. If, on the other hand, one finds that there are direct FDI-specific positive effects.

In the following section, provides a discussion of potential channels through which FDI may affect exports.

Effects of FDI on Exports—Theoretical Arguments

This section discusses some theoretical arguments regarding the different potential effects of FDI on the host country's exports.

Theory of Multinational Enterprise

The theory of multinational enterprise (MNE) examines conditions under which firms may undertake FDI and become MNEs. Such decisions may have consequences for host country's exports and it is a goal of this section to review parts of this theory that predict effects of inward FDI on host country's exports.

Overall, the theory indicates that positive effects of inward FDI on a host country's exports may be expected when the host country and a home country have different factor intensities. In this case, the MNE may outsource some segments of its production process to the host country and export these (intermediate) products back to the home country (as well as other countries). Similarly, when the host country has a cost advantage and costs of trade are low (as compared to the trade costs of the home country), the host country may be used by the MNE as an export platform for serving its home market, as well as other markets.

The starting point for the theory of MNE is the idea that firms must have certain advantages in order to become multinational companies. Dunning (1993) organised these advantages in three basic groups: (1) Ownership advantage that refers to the case where the MNE has a product or a production process that provides it with market power in the foreign market, (2) Location advantage that indicates that the multinational needs to locate production abroad to maintain its competitive advantage, and (3) Internalisation advantage that suggests that the MNE has an incentive to exploit its ownership advantage internally.

In order to analyse the effects of FDI on a host country's exports, it is useful to distinguish between horizontally and vertically integrated multinational firms. In the case of horizontal integration, the MNE produces the same product in multiple plants located in more than one country, while vertical integration implies that different segments of the production process are carried out in different countries. Horizontally integrated firms often arise because of trade barriers in the form of tariffs ('tariff jumping investment'), or high transport costs. The multinational firm basically faces the dilemma of either building an additional plant in the host country (FDI) to supply the host country's market, or exporting to host country from the (existing) plant in the home country. In a model with oligopoly competition, FDI is favoured relative to exports (of home country) under three conditions: (i) high transport and tariff costs, (ii) relatively large firm-level economies of scale, compared to those of plant-level economies, and (iii) countries similar in size and their relative endowments (Markusen and Venables, 1998; Markusen, 2002, p. 103).

In the analysis of vertically integrated MNEs, which includes trade in intermediary products, models suggest that the production process is likely to be geographically fragmented if the countries have factor-price differences and the stages of production are associated with different factor intensities) Since the segments of the production process occur in different countries, intermediate products need to be traded. As the portion of intermediate products produced by the foreign affiliates in the host country is typically shipped back to the home country (Zhang and Markusen, 1999; Markusen, 2002, p. 189), it is expected that FDI has a direct positive effect on host country's exports, which arises endogenously under specific conditions within the formal models of vertically integrated FDI.

Most of the models on MNE investigate the effect of FDI on trade flows between home and host countries. However, it is quite often that a foreign subsidiary of MNE is used to supply the markets of third countries. For example, a US MNE may set-up a plant in Hungary and supply all the Central European markets from this production site. In this case, Hungarian exports to third countries would increase. Ekholm *et al.* (2003) analyse such situation in which the MNE invests in one country and uses this production site as an export platform for supplying other markets.

Potential Indirect Effects on Host Countries' Exports

This section describes other channels through which FDI may affect host country's exports, in addition to those described in the theory of MNE.

The impact of FDI on host country exports is not only direct, through the exports of the foreign affiliates, but there may be important side effects, which may influence the export performance of domestic producers indirectly. The extent of the spillovers and indirect effects of FDI on exports may depend (at least in some industries) on the initial technological and human capital level of the domestic producers (Girma *et al.*, 2007; Barrios *et al.*, 2005), on the intensity of competition in domestic markets, as well as on the government policies promoting linkages between domestic and foreign firms (Barry and Bradley, 1997).

As noted in Helpman *et al.* (2004), MNEs tend to have higher productivity than other companies, including exporters, which are, on the other hand, more productive than non-exporters. This higher productivity of MNEs may be viewed as a reflection of their firm-specific competitive assets, which create the ownership advantage of MNEs. Such assets, which include production process, innovative products, human capital of employees, or patents, are often referred to as MNEs' superior technology or knowledge (Girma *et al.*, 2007; Markusen, 2002, p. 18). Thus, when an MNE transfers its competitive assets to its affiliate in the host economy, there is the possibility of knowledge spillovers to domestic firms in the host country (indirect effect, which is specific for FDI). One specific channel through which domestic firms may increase their productivity and export competitiveness in tradable goods and services industries is simply by copying the operations of the foreign producer. This may be facilitated by the mobility of workers previously trained in the MNE's affiliate.

Some of the other potential channels of MNE's influence on domestic companies have been analysed theoretically, but not in the specific context of exporting domestic companies. One of the potentially important indirect MNE's effects on domestic producers is the competition effect. The entry of an MNE in one sector of the host economy increases the intensity of competition in this sector, which may force some domestic companies to leave the market (Markusen and Venables, 1999; Barrios *et al.*, 2005). Such an effect is less pronounced with export-oriented MNEs and domestic producers; but, in the case of exporting domestic companies, this may lead to negative effects of inward FDI if the loss of exports by domestic companies is not compensated for by new exports of the MNE's local affiliate.

However, MNE entry may also have positive indirect effects on the export performance of domestic companies. For example, an additional channel through which productivity of local firms may be increased is the so-called forward linkages, which occur when foreign affiliates sell goods or services to domestic firms. Improved products and services (and/or lower prices) in the downstream sector of a domestic firm (incurred through more intense competition due to an MNE's entry in that sector, or because of higher quality of inputs produced by foreign producer) may improve the domestic firm's own productivity and competitiveness as well. This implies that FDI inflows into a non-exporting sector may improve performance of domestic exporters.

Comparison with other Studies

By briefly summarising empirical evidence from related studies and comparing it to our findings. The papers from Sun (2001), Zhang and Song (2000), and from Goldberg and Klein (2000) are especially related to this study, because they try to capture the overall effects of FDI on trade at the macroeconomic level. Sun (2001) examines the different impact of foreign investment on exports in three regions of China in a period from 1984 to 1997 and finds that the effects of FDI vary across the three regions. The impact is positive and the strongest in the coastal region. Zhang and Song (2000) address the same research question for China at the provincial level. They also find that higher levels of FDI are consistent with higher provincial exports. It is worth noting that the positive effect of FDI on exports in China has mostly been due to the fact that China has largely been used as an export platform by MNEs. Goldberg and Klein (2000), on the other hand, analyse the impact of FDI from the United States in the manufacturing sectors of individual Latin American countries on the net exports of those and other sectors. The results vary across sectors and host countries, reflecting the importance of the specific conditions in individual countries and industries. The fact that the results are mixed makes it impossible for the authors to draw a strong and clear conclusion on the relationship between the FDI flows and trade.

Two recent studies of indirect effects of FDI on domestic producers are especially important in the context of this study. Girma *et al.* (2007) explicitly test the effect of inward FDI on the productivity of exporters in the UK that have been acquired by the foreign companies. This is important since much of the FDI inflow in the transition countries was for the acquisition of existing companies (mostly through privatisation). This study shows that FDI affects the productivity of acquired firms; however, the magnitude and significance of this impact depends on the time elapsed since acquisition. Without controlling for the initial productivity, Girma et al. (2007) find that, 1 year after acquisition, FDI has had significant and positive influence on average productivity growth of acquired companies (no significant effect was found in the year of acquisition). When controlling for pre-acquisition productivity, only the acquired firms with relatively high productivity before acquisition experienced productivity gains in the year of acquisition, reflecting the importance of absorptive capacity for (immediately effective) effects. The companies with lower initial productivity, on the other hand, benefited more from FDI 2 years after acquisition. This shows that it takes time for the acquired firms to benefit from FDI, especially for the domestic firms with lower initial productivity, which is important in the context of the present study. In addition to Girma et al. (2007), we would like to stress the empirical findings of Barrios et al. (2005). They tested their theoretical prediction that, at first, negative competition effect from FDI is stronger, but with more inward FDI, the positive externalities dominate the initial negative effect (the u-curve overall effect of FDI on domestic companies). This is empirically confirmed on their sample of Irish companies implying that the sufficient accumulation of foreign capital plays a crucial role for the effectiveness of indirect effects on domestic companies.

Analysis of Foreign Trade Performance

Table 1 shows that the engineering goods growth 38.38 per cent. Engineering goods play a major role next to agri and allied products.

Table 1: System on Foreign Trade Performance Analysis (FTPA) Export of Principal Commodities Groups (Dated: 14/1/2011)

(Values in Rs. Crores)

Commodity	Apr.-Sep. 2009	Apr.-Sep. 2010 (P)	% Growth	% Share
1	2	3	4	5
(A) Plantation	2,214.75	2,694.25	21.65	0.56
(B) Agri & allied products	28,409.79	31,107.14	9.49	6.41
(C) Marine products	4,174.93	4,962.97	18.88	1.02
(D) Ores & minerals	15,937.84	20,183.15	26.64	4.16
(E) Leather & manufacturers	7,817.64	8,457.39	8.18	1.74
(F) Gems & jewellery	66,780.68	72,261.46	8.21	14.89
(G) Sports goods	341.55	396.79	16.17	0.08
(H) Chemicals & related products	53,241.70	64,461.73	21.07	13.29

(Contd.)

	1	2	3	4	5
(I)	Engineering goods	76,641.08	106,055.49	38.38	21.86
(J)	Electronic goods	15,375.12	15,975.45	3.90	3.29
(K)	Project goods	331.64	136.16	-58.94	0.03
(L)	Textiles	45,148.91	47,049.30	4.21	9.70
(M)	Handicrafts	498.25	389.70	-21.79	0.08
(N)	Carpets	1,551.34	1,972.80	27.17	0.41
(O)	Cotton raw including waste	1,360.96	1,727.28	26.92	0.36
(P)	Petroleum products	52,268.26	82,295.62	57.45	16.96
(Q)	Unclassified exports	21,167.74	25,080.09	18.48	5.17
	Total	393,262.20	485,206.77	23.38	100.00

(P) Provisional.
Data Source: DGCIS, Kolkata, DOC-NIC.

Table 2 shows that the growth in exports by regions to America place the growth of share to 37.41 per cent. Next to other Asian countries.

Table 2: System on Foreign Trade Performance Analysis (FTPA) Export by Region (Dated: 14/1/2011)

(Values in Rs. Crores)

	Region	Apr.-Sep. 2009	Apr.-Sep. 2010 (P)	% Growth	% Share
	1	2	3	4	5
(1)	Europe	83,809.38	97,998.08	16.93	20.20
	1.1 EU Countries (27)	78,310.12	90,403.17	15.44	18.63
	1.2 Other WE Countries	5,244.20	7,309.40	39.38	1.51
	1.3 East Europe	255.06	285.51	11.94	0.06
(2)	Africa	24,154.79	32,271.60	33.60	6.65
	2.1 Southern Africa	7,790.30	13,110.93	68.30	2.70
	2.2 West Africa	7,094.45	8,407.88	18.51	1.73
	2.3 Central Africa	808.21	944.44	16.86	0.19
	2.4 East Africa	8,461.82	9,808.35	15.91	2.02
(3)	America	58,136.43	79,884.54	37.41	16.46
	3.1 North America	46,357.21	56,652.53	22.21	11.68
	3.2 Latin America	11,779.22	23,232.01	97.23	4.79
(4)	Asia & ASEAN	212,078.95	259,503.10	22.36	53.48
	4.1 East Asia	4,031.82	4,131.69	2.48	0.85
	4.2 ASEAN	42,609.73	53,450.06	25.44	11.02
	4.3 WANA	91,757.26	108,253.73	17.98	22.31
	4.4 NE Asia	55,668.77	71,617.36	28.65	14.76
	4.5 South Asia	18,011.37	22,050.26	22.42	4.54

1	2	3	4	5
(5) CIS & Baltics	3,496.83	5,432.96	55.37	1.12
5.1 CARs Countries	627.12	597.36	-4.74	0.12
5.2 Other CIS Countries	2,869.72	4,835.60	68.50	1.00
(6) Unspecified Region	11,585.80	10,116.49	-12.68	2.08
Total	393,262.19	485,206.77	23.38	100.00

(P) Provisional.
Data Source: DGCIS, Kolkata, DOC-NIC.

Table 3 gives a detail picture of the top five commodities of export, and the highest growth of 57.45 per cent of petroleum (crude & products) products next to transport equipments of 53.26 per cent of growth.

Table 3: System on Foreign Trade Performance Analysis (FTPA) Top 5 Commodities of Export (Dated: 14/1/2011)

(*Values in Rs. Crores*)

Rank	Commodity	Apr.-Sep. 2009	Apr.-Sep. 2010 (P)	% Growth	% Share
1	Petroleum (Crude & Products)	52,268.26	82,295.62	57.45	16.96
2	Gems & Jewellary	66,780.68	72,261.46	8.21	14.89
3	Transport Equipments	26,373.11	40,420.43	53.26	8.33
4	Other Commodities	21,164.23	25,059.44	18.40	5.16
5	Machinery and Instruments	22,374.10	23,429.92	4.72	4.83
	Total	393,262.20	485,206.77	23.38	100.00

(P) Provisional.
Data Source: DGCIS, Kolkata, DOC-NIC.

Table 4: System on Foreign Trade Performance Analysis (FTPA) Top 5 Countries of Export (Dated: 14/1/2011)

(*Values in Rs. Crores*)

Rank	Country	Apr.-Sep. 2009	Apr.-Sep. 2010 (P)	% Growth	% Share
1	United Arab Emts	54,091.95	65,711.07	21.48	13.54
2	USA	43,703.73	53,942.97	23.43	11.12
3	China PRP	19,896.09	25,613.23	28.73	5.28
4	Hong Kong	18,049.52	22,034.84	22.08	4.54
5	Singapore	17,593.41	21,353.02	21.37	4.40
	Total	393,262.19	485,206.77	23.38	100.00

(P) Provisional.
Data Source: DGCIS, Kolkata, DOC-NIC.

Table 4 shows that the china have a growth of 28.73 percent and next comes USA 23.43 per cent of growth.

Our results show that, as in China, Ireland, or in some industries in some Latin American countries (Sun, 2001; Zhang and Song, 2000; Barry and Bradley, 1997; Goldberg and Klein, 2000), FDI contributed to increasing exports of host transition economies. Since other studies do not differentiate between supply-increasing and FDI-specific effects of FDI inflows on exports, a direct comparison of results is not possible. Our results on FDI-specific impact, which is significant only in NEU countries, reveal the importance of findings by Girma *et al.* (2007) and Barrios *et al.* (2005), which suggest that indirect impact of FDI on host countries (which, to some extent, should coincide with FDI-specific effects) depends on the initial situation in the host economies, that is, initial productivity of acquired firms (Girma *et al.*, 2007), and on the accumulated amount of FDI inflows (Barrios *et al.*, 2005). Since NEU countries are, on average, more developed than the Southeast European countries, they are expected to have relatively more productive companies. Also, they have received more FDI, which can additionally (at least partly) explain why such effects are significant only for this group (NEU) of countries.

The results imply that, for all the countries in our sample, FDI has significantly contributed to higher exports, through increased supply capacity, that is, potential output. When potential output is controlled for, the contribution of FDI is statistically significant only for the group of new EU countries, however. This implies that, for these countries, the positive impact of FDI goes beyond increasing supply capacity in that there are additional indirect, positive effects from inward FDI.

Conclusion and Suggestions for Further Research

In this paper, we estimate the impact of FDI inflows on export performance in different regions of transition economies, including some new member states of the EU. FDI can contribute to higher exports by increasing supply capacity and/or through FDI-specific effects as MNEs may have better knowledge about foreign markets, superior technology, and better ties to the supply chain of the parent firm than do local firms. It is important to distinguish between these types of effects, since the supply-increasing effects may arise as a consequence of domestic investment as well, making an FDI-promoting policy reluctant in the absence of FDI-specific impact.

On the other hand, evidence for FDI-specific effects is mixed. The results suggest that this effect has been present mainly for the new EU member states, reflecting, among other things, the higher amount of FDI inflows received by these countries relative to Southeast European countries, as well as the potentially higher initial productivity of domestic companies acquired by MNEs.

Our results have important implications for policymakers and other transition economies. First, our results support the notion that the MNE has an important advantage over local firms that it brings to the host economy. Hence, policy-makers need to support FDI inflows by designing appropriate policies and reforms. However, it seems that the amount of FDI stock accumulated over time matters for the positive FDI-effects on exports. In our sample of countries, the new EU countries received the larger amount of FDI relative to other transition economies and hence have been able to better take advantage of the FDI-specific effects than the rest of the countries, leading to more exports.

An important issue that the researcher did not study in this paper is the impact of FDI inflows on import behaviour. If the FDI is a substitute for imports of goods or services, it should further improve the balance of trade of the host country by reducing imports. We believe that this is an important research agenda that we plan to tackle in the near future.

The definition of FDI used in this paper is that of the IMF. FDI is '... international investment in which a resident entity in one economy (the direct investor) acquires a lasting interest in another economy (the direct investment enterprise)' (IMF, 1996). A lasting interest is implied if 10 per cent or more of the ordinary shares or voting power is acquired by the investor. Only trade and exports of goods is considered in this paper (as in most of the related literature), while trade in services is omitted. On the other hand, total FDI, that is, FDI in all sectors of the host economy is relevant.

REFERENCES

Barrios, S., Gorg, H. and Strobl, E. (2005), Foreign direct investment, competition and industrial development in the host country, *European Economic Review*, 49: 1761-84.

Barry, F. and Bradley, J. (1997), FDI and trade: The Irish host-country experience, *The Economic Journal*, 107: 1798-1811.

Brada, J., Kutan, A.M. and Yigit, T. (2006), The effects of transition and political instability on foreign direct investment inflows: Central Europe and the Balkans, *Economics of Transition*, 14: 649-80.

Dunning, J.H. (1993), Multinational enterprises and the global economy, Addison-Wesley Publishing Company: Reading, MA.

Ekholm, K., Forslid, R. and Markusen, J.R. (2003), Export-platform foreign direct investment, *NBER Working Paper No. 9517.*
Fan, E.X. (2002), Technological spillovers from foreign direct investment—A survey. *Asian Development Bank Working Paper No. 33.*
Galego, A., Vieira, C. and Vieira, I. (2004), The CEEC as FDI attractors: A menace to the EU Periphery? *Emerging Markets Finance and Trade,* 40: 74-91.
Ministry of Commerce web site.
Economic Survey.

FDI and Export Performance in India

S. SARAVANAN AND G. SARAVANAN

Introduction

FDI in India

There have been significant changes in the growth models of developing economies during the past two decades. Many of these economies, including India, have moved away from inward-oriented import substitution policies to outward oriented and market-determined export-oriented strategies. The skepticism about the role of FDI in reinforcing domestic growth has given way to greater openness to FDI, with a view to supporting investment and productivity of the host countries. While developing countries have started accepting FDI inflows with some caution, which is obvious, the developed countries have moved their investments to foreign locations, subject to safety and profitability of their business operations in foreign lands.

FDI plays an important role in the transmission of capital and technology across home and host countries. Benefits from FDI inflows are expected to be positive, although not automatic. A facilitating policy regime with minimal interventions may be ideal to maximize the benefits of FDI inflows. The debate on its pros and cons has not yet been settled and is likely to continue. It is not possible to reach a decisive value judgment on whether FDI is good or bad for the developing country/host economy. It may or may not have the desired and expected growth-enhancing impact on the host economy. Even more difficult is the question of whether it brings about equity along with growth effects.

FDI might enter a labour-abundant country with capital-intensive technologies; however, if the labour laws are not flexible, this would have a relatively small impact on employment generation. On the other hand, the entry of FDI in labor-intensive firms would have a positive impact on equity and poverty reduction if the FDI-enabled firms choose to locate close to suburban/rural areas.

The history of capital flows shows that large amounts of FDI crisescrossed the high-income countries and benefited their economies. The newly industrialized economies (NIEs) constitute important case studies.

Many developing countries, including India, have started receiving significant amounts of FDI in the past two decades. A large quantum of such FDI originates from high-income countries including the United States and the EU, while south-south FDI flows have also been increasing.

In order to fulfil sufficient conditions, the host country has to ensure that it creates absorptive However, nothing comes for free. Mere openness to FDI inflows may be a necessary but insufficient condition and the host economy needs to provide a sufficiently enabling environment to attract foreign investor's capability to make the best use of the FDI it receives. It needs to create a level playing field through developing an efficient, competitive and regulatory regime, such that both domestic and foreign invested companies play a mutually reinforcing role within a healthy competitive environment.

Investment Outlook

A number of studies in the recent past have highlighted the growing attractiveness of India as an investment destination. According to **Goldman Sachs (2003)**, the Indian economy is expected to continue growing at the rate of 5 per cent or more until 2050.

According to the **A.T. Kearney (2007)**, India continues to rank as the second most attractive FDI destination, between China at number one and the United States at number three. India displaced the United States in 2005 to gain the second position, which it has held since then. FDI inflows in 2006 touched $19.6 billion and in 2007, total FDI inflows.

FDI Performance and Potential Index

UNCTAD ranks countries by their Inward FDI Performance and Inward FDI Potential Indices. While India is the second most attractive country in terms of the foreign investors' confidence index, it does not rank high on either the performance or potential indices. UNCTAD

(2008) provides a matrix of four groups of countries based on their FDI performance and potential:

(a) *Front runners:* countries with both high FDI potential and performance.
(b) *Above potential:* countries with low FDI potential but strong performance.
(c) *Below potential:* countries with high FDI potential but low performance.
(d) *Under-performers:* countries with both low FDI potential and performance.

While countries like Chile, Hong Kong, Malaysia, Singapore and Thailand are "front runners", and China is below potential, all the major South Asian countries, viz., Bangladesh, India, Nepal, Pakistan and Sri Lanka are "underperformers".

India's FDI Performance Index in 2007 ranked at 106 (China was 88) out of 141 countries. However, it has a relatively high FDI Potential Index at 84 (China is 32). India's outward FDI Performance Index in 2007 is also high at the 50th position (China was 59th).

Global Competitiveness of India's FDI

Another method of assessing the investment potential of an economy is its rank on global competitiveness. The Global Competitiveness Index (GCI) is a comprehensive index developed by the World Economic Forum (WEF) to measure national competitiveness and is published in the Global Competitiveness Report (GCR). It takes into account the micro- and macro-economic foundations of national competitiveness, in which competitiveness is defined as the set of institutions, policies and factors that determine the level of productivity of a country and involves static and dynamic components. The overall GCI is the weighted average of three major components: (a) basic requirements (BR); (b) efficiency enhancers (EE); and (c) innovations and sophistication factors (ISF).

Within the information available for 131 countries, the United States is ranked the highest, with an overall index of 5.67, and Chad is ranked the lowest with an overall index of 2.78; the overall index is 107 for Bangladesh, 92 for Pakistan and 70 for Sri Lanka. The overall rank of India at 48 is still below that of China at 35. In terms of the components, India holds a relatively low rank for BR (74), but higher ranks for EE (31) and even higher for ISF (26). Compared to China, India's BR rank is lower, but it is higher than China's on EE and ISF.

Trends in FDI Scenario in India

Foreign direct investment (FDI) refers to cross-border investment made by a resident in one economy (the direct investor) with the objective of establishing a lasting interest in an enterprise (the direct investment enterprise) that is resident in a country other than that of the direct investor (OECD 2008). The motivation of the direct investor is strategic "lasting interest" in the management of the direct investment enterprise with at least 10 per cent voting power in decision making.

The host country aspires to receive FDI inflows because of the potential benefits, the most established benefit being that FDI supplements the domestic savings of a nation. Other payoffs include access to superior international technologies, exposure to better management and accounting practices, and improved corporate governance. FDI is likely to expand and/or diversify the production capacity of the recipient country which, in turn, is expected to enhance trade. On the other side, foreign investors are motivated by profits and access to natural resources. Therefore, large and growing domestic markets are likely to receive more FDI. Countries with abundant natural resources such as mines, oil reserves and manpower appear prominently on the investment maps of foreign investors.

While the objectives of FDI can be different from the home and the host country's perspectives, one of the major aims of attracting FDI is overall development of the recipient country keeping some specific strategy in view. This can be done by achieving higher FDI inflows (China, Malaysia and Singapore), maximising technology spill-over into the domestic economy (South Korea and Taiwan), or imposing local content requirements (East and South-East Asia).

The year 2007 posted 30 per cent growth in global FDI inflows, which touched $1,833 billion, i.e., about $400 billion above the previous record in the year 2000. About two-third of the inflows ($1,248 billion) was received by developed economies, while developing economies received about $500 billion FDI inflows—a 21 per cent increase over the year 2006. $500 billion FDI inflows into developing countries included about $13 billion for the least developed countries (LDCs). The transition economies of South-East Europe and the Commonwealth of Independent States (CIS) received about $86 billion worth of FDI. India received $23 billion of FDI inflows in 2007, up from $20 billion in 2006.

India has inward FDI stock worth $76.2 billion (compared with $327.1 billion in China) and outward FDI stock of $29.4 billion (compared with $95.8 billion of China). The FDI inflows received by

India accounted for 3 per cent of gross fixed capital formation (GFCF) in 2005, 6.6 per cent in 2006 and 5.8 per cent in 2007. The corresponding figures for China are 7.7, 6.4 and 5.9 per cent, respectively. Thus, the share of FDI in GFCF for India in 2007 was almost the same as that of China. The share of inward FDI stock of India was 0.5 per cent of GDP in 1990, 3.7 per cent in 2000 and 6.7 per cent in 2007. The corresponding figures are much higher for China, viz., 5.1, 16.2 and 10.1 per cent, respectively. The sales of India's mergers and acquisitions (M&A) reached $5,580 million in 2007 and stood at $2,254 million in January-June 2008. Similarly, India's purchases of M&As reached $30,414 million 2007 and stood at $8556 million in January-June 2008.

Trends in FDI inflows into India

FDI inflows grew steadily through the first half of the 90s but stagnated between 1996-97 and 2003-04 (Table 1). The year-on-year fluctuations until 2003-04 make it difficult to identify a clear trend; however, inflows have been increasing continuously since 2004-05. During 2008-09, India registered FDI inflows of $33.6 billion and total cumulative inflows from August 1991 to March 2009 have been to the tune of $155 billion.

Table 1: FDI Inflows (August 1991 to November 2008)

Year	Amount of FDI inflows		Annual Growth
	Rs. Crore	US$ million	
1	2	3	4
1991-92	375	129	—
1992-93	1051	315	144.2
1993-94	2041	586	86.0
1994-95	4241	1314	124.2
1995-96	7317	2144	63.2
1996-97	10170	2821	31.6
1997-98	13317	3557	26.1
1998-99	10550	2462	-30.8
1999-2000	9409	2155	-12.5
2000-01	18404	4029	87.0
2001-02	29269	6130	5.21
2002-03	24681	5035	-17.9
2003-04	19830	4322	-14.2
2004-05	27234	6051	40.0
2005-06	39730	8961	48.1

(Contd.)

1	2	3	4
2006-07	103037	22826	154.7
2007-08 (P)+	137935*	34362	50.5
2008-09 (P)+	159354^	33613	-2.2
August 1991 to March 2000	58471	15483	
April 2000 to March 2009	559474	125329	
August 1991 to March 2009	617945	140812	

Note: +RBI has included the amount of US$ 492 million for the month of April 2007.
*Partially Revised.   ^: Preliminary.   P: Provisional.
Sources: Secretariat for Industrial Assistance, Various FDI Fact Sheets, NACER, 2010.

FDI Outflows from India

Indian companies are reaching overseas destinations to tap new markets and acquire technologies. While some of the investment has gone into greenfield projects, a major portion of Indian overseas investment went into acquiring companies abroad. Acquisitions bring with them major benefits such as existing customers, a foothold in the destination market and the niche technologies they require. Due to the rapid growth in Indian companies' M&A activity, Indian companies are acquiring international firms in an effort to acquire new markets and maintain their growth momentum, buy cutting-edge technology, develop new product mixes, improve operating margins and efficiencies, and take worldwide competition head-on. It has emerged as the most acquisitive nation in emerging nations, according to global consultancy KPMG (2008) in their Emerging Markets International Acquisitions Tracker.

Table 2 shows that FDI outflows from India have increased consistently since 2000 at US$18.5 billion in 2008-09, compared to only US$1.4 billion in 2001-02.

FDI: Definition Issues

FDI statistics in India are officially monitored and published by the Reserve Bank of India (RBI) and the Secretariat for Industrial Assistance (SIA), Ministry of Commerce and Industry. While the IMF's definition of FDI incorporates equity capital, reinvested earnings (retained earnings of FDI companies) and 'other direct investment capital' (intra-company loans or intra-company debt transactions), FDI statistics compiled by the RBI in the Balance of Payments prior to 2000 included only equity capital. This led to an underestimation of FDI inflows. The accounting system was revised in 2000 in order to align the FDI data-reporting system with international best practices. Table 3 presents the revised inflows from the year 2000-01.

Table 2: India's FDI Outflows (Debit)

Year	FDI Outflows (US$ million)
2000-01	829
2001-02	1,490
2002-03	1,892
2003-04	2,076
2004-05	2,309
2005-06	6,083
2006-07	15,810
2007-08 (PR)	21,312
2008-09 (P)	18,596

Note: P: Preliminary; PR: Partially Revised.
Sources: Reserve Bank of India (2007, 2008). Handbook of Statistics on Indian Economy, *RBI Bulletin*, July 2009. NACER, 2010.

Table 3: Revised FDI Inflows Data (Equity + Additional Components)

(*in US$ million*)

Year	Equity	Equity capital for incorporated bodies	Equity capital of unicorporated bodies#	Re-invested earnings+	Other capital++	Total FDI Inflows
2000-01	2,400	2,339	61	1,350	279	4,029
2001-02	4,095	3,904	191	1,645	390	6,130
2002-03	2,764	2,574	190	1,833	438	5,035
2003-04	2,229	2,197	32	1,460	633	4,322
2004-05	3,778	3,250	528	1,904	369	6,051
2005-06	5,975	5,540	435	2,760	226	8,961
2006-07	16,481	15,585	896	5,828	517	22,826
2007-08 (P)	26,867	24,575	2,292	7,168	327	34,362
2008-09 (P)	27,973	27,307	666	6,426	747	35,146
Cumulative Total (April 2000 to March 2009)	82,562	87,271	5,291	30,374	3,926	126,862

Note: #Figures for equity capital of Unincorporated bodies for 2006-07 and 2007-08 are estimates.
+Data for 2006-07 and 2007-08 are estimated as average of previous two years.
++Data pertain to inter-company debt transactions of FDI entities.
(P): Provisional.
Sources: RBI Bulletin, July 2009. NACER, 2010.

The revised practice of reporting FDI statistics addressed the issue of underestimated FDI flows into India. Following the new exercise that included figures on reinvested earnings and other capital, the additional FDI in a given year was found to be as high as 72 per cent for the year 2000-01 and 57 per cent in 2001-02 (Table 3).

The equity inflows have been differentiated under equity inflows of incorporated bodies and equity inflows of unincorporated bodies. A comparison between the earlier period of 2000-01 and the latest available period of 2008-09 shows that the equity capital inflows of incorporated bodies continue to dominate the scene. The share increased to 86 per cent of total FDI inflows in 2008-09, as against 58 per cent in 2000-01. The reinvested earnings are the second most important component, though their significance has declined almost continuously over the period. In 2008-09, reinvested earnings constituted 14 per cent of the total FDI inflows compared to 33.5 per cent in 2000-01. Inflows through other capital (which include short-term and long-term inter-corporate borrowings, trade and supplier credit, financial leasing, financial derivatives, debt securities, and land and buildings) constituted 3.2 per cent in 2008-09 as against 6.9 per cent during 2000-01. The equity capital inflows of incorporated bodies continue to be nearly the same, at about 2 per cent or less of the total FDI inflows. Therefore, inflows through equity capital of the unincorporated bodies are the most significant component for India.

Table 4: Route-wise FDI Inflows

(in US$ million)

Year (Jan.-Dec.)	FIPB & SIA route	RBI's Automatic route	Inflows through acquisition of existing shares[#]	RBI's Various NRI schemes[*]	Total
1	2	3	4	5	6
1991 (Aug.-Dec.)	78	-	-	66	144
1992	188	18	-	59	264
1993	340	79	-	189	608
1994	511	116	-	365	992
1995	1264	169	-	633	2065
1996	1677	180	88	600	2545
1997	2824	242	266	290	3621
1998	2086	155	1028	91	3359
1999	1474	181	467	83	2205
2000	1474	395	479	81	2428
2001	2142	720	658	51	3571

1	2	3	4	5	6
2002	1450	813	1096	2	3361
2003	934	509	637	-	2079
2004	1055	1179	980	-	3213
2005	1136	1558	1661	-	4355
2006	1534	7121	2465	-	11120
2007	2586	8889	4447	-	15921
2008	3209	23651	6169		33029
2009 (Jan.-Mar.)	1992	3528	635		6155
Total (as on March 31, 2009)	27867	48343	21012	2509	99732

Notes: 1. Inflows through ADRs/GDRs/FCCSs against FDI approvals have not been included.
2. #Data Prior to 1996 not provided by the RBI.
3. From 2003, RBI's various NRI schemes inflows included under the heading RBI's Automatic Route.

Source: SIA Newsletter, April 2009. http://siadipp.nic.in/publical/newsittr/aug2008/index.htm. NACER 2010.

When the components of FDI inflows are studied over a period of time, we find that the value of equity inflows of incorporated bodies declined between 2001-02 and 2003-04, but have been on an uptrend thereafter (Table 4). Inflows through reinvested earnings increased continuously through this period, with only 2003-04 as an exceptional year. Annual fluctuations were observed for the inflows under equity capital of unincorporated bodies. However, the value of inflows through other capital stagnated during this period.

There are two main channels for the entry of FDI into India: the SIA/FIPB Route and the RBI Automatic Approval Route. From the inception of economic reforms in India in 1991 until the year 2000, most of the FDI came through the government route as there was strict monitoring of the approvals; therefore, FDI coming through the SIA/FIPB route was greater than the FDI coming through the RBI route (Table 4). However, there has been a dilution of this trend in the past five years. With the investment boom in India and different states competing for FDI, the government has eased foreign investment regulations leading to a spurt in FDI coming through the RBI route, which is a positive sign.

During 1991, as much as 54.1 per cent of total FDI was channeled through the SIA/FIPB route in contrast to 45.9 per cent through the

RBI route. No inflows on account of acquisition of existing shares were recorded for this year. The route-wise FDI inflows fluctuated till 1998. During 1998, the FDI inflows through the SIA/ FIPB route accounted for 62.1 per cent of the total FDI inflows, while those through the RBI's automatic route touched an all-time low of only 7.3 per cent. However, by this year, inflows through acquisition had gained a significant share of 3.06 per cent in total FDI inflows. The following period until 2007, for which the latest figures are available, recorded an increase in share of inflows through the RBI's automatic route, a decrease in the shares of inflows through the FIPB, while SIA the share of inflows through acquisition banded between 30 to 20 per cent.

Sector-wise FDI Inflows

Over the recent past, the sector-wise inflows of FDI have undergone a change. This is clear from the variation in the sector ranks based on their share in total FDI inflows. For comparison, we divide the period from August 1991 to March 2009 into two sub-periods of approximately the same length: the initial period of August 1991 to December 1999 and the second sub-period of 2000 to the latest available (which is the reference period of this study).

Table 5 presents the ranks, names and shares of FDI inflows for the top 20 sectors and miscellaneous industries (and, therefore, 21 industries in total), as reported in SIA publications. The figures are reported for the two cumulative periods and the year 2008 for which the latest information is available. The FDI inflows appear to be concentrated among the 21 industries. During the initial sub-period, namely, August 1991 to December 1999, the 21 sectors constituted 69.3 per cent of total FDI inflows, whereas during the second sub-period, namely, January 2000 to March 2009, these sectors constitute 84.3 per cent of the total FDI inflows. The emergence of the service sector is clear from a comparison of the shares over the two sub-periods. Other new sector entrants in the list of top five recipient sectors include computer software and hardware, construction activities and housing and real estate. The changing significance of the top five recipient sectors is shown in Exhibits 1 and 2.

FDI Inflows in Manufacturing

The manufacturing sector plays a significant role in the Indian economy, contributing nearly 17 per cent to the GDP (in 2008-09). Encouraged by the increasing presence of multinationals, the scaling up of operations by domestic companies and an ever expanding

Table 5: Sector-wise Break-up of FDI Inflows (August 1991 to October 2008)

Rank	Sector (Share as % of total investment)		
	Aug. 1991 to Dec. 1999	Jan. 2000 to March 2009	2008
1	Transporation industry (8.9)	Services sector (21.2)	Services sector (24.3)
2	Electrical Equipment (including S/W & Elec.) (8.0)	Computer Software & Hardware (9.9)	Telecommunications (8.3)
3	Service sector (7.0)	Telecommunications (7.1)	Housing & Real Estate (including Cineplex, Multiplex, Integrated Townships & Commercial Complexes) (8.1)
4	Telecommunications (6.9)	Housing & Real Estate (including Cineplex, Multiplex, Integrated Townships & Commercial Complexes, etc.) (6.1)	Construction Activities (7.4)
5	Chemicals (other than fertilisers) (6.9)	Construction Activities (5.7)	Computer Software & Hardware (5.6)
6	Fuels (Power & Oil Refinery) (6.3)	Automobile industry (3.9)	Metallurgical industries (4.5)
7	Food-Processing industries (4.1)	Power (3.6)	Ports (4.0)
8	Paper and Pulp (including Paper Products (1.5)	Metallurgical industries (3.0)	Petroleum & Natural Gas (4.0)
9	Miscellaneous, Mechanical & Engineering (1.4)	Petroleum & Natural Gas (2.6)	Power (3.9)
10	Textiles (including Dyed, Printed) (1.4)	Chemicals (other than fertilisers) (2.4)	Automobile industry (3.4)
11	Drugs and Pharmeceuticals (1.4)	Cement and Gypsum Products (1.9)	Cement and Gypsum Products (2.1)
12	Trading (1.1)	Ports (1.7)	Trading (2.0)
13	Metallurgical industries (1)	Trading (1.7)	Chemicals (other than fertilisers) (1.9)

(Contd)

Table 5: (Contd.)

Rank	Sector (Share as % of total investment)		
	Aug. 1991 to Dec. 1999	Jan. 2000 to March 2009	2008
14	Glass (0.9)	Drugs & Pharmaceuticals (1.7)	Information & Broadcasting (including Print Media) (1.6)
15	Commercial, Office & Household Equipment (0.9)	Electrical Equipment (1.6)	Hotel & Tourism (1.6)
16	Industrial Machinery (0.6)	Information & Broadcasting (including Print Media) (1.5)	Fermentation Industries (1.1)
17	Rubber Goods (0.5)	Hotel & Tourism (1.4)	Consultancy Services (1.1)
18	Hotel & Tourism (0.5)	Consultancy Services (1.4)	Hosptial & Diagnostic Centres (1.0)
19	Agricultural Machinery (0.3)	Food-Processing industries (0.9)	Electrical Equipment (0.8)
20	Ceramits (0.2)	Electronics (0.8)	Drugs & Pharmaceuticals (0.8)
21	Miscellaneous industries (9.5)	Miscellaneous industries (5.0)	Miscellaneous industries (4.9)

Source: SIA Newsletters, January 2005 and November 2008. NACER, 2010.

Exhibit 1: Sector-wise FDI Inflows (August 1991 to December 1999)

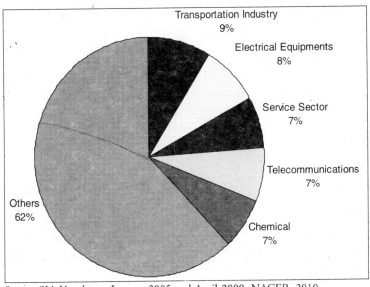

Source: *SIA Newsletters*, January 2005 and April 2009, NACER, 2010.

Exhibit 2: Sector-wise FDI Inflows (January 2000 to March 2009)

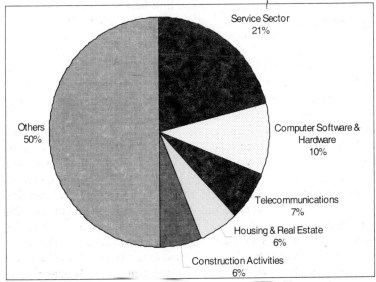

Source: *SIA Newsletters*, January 2005 and April 2009, NACER, 2010.

domestic market, the Indian manufacturing sector has been averaging 9 per cent growth in the past four years (2004-08), with a record 12.3 per cent in 2006-07. Industry and manufacturing were the major contributors to the economy, having a consistently high GDP growth rate in the past two years, making India one of the fastest growing economies in the world. India has all the requisite skills in product, process and capital engineering, due to its long manufacturing history and higher education system. India's cheap, skilled manpower is attracting a number of companies across diverse industries, making India a global manufacturing powerhouse. FDI inflows into manufacturing have been computed based on FDI records provided by DIPP.

Methodology

This study examine impact of FDI on India's Foreign trade particularly export performance. Though, export performance is influenced by both foreign demand and domestic supply factors we restrict our study with relation to supply factors by employing multiple regression model to explain India's export performance.

On the basis of theoretical reasoning one would expect a rise in export supply when the export prices rise relative to domestic prices and *vice versa*. Increase in domestic demand diverts export supply towards domestic consumption, leading to a fall in exports. This leads us to believe that there is a negative link between domestic demand and export supply (Joshi and Little, 1994). The role of FDI in export promotion in developing countries is ambiguous and crucially depends on the motive behind such investment. If the motive behind such investment is to by pass trade barriers in the host country, then it is highly unlikely that such investment would result in better export performance. However, if FDI is motivated by the country's comparative advantage, then it may contribute to export growth. Thus, the nature of the link between FDI and export performance is not clear. Reliable and efficient infrastructure facilities are essential for reducing costs, ensuring timely supply of exports and thereby improving export performance (Srinivasan, 1998). However, many developing countries including India lack reliable and efficient infrastructure facilities due mainly to under-investment and the public sector intervention. This contributes to higher costs and poor export performance. Thus, we expect a positive link between improved infrastructure facilities and export supply. The above discussions lead to the following specifications of export supply functions, with expected signs given in parenthesis:

$$XS = f(PX/P, DD, FDI, INF, LXS,) \qquad \text{(eq. 1)}$$
$$(+) \quad\; (-) \quad (?) \quad\; (+)$$

where:
- XS = Export supply, measured as total export volume index.
- PX/P = Indian export prices relative to domestic prices where PX is the export unit index while P is the wholesale price index for India.
- DD = Domestic demand pressure, proxied by the gross fiscal deficit of the Central Government as a percentage of GDP.
- FDI = Foreign direct investment, measured as the net inflows of FDI in US$.
- INF = Infrastructure facilities, measured by infrastructure index of India.
- LXS = Log of lagged export supply.

Analysis and Interpretation

Models specified in equation 1 are estimated using annual data for 12 years period from 1996 to 2007. The coefficient of relative price of export to domestic price is 0.610, which is significant at 10 percent level. This positive significant coefficient implies that there is improved export supply when relative price of export is more than domestic price. The coefficient of domestic demand pressure is -0.044 and which is insignificant. Though, it is insignificant which can be taken to reveal that exports supply declines as domestic demand increases. The coefficient value of FDI is 0.020 which is positive and insignificant, and exhibits insignificant contribution of FDI inflows towards export

Table 6: Results for Export Supply Function

Particulars	Co-efficient	t- Statistics
Constant	-9.909**	-2.17
Log of relative price of exports	0.610*	1.76
Log of domestic demand pressure	-0.044	-0.290
Log of Foreign direct investment	0.020	0.296
Log of infrastructure investment	2.151**	2.019
Log of lagged exports	0.402	1.200
R-squared	0.984	
Adjusted R-squared	0.971	
Durbin-Watson Stat.	2.129	
No. of observations	12	

** and * represent significant at 5% and 10% respectively.

performance. This might be because of role of greater domestic consumption and inward oriented policy that India has been perusing for long period which may have discouraged export-oriented foreign investment. The coefficient of infrastructure index is 2.151 with significant level of 5 percent this reveals the improvement in provision of adequate infrastructure in India leads to increase the export performance besides attraction of FDI inflows.

Conclusion

As a result of introduction of LPG in India in 1991, it witnessed increased exports performance much faster than GDP. Several factors appear to have contributed this increasing trend in india's export inculding FDI. However, very few studies have been made an attempt to investigate the role FDI in india's export performance. So, this study made an attempt to investigate this phenomenon using annual data for the period 12 years from 1996 to 2007. To investigate this problem our study have used multiple regression framework. Findings of this study reveal that the export supply is positively related to the domestic relative price of exports and a higher domestic demand reduces export supply. This suggest that dyanamic monetary and fiscal policies are necessary especially at the time of high growth to check domestic prices and demand pressure. And insignificant contribution of FDI inflows towards export performance might be because of role of greater domestic consumption and inward-oriented policy that India has been perusing for long period which may have discouraged export-oriented foreign investment. Further, the postive relatrionship between infrastructure and export reveals the improvement in provision of adequate infrastructure in India leads to increase in export performance besides attraction over FDI inflows.

REFERENCES

Ahluwalia, I.J., R. Mohan and C. Oman (1996), *Policy Reform in India* (Paris: Organisation for Economic Co-operation and Development).

Balasubramanyam, V.N., M. Salisu and D. Spasford (1996), 'Foreign Direct Investment and Growth in EP and IS Countries', *The Economic Journal*, Vol. 106, pp. 92 105.

Bhagwati, J. (1993), *India in Transition* (Oxford: Clarendon Press).

Bhagwati, J. and T.N. Srinivasan (1975), *Foreign Trade Regime and Economic Development—India* (New York: National Bureau of Economic Research).

Bhagwati, J. (1978), *Anatomy and Consequences of Exchange Rate Regime*, Vol. 1, Studies in International Economic Relations, No. 10 (New York: National Bureau of Economic Research).

Brahmbhatt, M., T.G. Srinivasan and K. Murell (1996), 'India in Global Economy' (World Bank: International Economics Department) (processed).

Chen, C., L. Chang and Y. Zhang (1995), 'The Role of Foreign Direct Investment in China's Post-1978 Economic Development', *World Development*, Vol. 23(4), pp. 691-703.

Domestic demand pressure. It is proxied by the gross fiscal deficit of the Central Government as a percentage of GDP. *Handbook of Statistics on Indian Economy*, Reserve Bank of India, 1999.

Economists Intelligent Unit (1999), India: Country Report, 3rd quarter, UK.

Economic and Social Commission for Asia and the Pacific (1998), *Foreign Direct Investment in Selected Asian Countries: Policies, Related Institution-building and Regional Co-operation* (New York: United Nations).

Export subsidies. Joshi and Little (1994) for 1970-88 data and the rest from *Economic Survey*, various issues, GOI.

Export unit price index for India and the rest of the world. *International Financial Statistics* (CD ROM), International Monetary Fund, 2000. World income. *World Development Indicators* (CD ROM), World Bank, 1999.

Export volume index. *Monthly Statistics of Foreign Trade of India*, Directorate General of Commercial Intelligence and Statistics, and *Economic Survey*, 1992-93 and 1993-94, Government of India (GOI).

FDI. *World Development Indicators* (CD ROM), World Bank, 1999. This is deflated by the Wholesale price index of India, IMF, 2000. Infrastructure facilities. It is proxied by infrastructure investment as a percentage of GDP.

Government of India, Ministry of Finance, *Economic Survey*, 1992-93 and 1993-94, New Delhi.

Government of India, Directorate General of Commercial Intelligence and Statistics, *Monthly Statistics of Foreign Trade of India*, various issues, Calcutta.

Gulati, I.S. and S.K. Bansal (1980), 'Export Obligation, Technology Transfer and Foreign Collaboration in Electronics', *Economic and Political Weekly*, Vol. 25, Special Number, October.

International Monetary Fund (2000), *International Financial Statistics* (CD ROM), Washington, D.C.

Joshi, V. and I.M.D. Little (1994), *India: Macroeconomics and Political Economy 1964-91* (Washinton, D.C.: The World Bank).

Joshi and Little (1994) for 1970-90 data and *Expenditure Budget*, 1997-98, GOI for 1991-98 data.

Kumar, N. (1994), *Multinational Enterprises and Industrial Organization: The Case of India* (New Delhi: Sage Publication).

REER. *Handbook of Statistics on Indian Economy*, Reserve Bank of India, 1999.

Reserve Bank of India (1999), *Handbook of Statistics on Indian Economy*, India.

Srinivasan, T.N. (1998), 'India's Export Performance: A Comparative Analysis' in I.J. Ahluwalia and I.M.D. Little (eds.), *India's Economic Reforms and Development Essay for Manmohan Singh* (Delhi: Oxford University Press).

Virmani, A. (1992), 'Demand and Supply Factors in India's Trade', *Economic and Political Weekly*, 26 (6), February.

Wholesale price index of India. *International Financial Statistics* (CD ROM), International Monetary Fund, 2000.

World Bank (1999), *World Development Indicators* (CD ROM), Washington, D.C.

World Bank (1998), *Global Development Finance: Analysis and Summary Tables*, Washington D.C.

World Bank (1996), *India: Five Years of Stabilization and Reform and the Challenges Ahead,* Washington, D.C.

World Bank (1993), *The East Asian Miracle* (London: Oxford University Press).

A Study of Role of FDI in Economic Growth and Employment Generation in India

K.S. Santha Kumar

Introduction

Foreign direct investment is defined as investment, which is made to serve the business interests of the investor in a company, which is in a different nation distinct from the investor's country of origin. Private investment, both domestic and foreign, is viewed as the driving force of the economy. FDI is seen to complement scarce domestic financial resources. Attracting foreign direct investment (FDI) has been the key aspect of outward-oriented development strategy for many developing countries, as investment is considered as a crucial element for output growth and employment generation. Besides growth, it is also assists to modernize production by transferring know-how and technology, while increasing domestic productivity and competition and improving international competitiveness.

Foreign direct investment can increase the economic growth of a country and the government of India realized this fact and this might be the reason for the implementation of a series of financial and economic reforms in the country in 1991. In 2003, the Indian government started the second generation reforms in order to increase the flow of foreign direct investment in the country which in turn, helped to integrate the country's economy with the economy of the world. The Indian government has assured to release an improvised

FDI policy in every six months regarding the sanction of FDI tenders. The various countries investing in India includes Japan, USA, UK, Singapore, Switzerland, France, Mauritius, Netherlands, South Korea and Germany.

FDI in India can take the following forms of investments into the economy:

- Through financial collaborations.
- Through joint ventures and technical collaborations.
- Through capital markets via Euro issues.
- Through private placements or preferential allotments.

FDI is not permitted in the following industrial sectors:

- Arms and ammunition.
- Atomic Energy.
- Railway Transport.
- Coal and Lignite.
- Mining of iron, manganese, chrome, gypsum, sulphur, gold, diamonds, copper, zinc.

Why India Really Needs FDI?

FDI usually is associated with export growth in the sense that it endorses vast investment in order to increase export potential and competitiveness of domestic industries in the world market. IT, BPO, Auto Parts, Pharmaceuticals, unexplored service sectors including accounting, drug testing, medical care, etc. are key sectors for foreign investment. Manufacturing industries requires a brick and mortar investment which is of permanent nature and stays in the country for a very long time. Huge investments are needed to set this industry. It is also expected to provide employment to both skilled and semi-skilled workers because Indian service sector observes only fewer but highly skilled workers.

Recent Trends of FDI in India

1. India has been ranked at the third place in global foreign direct investments in 2009 and will continue to remain among the top five attractive destinations for international investors during 2010-11, according to **United Nations Conference on Trade and Development (UNCTAD)** in a report on world investment prospects titled, **'World Investment Prospects Survey, 2009-2011'** released in July 2009.
2. The 2009 survey of the **Japan Bank for International**

Cooperation released in November 2009, conducted among Japanese investors continues to rank India as the second most promising country for overseas business operations after China.

3. A report released in February 2010 by **Leeds University Business School, commissioned by UK Trade & Investment (UKTI)**, ranks India among the top three countries where British companies can do better business during 2012-14.
4. According to **Ernst and Young's 2010 European Attractiveness Survey**, India is ranked as the 4th most attractive foreign direct investment (FDI) destination in 2010. However, it is ranked the 2nd most attractive destination following China in the next three years.
5. Moreover, according to the **Asian Investment Intentions survey** released by the Asia Pacific Foundation in Canada, more and more Canadian firms are now focusing on India as an investment destination. From 8 per cent in 2005, the percentage of Canadian companies showing interest in India has gone up to 13.4 per cent in 2010.
6. India attracted FDI equity inflows of US$ 2,214 million in April 2010. The cumulative amount of FDI equity inflows from August 1991 to April 2010 stood at US$ 134,642 million, according to the data released by the **Department of Industrial Policy and Promotion (DIPP)**.
7. The services sector comprising financial and non-financial services attracted 21 per cent of the total FDI equity inflow into India, with FDI worth US$ 4.4 billion during April-March 2009-10, while construction activities including roadways and highways attracted second largest amount of FDI worth US$ 2.9 billion during the same period. Housing and real estate was the third highest sector attracting FDI worth US$ 2.8 billion followed by telecommunications, which garnered US$ 2.5 billion during the financial year 2009-10. The automobile industry received FDI worth US$ 1.2 billion while power attracted FDI worth US$ 1.4 billion. During April-March 2009-10, according to data released by DIPP.
8. In April 2010, the telecommunication sector attracted the highest amount of FDI worth US$ 430 million, followed by services sector at US$ 355 million and computer hardware and software at US$ 172 million, according to data released by DIPP. During the financial year 2009-10, Mauritius has led

investors into India with US$ 10.4 billion worth of FDI comprising 43 per cent of the total FDI equity inflows into the country. The FDI equity inflows in Mauritius is followed by Singapore at US$ 2.4 billion and the US with US$ 2 billion, according to data released by DIPP.
9. During April 2010, Mauritius invested US$ 568 million in India, followed by Singapore which invested US$ 434 million and Japan that invested US$ 327 million, according to latest data released by DIPP.

Objectives and Methodology

The main objective of the paper is to analyse the role of FDI in economic growth and employment generation in India from 1995-96 to 2007-08. The necessary data for the purpose was collected from *Economic Survey*, 2009 and *RBI Bulletin*, 2010, Govt. of India. Average Annual Growth Rate (AAGR) and Compound Growth Rate (CGR) was used to measure the growth of FDI and the selected indicators of economic growth and employment generation viz., Gross National Product (GNP) at current prices and total employment in the organized sector both public and private sector combined. Correlation analysis was used to find out the nature of relationship that exists between selected variables. Regression analysis was used to find out the response of growth of FDI in the growth of GNP and total employment.

Findings of the Study

The following are the major findings of the study:

FDI and Economic Growth in India

1. In the study, Economic growth is measured in terms of GNP at current prices which mean that the total value of goods and services produced during a year in a country including net income from abroad.
2. On an average, FDI and GNP in India had grown at a similar compound growth rate of 1.21 and 1.12 per cent per annum respectively during the period of the study (Table 1).
3. The estimated AAGR indices showed that GNP has fluctuated in a unique manner but FDI has shows large variations in its trends (Table 1 and Figure 1).
4. The results of correlation analysis inferred that there is positive relationship existing between growth of FDI and GNP in India i.e., .865 (Table 3).

Table 1: Growth of FDI and GNP from 1995-96 to 2007-08 in India

Year	FDI Inflows (in Millions)	AAGR	Growth Indices	GNP at current prices (in Millions)	AAGR	Growth Indices
1995-96	96801.6	-	-	10,69,805	-	-
1996-97	127368.2	31.58	100	12,47,628	16.62	100
1997-98	160598.6	26.09	82.61558	13,88,729	11.31	68.05054
1998-99	111159.3	-30.78	-97.4668	16,01,114	15.29	91.99759
1999-00	97298.25	-12.47	-39.487	17,71,094	10.62	63.89892
2000-01	181909.4	86.96	275.3642	19,02,284	7.41	44.58484
2001-02	276769.5	52.15	165.1362	20,77,658	9.22	55.47533
2002-03	227330.3	-17.86	-56.5548	22,44,725	8.04	48.37545
2003-04	195138.3	-14.16	-44.8385	25,17,462	12.15	73.10469
2004-05	273202.7	40.01	126.6941	28,55,326	13.42	80.74609
2005-06	404589.2	48.09	152.2799	32,56,269	14.04	84.47653
2006-07	1030594	154.73	489.962	37,49,607	15.15	91.15523
2007-08	1572800	52.61	166.5928	42,97,047	14.60	87.84597
CGR	1.21			1.12		

Source: Economic Survey, 2009.

Figure 1: Movement of Growth Indices of FDI and GNP in India

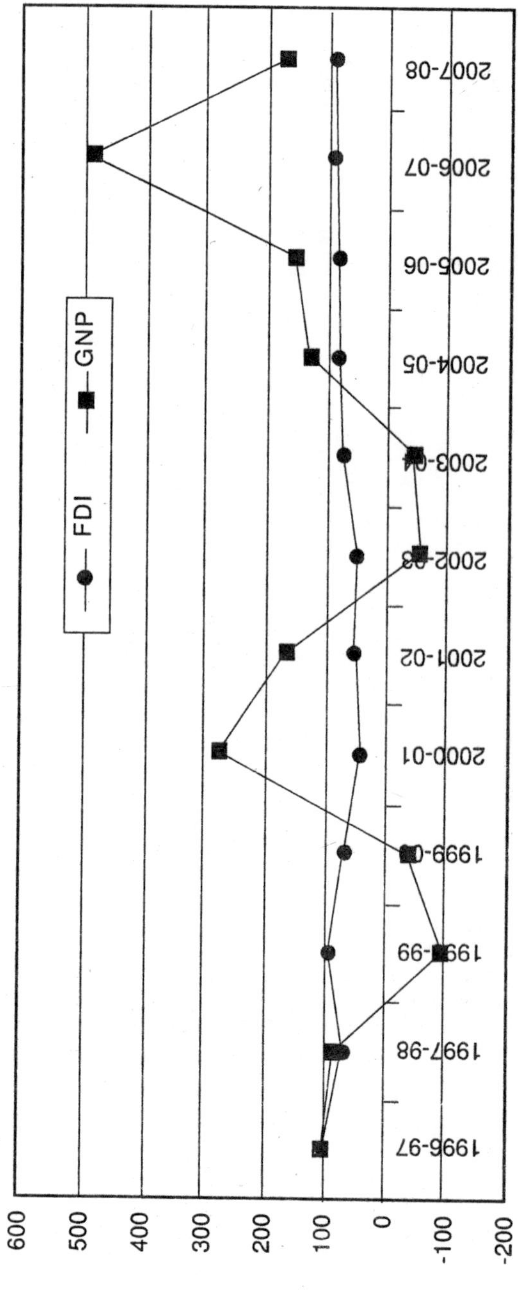

5. The regression results proved that FDI is a significant determinant of GNP in India and thereby economic growth. Hence, it was observed that the estimated regression co efficient of FDI was statistically significant at 5 per cent level and unit change in FDI causes to change 1.956 units in GNP in India. Moreover, estimated R^2 implies that FDI causes 85 per cent variation in GNP thereby economic growth (Table 4).

FDI and Employment Generation in India

1. On an average, FDI in India has grown at a compound growth rate of 1.21 per cent per annum during 1995-96 to 2007-08 while the employment in India including both in private and public sector has grown at a rate of 1.00 per cent per annum during the reference period. This means that, on an average both FDI and Employment in India were grown at a similar percentage annually.
2. The calculated AAGR showed that the rate of growth between FDI and Employment was dissimilar but the movement of growth has showing a similar trend during the reference period (Table 2 and Figure 2).
3. The estimated correlation results inferred that there is negative relationship between growth of FDI and Total Employment in India i.e., -.668 (Table 3). This may be due to the fact that it creates employment only to the skilled workers and thrown out the large part of unskilled workers to remain unemployed. According to the *Economic Survey*, 2009, 52 per cent of the total workforce was still engaged in agricultural sector.
4. The regression results showed that FDI has no significant influence on total employment in India. This is because the estimated regression co efficient of FDI was not statistically significant and showing a negative value which confirms the findings of correlation analysis of negative relationship (Table 4).

Conclusion

FDI has been a booming factor that has bolstered the economic life of India, but on the other hand it is also being blamed for ousting domestic inflows. Some of the advantages of FDI enjoyed by India are Economic growth, Trade, Employment and skill levels, Technology diffusion and knowledge transfer, Linkages and spillover to domestic firms. From the findings made in the study it was concluded that FDI

Table 2: Growth of FDI and Employment Growth from 1995-96 to 2007-08 in India

Year	FDI Inflows (in Millions)	AAGR	Growth Indices	Employment in Organized Sector	AAGR	Growth Indices
1995-96	96801.6	-	-	2,73,75,000	-	-
1996-97	127368.2	31.58	100	2,75,25,000	0.55	100
1997-98	160598.6	26.09	82.61558	2,79,41,000	1.51	274.5455
1998-99	111159.3	-30.78	-97.4668	2,82,45,000	1.09	198.1818
1999-00	97298.25	-12.47	-39.487	2,81,66,000	-0.28	-50.9091
2000-01	181909.4	86.96	275.3642	2,81,13,000	-0.19	-34.5455
2001-02	276769.5	52.15	165.1362	2,79,60,000	-0.54	-98.1818
2002-03	227330.3	-17.86	-56.5548	2,77,90,000	-0.61	-110.909
2003-04	195138.3	-14.16	-44.8385	2,72,05,000	-2.11	-383.636
2004-05	273202.7	40.01	126.6941	2,70,01,000	-0.75	-136.364
2005-06	404589.2	48.09	152.2799	2,64,43,000	-2.07	-376.364
2006-07	1030594	154.73	489.962	2,64,59,000	0.06	10.90909
2007-08	1572800	52.61	166.5928	2,66,44,000	0.70	127.2727
CGR	1.21			1.00		

Source: Column 2 in Economic Survey, 2009 and Column 5 in RBI Bulletin, 2010.

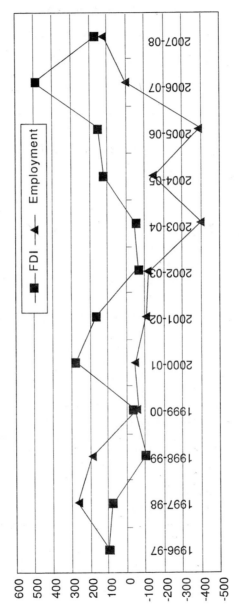

Figure 2: Movement of Growth Indices of FDI and Employment in India

Table 3: Correlation Matrix

	Correlation between Vectors of Values		
	FDI	EMPT	GNP
FDI	1.000	-.668	.865
EMPT	-.668	1.000	-.782
GNP	.865	-.782	1.000

Table 4: Regression Coefficients and Level of Significance

S.No.	Dependent Variable	Independent Variable	Regression Co-efficient	R^2	F-Value
1.	GNP	FDI	1.956 (5.721*)	.865	32.735*
2.	Employment	FDI	-.995 (14.109)	.668	8.851*

*Singnificant at 5 per cent level.

had a significant impact on economic growth and less impact on employment generation in the economy because it creates employment to the particular group of workers and not for the whole.

REFERENCES

Alfaro, L., A. Chanda, S. Kalemi-Ozcan and S. Sayek (2004), "FDI and Economic Growth: The Role of Local Financial Markets", *Journal of International Economics*, Vol. 64, pp. 89-112.

Blomström, M. and A. Kokko (2003), "The Economics of Foreign Direct Investment Incentives", *Working Paper No. 9489*, NBER.

Government of India (GOI), (2006), Foreign Direct Investment Policy, Ministry of Commerce and Industry, Department of Industrial Policy and Promotion.

Christoph Ernst (2005), "The FDI—employment link in a globalizing world: The case of Argentina, Brazil and Mexico", Employment Analysis Unit, Employment Strategy Department, pp. 1-45.

Robert E. Baldwin (1994), "The Effects of Trade and Foreign Direct Investment on Employment and Relative Wages", *OECD Economic Studies*, No. 23, pp. 7-54.

Effect of FDI on Spillovers and Productivity: Evidence from India

SUMAN SHARMA

1. Introduction

Foreign Direct Investment (FDI) is assumed to play a crucial role in economic restructuring and enhancing growth in the developing countries. In the context of developing economies, we expect that FDI will raise productivity. This is referred to as the direct effect of FDI. The positive direct effect of foreign ownership has been confirmed empirically in a large number of studies. Next to a direct effect, there exist a number of externality effects, by which FDI affects other firms in the same sector or even in other sectors. These indirect effects are referred to as spillover effects. These originate from several sources. First, FDI could generate a beneficial transfer of know-how and technology. Second, the injection of capital and technology certainly stimulates competition in the local market.

Among the developing countries India is also showing interest for FDI after 1991. FDI Inflows to Drugs and Pharmaceuticals industry in India has grown over the last few years due to the several incentives that have been provided by the Indian government. The increase in FDI inflows to Drugs and Pharmaceuticals industry in India has helped in the expansion, growth, and development of the industry. This in its turn has led to the improvement in the quality of the products from the drugs and pharmaceuticals industry. As per the estimates of Oct. 2010 the drugs and pharmaceuticals industry of India was worth 1,846.57 million US dollars, contributing 1.51% to India's FDI Inflows.

The domestic market in the drugs and pharmaceuticals industry in India is worth more than US$ 4.8 billion. The industry of drugs and pharmaceuticals in India is highly fragmented with more than 3,000 medium and small sized producers. The major domestic companies in the drugs and pharmaceuticals industry of India are Ranbaxy, Dr. Reddy's, and Cipla. The major international companies having presence in the industry of drugs and pharmaceuticals in India are Johnson & Johnson, Novartis, Pfizer, and Glaxo SmithKline. The government of India has allowed foreign direct investment up to 100% through the automatic route in the drugs and pharmaceuticals industry of the country, on the condition, that the activity should not fall into the categories that require licensing.

With this background this paper examines the relationship between the presence of foreign firms and local productivity growth in Indian pharmaceutical industry. We specifically look at the main issue, whether the productivity levels of local firms improved by the presence of foreign firms? Understanding of these questions is of crucial importance to the policy-makers for improving the productivity of domestic sector and managing FDI policy effectively concerning the industry.

This paper has been structured as follows. Section 2 conceptualizes the link between FDI spillovers and local productivity growth. The model and hypotheses to be tested has been developed in the section 3. Section 4 describes the data source and presents results from empirical analysis. Section 5 concludes the paper.

2. Theory and Related Literature

Foreign firms are assumed to have inherent advantages, in scale and technological knowledge and in access to international markets, which allow them to overcome the cost of setting up in a different country and to produce more efficiently (Blomstrom and Kokko, 1998; Hymer, 1976). Often, these advantages take the form of proprietary assets, technology and marketing practices. These imply higher productivity of foreign-owned firms themselves. Moreover, productivity spillovers may have positive effects on local firms. Productivity spillovers generally take place when the entry of foreign firms leads to efficiency or productivity benefits for domestic firms that are not fully internalized by the foreign firm (Blomstrom and Kokko, 1998).

There are several mechanisms through which these spillover effects occur. These can be split into competition and demonstration effects (Girma, Greenway & Wakelin, 2001). The presence of more efficient foreign firms in an industry may increase competition in domestic industries as foreign firms tend to populate industries where the initial cost of entry is high (Caves, 1974). They may also break up domestic monopolies by lowering excess profits and generally improving allocative efficiency. Local firms can also improve their productivity by copying technology from multinational firms in their industry. Foreign firms may not be able to internalize all the gains of their technology and domestic firms may benefit through their contact with foreign firms, either as suppliers, consumers or competitors. On the other hand, entry of foreign firms may crowd out domestic firms, reducing their scale and thus their productivity. The extent to which spillovers occur helps determine the productivity effect for local firms from the presence of foreign firms in the same or related industries.

Table 1: Productivity Spillovers from FDI in Selected Economies

Sl. No.	Author(s)	Year(s)	Result
	Developing Countries		
1.	Blomström and Persson (1983)	1970	+
2.	Blomström (1986)	1970/75	+
3.	Blomström and Wolff (1994)	1970/75	+
4.	Kokko (1994)	1970	+
5.	Kokko (1996)	1970	+
6.	Haddad and Harrison (1993)	1985-89	?
7.	Kokko et al. (1996)	1990	?
8.	Blomström and Sjoholm (1999)	1991	+
9.	Sjoholm (1999a)	1980-91	+
10.	Sjoholm (1999b)	1980-91	+
11.	Chuang and Lin (1999)	1991	+
12.	Aitken and Harrison (1999)	1976-89	-
13.	Kathuria (2000)	1976-89	?
14.	Sasidharan and Ramanathan (2007)	1994-02	?, -
15.	Kokko et al. (2001)	1988	?
16.	Wei and Liu (2001)	1996-98	+
17.	Li, et al. (2001)	1995	+
18.	Liu (2002)	1993-98	+
19.	Liu (2008)	1995-99	-/+
	Developed Countries		
20.	Caves (1974)	1966	+
21.	Globerman (1979)	1972	+
22.	Liu et al. (2000)	1991-95	+
23.	Driffield (2001)	1989-92	+
24.	Girma et al. (2001)	1991-96	?

(Contd.)

Sl. No.	Author(s)	Year(s)	Result
25.	Girma and Wakelin (2000)	1988-96	?
26.	Girma and Wakelin (2001)	1980-92	?
27.	Harris and Robinson (2003)	1974-95	?
28.	Griffith et al. (2003)	1980-92	+
29.	Haskel et al. (2007)	1973-92	+
30.	Ruane and Ugur (2004)	1991-98	?
31.	Barry et al. (2005)	1990-98	-
32.	Piscitello and Rabbiosi (2005)	1994-97	+
33.	Barrios and Strobl (2002)	1990-94	?
34.	Dimelis and Louri (2001a)	1997	+
35.	Dimelis and Louri (2004b)	1997	+
36.	Dimelis (2005)	1992/97	+
37.	Siler et al. (2003)	1992-95	+
	Transition Countries		
38.	Djankov and Hoekman (2000)	1993-96	-
39.	Kinoshita (2001)	1995-98	?
40.	Bosco (2001)	1993-97	?
41.	Konings (2001)	1993-97, 1994-97	-
42.	Damijan et al. (2003)	1994-98	?
43.	Yudaeva, et al. (2003)	1993-97	-/+
44.	Sinani and Meyer (2004)	1994-99	+

Source: Author's adapation from Ludo Cuyvers, Reth Soeng, Joseph Plasmans & Daniel Van den Bulcke (2008), Figure 2, pp.15-16.

Table 1 provides a summary of studies on FDI spillovers. The results, however, are far from conclusive. FDI spillovers may be positive or negative. Net result therefore depends upon the relative strength of these two effects. Further, the impact of FDI firms on the productivity growth of domestic firms is not only sector specific but also firm specific as postulated by the technology gap hypothesis. As the knowledge brought in by foreign firms involves tacit elements difficult for imitation, domestic firms need to incur R&D to apprehend FDI spillovers. The domestic firms with a lower technology-gap vis-à-vis foreign firms are relatively better placed to benefit from spillovers than those with a wider technology-gap. Hence, the spillover impact of FDI is ambiguous in nature.

The positive spillovers that FDI firms may generate in the development process can occur through many channels but important are the followings:

- *Competitive effect*: Caves (1974) argues that the entry of a foreign firm into local markets can force more active rivalry and an improvement in performance than would a domestic firm at the same scale. This is because FDI is thought of as a vehicle for disseminating the transfer of technology, including a higher level of technical efficiency.

- *Human capital effect*: Inward FDI can cause spillovers to local firms through labor market turnover whereby skilled workers who once worked for the FDI firms move to local firms, it results in local productivity growth (Blomström and Persson, 1983; UNCTAD, 1999)
- *Demonstration effect*: FDI can generate a "demonstration effect." The mere presence of foreign products in domestic markets can stimulate local firms' creative thinking and thus help generate blueprints for new products and processes. The technologies that FDI firms bring in have already been tested by consumers in the foreign markets, similar products and technologies will likely work well for the host country as well.
- *Linkage effect*: FDI can influence the economy of the host country via inter-firm linkages. To the extent that foreign subsidiaries establish links with local suppliers for locally-produced materials and parts. FDI can help to provide local firms with increased opportunities that in turn affect their employment and income positions. These are called backward linkages. Forward linkages can also be established for distribution purposes (World Bank, 1997).

While FDI is associated with these positive externalities, this does not rule out negative externalities from it. This aspect of spillovers is often discussed in the context of crowding out from FDI, which can occur through one or both of the following two channels:

- *Product market*: Reuber et al. (1973) argue that FDI may 'preempt the development of indigenous firms and managers capable of establishing and maintaining a strong countervailing influence'. In this case, there would be a worsening of market concentration and the possibility to worsening industrial performance. Moreover, Reuber et al. argue that the entry of foreign subsidiaries might raise the level of concentration in the host country because their presence might exert pressure for mergers among local firms. Newfarmer and Mueller (1975) present evidence from Mexico and Brazil supporting the proposition that the entry of MNCs significantly speeds up

the process of oligopolization in developing host countries.
- *Financial market*: Lall and Streeten (1978) cast doubt on the ability of FDI to perform the function of providing capital, for at least three reasons. First, direct investment is a relatively expensive source of foreign capital. Second, the actual capital inflow provided by the MNC may not be very large. Indeed, MNC can, through their market power, raise cheap funds and crowd out other socially desirable activities in the host country. Third, the capital contribution of the MNC may take the form of machinery or capitalized intangibles, such as know-how and goodwill. For these reasons, FDI provides little, and expensive, capital.

3. Empirical Methodology, Hypotheses and Data Source

The productivity of domestic enterprises depends on several firm-specific factors besides the spillover effects from the presence of FDI firms. Firm-level productivity growth is a composite measure of the efficiency improvements in the firm including technical progress, learning-by-doing, improved skills, and enhanced utilization of capacities, etc. (Pradhan, 2004). The study has considered the following possible factors to explain the firm-level productivity growth:

3.1 Technology

Foreign investment brings with it technological knowledge while transferring machinery and equipment to developing countries. As the foreign-owned enterprise comes into competition with the local firms, the latter category of enterprises are forced to improve their technology and standards of product quality. Further, the foreign-owned enterprises pressurize and assist the local support industries to improve the quality of their products and ensure greater reliability of delivery, both of which make it necessary for the support industries to upgrade their technology. In the present study, the technological capability of a firm has been measured by a group of three variables: the in-house R&D expenditure (RDINT), the technological payments made overseas (TECHIM) and the imports of capital goods (EMTECH), all expressed as a percentage share of sales. RDINT measures the firm's own efforts to create and strengthen indigenous innovative capacity. TECHIM and EMTECH respectively measures embodied and disembodied channels of technology imports like know-how licenses and import of plant and machinery. All these three measures of firm-specific technical capability are predicted to affect positively the productivity growth of domestic firms. However, as the relationship between productivity and technology is likely to exhibit bi-way causation, the study has introduced measures of technology in one period lagged form.

3.2 Firm Age

A firm's efficiency is also dependent upon the age of the firm. Younger firms are probable to be more efficient than their older counterparts, as the scope for productivity growth from learning by doing effects is greater for them. Hence, other things being equal the efficiency of the firm is predicted to depend negatively upon its age (AGE).

3.3 Capital Intensity

A higher firm's efficiency is associated with higher capital intensity (KINT) of operations as the capital goods incorporate latest knowledge and innovations which in turn affects technical change and productivity growth at the firm level. The KINT is measured as the ratio of capital stock to labour.

3.4 Import

After 1991 Government of India has phased out many restrictions on imports which have provided an easy access to imports of capital goods, raw materials and components. Due to these changes new import is increasing which is technologically and qualitatively better than local alternatives. The import intensity (IMINT) of a firm can be expected to determine its productivity performance.

3.5 Exporting

FDI can help the host country improve its export performance. By raising the level of efficiency and the standards of product quality, FDI makes a positive impact on the host country's export competitiveness. Further, because of the international linkages of MNCs, FDI provides to the host country better access to foreign markets. Also, where the foreign investment has been made with the specific intention of sourcing products from host country to take advantage of low cost conditions, FDI contributes to exports directly. Enhanced export possibility contributes to the growth of the host economies by relaxing demand side constraints on growth. Thus, the export intensity of a firm (EXPOINT) is hypothesized to have a positive impact on its productivity growth. As the relationship between exporting and productivity may be subject to bi-way causality, EXPOINT has been introduced as one period lagged variable.

3.6 Foreign Presence

In the literature, it is often argued that the most important benefits to the host country from the foreign presence are a variety of spillovers. There are several channels through which knowledge and technology are spilled over from the foreign-owned to domestically-owned firms in host economies. Kokko (1992), Blomström and Kokko (1998), Blomström *et al.* (2000), and Saggi (2002) show that benefits from multinational firms are:

- contribute to higher productive efficiency and to a better use of existing technology and resources;
- break down local monopolies, and lead to fiercer competition and higher efficiency;
- introduce new know-how by demonstrating new technologies and provide on-the-job training to employees who might transfer important knowledge, skills and information to local firms by shifting employers;
- force domestic firms to increase their managerial efforts, to adopt some of the marketing techniques used by their foreign counterparts, and to search for new, modern technologies; and
- transfer technology to the firms that are potential suppliers of intermediate goods or buyers of other own products.

On the other hand, it may also result in crowding out of local capabilities through blocking information flows, less local linkages, market and credit rationing for domestic firms. Hence, the impact of spillover variable on the productivity growth of local firms is theoretically ambiguous. The study has used two proxy variables for the presence of FDI firms in the industry: (1) the share of sales of FDI firms to total industry sales (SPIL1), and (2) the share of R&D expenditure of FDI firms to total industry R&D expenditure (SPIL2). The first and second measures respectively capture foreign participation in the product market and technological efforts in the industry.

However, not all domestic firms get equally affected by the presence of foreign firms in an industry. As far as the efficiency caused by competitive pressures from the foreign share of an industry's sales is concerned, the effect can be expected to depend upon the relative variation in inter-firm market power. A domestic firm with higher market power proxied by the size of its sales may be more sensitive to the presence of foreign firms than a domestic firm with a fringe status.

To capture this phenomenon the study has constructed an interaction variable by interacting SPIL1 and size of the firm (SPIL1*SIZE). Likewise the spillovers benefits from foreign firm's innovative activity require a degree of technological capability on the part of the domestic firm. The fact that foreign firms bring in new technologies doesn't automatically guarantee that domestic firms may benefit as technology by definition is firm-specific, local, often tacit and partly appropriable knowledge. Domestic firms with higher innovative capability may benefit relatively more from knowledge spillovers from FDI than those with low level of technological capability. An interaction term between SPIL2 and R&D intensity (SPIL2*RDINT) of domestic firms has been included in the study to capture the inter-firm differences in the ability to de-codify and absorb the FDI spillovers.

Data and Empirical Methodology

The paper analyses the productivity spillovers from foreign direct investment in Indian Drugs and pharmaceutical industries as outlined in Cornwell, Schmidt and Sickles (1990). We begin with a production function with value-added Y, being a function of two inputs, labour (L) and capital (K)

$$\log Y_{it} = p_{it} + \alpha \log K_{it} + \beta \log L_{it} + \varepsilon_{it} \qquad (1)$$

where, Y_{it}, K_{it}, L_{it} are the logarithmic values of Net Value Added of the firm, labour input of the firm and capital input of the firm. ε_{it} is the usually normally distributed two sided noise term permitting random variation of the firms.

According to paper estimation involves two steps which are:

Step 1

The production function is estimated with fixed effects techniques of panel data and the residuals giving the joint estimate of the productive efficiency and the error term are obtained. This step gives the firm effects but assumes that the firm effects are constant over time.

Step 2

The residual for each firm are regressed on time t and t^2 to obtain the fitted values which give estimates of firm-specific efficiency denoted as p_{it} in order to relax the assumption that the firm effects are time-invariant. The change in the productive efficiency level $z_{it} = p_{it} - p_{it-1}$.

From the literature review, for our hypothesis testing, z_{it} can be represented as:

$$z_{it} = F(AGE_{it}, RDINT_{it-1}, TECHIM_{it-1}, EMTECH_{it-1}, KINT_{it}, IMINT_{it}, EXPOINT_{it-1}, SPIL1_t, SPIL2_t, SIZE_{it}) \qquad (2)$$

where,

Variables	Description
AGE_{it}	The age of ith firm in number of years
$RDINT_{it-1}$	Total R&D expenditure as a percentage of total sales of ith firm in $t-1$ year
$TECHIM_{it-1}$	Royalties, technical and other professional fees remitted abroad by ith firm as a percentage of sales in the year $t-1$
$EMTECH_{it-1}$	Imports of capital goods as a percentage of total sales of ith firm in $t-1$ year
$KINT_{it}$	The ratio of capital stock to labour
$IMINT_{it}$	Total imports as a percentage of total sales of ith firm in tth year
$EXPOINT_{it-1}$	Total exports as a percentage of total sales of ith firm in $t-1$ year
$SPIL1_t$	The percentage share of foreign firms in industry sales in tth year
$SPIL2_t$	The percentage share of foreign firms in industry R&D expenses in tth year
$SIZE_{it}$	Total sales of ith firm in tth year

The data for the study is obtained from the PROWESS database provided by the Centre for Monitoring Indian Economy (CMIE), a private company in India. The data is primarily drawn from the information in the firms' annual reports. Since our data is pertaining to the drug and pharmaceuticals industries, we obtain data for 134 domestic firms with 1073 observation. The data covers the period from 2001 to 2008. The summary of variables of production function is as follows:

Variable	Description
Output	The net value added (NVA) deflated by the wholesale price index for chemical industry (base1993-94=100) represent output.
Capital	The net fixed asset (NFA) deflated by the wholesale price index for machinery and machine tools (base 1993-94=100) represent capital input.
Labour	Labour has been obtained by dividing total wage bill of a firm by the average industry wage rate obtained from the Annual Survey of Industries (ASI).

4. Results

To derive firm-specific productive efficiency growth for domestic firms' first step is to estimate Cobb-Douglas production function specified in Model (1) with the panel data techniques with heteroscedasticity corrected t-statistics. The statistical package used for this purpose is stata. The results obtained from the estimation of the production function are shown in Table 2.

Table 2: Estimated Production Function

	Dependent Variable: Log Y
Log K	.687618***
	(37.50)
Log L	.3334717***
	(20.28)

***Significant at 1%.

The estimated elasticity of output with respect to capital and labor are 0.68 and 0.33 percent respectively. Both these partial elasticity coefficients are highly significant and suggest that over the study period for 1 percent increase in the capital input, holding the labor input constant, led on an average to about 0.68 percent increase in the output and that in the case of labor the increase in the output is .33 percent and the estimated model is quite satisfactory also.

After obtaining the output elasticity of capital and labor, the study proceeds to obtain residuals from the fixed effect estimation and then derive firm level productive efficiency growth for domestic firms as discussed previously. Finally, the productive efficiency growth relation as specified by the Model (1) has been estimated. Apart from correcting heteroscedasticity in the variance matrix, the study has also checked for problems of multicollinearity that can inflate standard errors of the estimates. Tests such as variance inflating factor (VIF) reveal that a moderate level of colinearity exists among independent variables not serious enough to mislead the estimated standard errors.

The results obtained from the estimation of equation 2 are shown in Table 3. It is clear that the overall significance is fairly high.

Table 3: Fixed Effects Regression of the Productive Efficiency

	Dependent Variable: z_{it}
AGE_{it}	-.0105776***
	(-7.08)
$RDINT_{it-1}$	-.0076046*
	(-1.98)
$TECHIM_{it-1}$	.0895129**
	(2.94)
$EMTECH_{it-1}$	-.0354373***
	(-5.09)
$KINT_{it}$	.231011**
	(3.11)
$IMINT_{it}$	-.0149404***
	(-8.22)
$EXPOINT_{it-1}$	-.0104881***
	(-9.23)
$SPIL1_t$	-.000085**
	(-1.49)
$SPIL2_t$	-.0136096***
	(-3.41)
$SIZE_{it}$	-.0035951*
	(-17.07)
$SPIL1SIZE_t$	.0000304*
	(1.85)
$SPIL2RDINT_t$	0.00000101***
	(3.78)

***—Significant at 1%, **—Significant at 5%, *—Significant at 10%.

AGE_{it} has a predicted negative and significant coefficient for both the estimations. This tends to suggest that younger firms in Indian pharmaceutical industry experience higher efficiency growth than their older counterparts. The relatively higher productivity growth of younger firms can be explained by their advantages of possessing new equipments and highly flexible organizational setup to be able to benefit more from the learning process. Among the three measures of firm's technological capabilities, $RDINT_{it-1}$ came out with a negative effect significant at 10 per cent level of significance whereas $TECHIM_{it-1}$ came out with a positive effect significant at 5 per cent level of significance; the import of capital goods represented by $EMTECH_{it-1}$ has consistently got a significantly negative coefficient in the efficiency growth regression. This seems to corroborate our hypothesis that efficiency growth crucially depends upon firm's own technological efforts and imports of foreign disembodied technologies like know-how, design, specification etc. However, the fact that $EMTECH_{it-1}$ is associated with statistically lower levels of efficiency indicates that Indian firms are not being able to efficiently absorb and utilize the imported capital goods into their production process.

The capital intensity, $KINT_{it}$, has a positive sign and turns statistically significant at 5 percent level. This is confirms to our hypothesis that firms with higher capital intensities are associated with higher performance of firm-specific efficiency. $IMINT_{it}$ has a negative sign and achieved the levels of statistical significance. Therefore, firm efficiency in Indian pharmaceutical industry seems to be not significantly affected by the intensity of firms to imports. $EXPOINT_{it-1}$ comes out with a negative effect on the efficiency of the firm and reaches a level of statistical significance. It would suggest that firms on the contrary to witness the predicted efficiency-enhancing benefits from exporting in fact tend to be less-efficient. More research is required to understand why exporting firms are not performing well on the efficiency front.

However our main focus in this paper is the spillover impact of foreign firms. We have tested two possible sources of spillover: SPIL1 and SPIL2. Our results clearly indicate that foreign presence has spillover impact on firms' productivity and a technological effort has strong spillover impact. From Table 2 we can see that the coefficient of SPIL1SIZE is negative and statistically significant at 10 per cent level. On the other hand SPIL2RDINT is negative and statistically significant 1 per cent. This is against our hypothesis that domestic firms with higher innovative capability may benefit relatively more from knowledge spillovers from FDI than those with low level of technological capability.

5. Conclusion

The experience of developing countries with foreign direct investment varies. Existing study found that the presence of foreign firms helps in improving productivity growth of the domestic sector and also support the view that openness to FDI is not only the solution to ensure the benefits from the FDI instead it depends on the absorptive capacity of the firms domestic firms.

Indian Drugs and pharmaceutical industry so far do not seem to benefit significantly from R&D spillovers because local firms are still less inclined to invest in uncertain risky in-house R&D activities. Our study shows that there is negative productivity spillover from exports for domestic firms because in India FDI act as a competitive spur for domestic exporters forcing them to innovate. Foreign firms aimed for the domestic market, allowing local firms to expand in export market. On the other hand, technology import has a favourable effect on the productivity performance. Therefore, in improving productivity and technological capability building, the policy-makers should focus on local technology generations, and provide more subsidies and tax concession on innovations. They should also ensure firms' easy access to new technology from overseas because it's crucial for enhancing efficiency of domestic enterprises.

References

Blomström, M. and A. Kokko (1998), "Multinational Corporations and Spillovers." *Journal of Economic Survey*, 12: 1-31.

Blomström, M. and H. Persson (1983), "Foreign Investment and Spillover Efficiency in an Underdeveloped Economy: Evidence from the Mexican Manufacturing Industry." *World Development*, 11: 493-501.

Blomström, M., A. Kokko, and M. Zejan (2000), "Foreign Direct Investment: Firm and Host Country Strategies." Hong Kong: Macmillan.

C. Ludo, Reth Soeng, Joseph Plasmans and Daniel Van den Bulcke (2008), "Productivity Spillovers from Foreign Direct Investment in the Cambodian Manufacturing Sector: Evidence from Establishment-Level Data." University of Antwerp Research Paper 2008-004.

Caves, R.E. (1974), "Multinational Firms, Competition, and Productivity in Host-Country Markets," *Economica*, 41: 176-93.

Cornwell, C., P. Schmidt and R.C. Sickles (1990), "Production Frontier with Cross-Section and Time-Series Variation in Efficiency Levels," *Journal of Econometrics*, 46: 185-200.

Girma, S., D. Greenway and K. Wakelin (2001), "Who benefits from foreign direct investment in the UK?" *Scottish Journal of Political Economy*, 48(2): 122-30.

Kokko, A. (1992), "Foreign Direct Investment, Host Country Characteristics and Spillovers." Stockholm: Economic Research Institute.

Lall, S. (1978), "Transnationals, domestic enterprises and Industrial Structure in LDSs: A Survey." *Oxford Economic Papers*, 30(2): 217-48.

Newfarmer, R.S. and W.F. Mueller (1975), "Multinational Corporation in Brazil and Mexico: Structural Sources of Economic and Non-economic Market Power." Report to the Sub-committee on Multinational Corporations of the Committee on Foreign Relations, US Senate (Washington, DC: US Government).

Pradhan, Jaya Prakash (2004), "FDI Spillovers and Local Productivity Growth: Evidence from Indian Pharmaceutical Industry," University Library of Munich MPRA Paper 17080.

Reuber, G., H. Crokell, M. Emersen and G. Gallais-Hamonno (1973), "Private Foreign Investment in Development," Oxford: Clarendon Press and OECD.

Saggi, K. (2002), "Trade, Foreign Direct Investment, and International Technology Transfer: A Survey," *World Bank Research Observer*, 17(2): 191-235.

UNCTAD (1999), "World Investment Report: Foreign Direct Investment and the Challenge of Development," New York.

World Bank (1997), "Malaysia: Enterprise Training, Technology and Productivity," *A World Bank Country Study*, Washington, D.C.

Index

Accelerated Economic Growth, 98
Ahamed, Fayaz, 136
Akaike Information Criterion (AIC), 38, 63, 116
Amitava, Krishna Dutt, 149
Analysis and Interpretation, 207
Angappapillai, A.B., 52
Annual Capital Flows, 60
Arul, P.G., 122
ASEAN market, 7
Asia Pacific Foundation in Canada, 213
Asian Investment Intentions Survey, 213
Augmented Dickey Fuller (ADF), 38, 91, 116
Average Annual Growth Rate (AAGR), 214

Balaji, B., 112
Banu, M. Thahira, 97
Banu, R. Vaheedha, 97
Basic Requirements (BR), 195
Bombay Stock Exchange (BSE), 175
BPM5 (Balance of Payments Manual 5th Edition), 147
Busenna, Pesala, 147

Capital Controls, 21
Capital Flows:
  Impact, 52
  Trends and Composition, 57
Capital Movements, 20
  Importance, 20
Cash Reserve Ratio (CR), 23
Central and Eastern Europe (CEE), 83
Centre for Monitoring Indian Economy (CMIE), 68

Chandra, Charkraborty, 148
Chidambaram, P., Minister of Finance, 79
Commercial Law and Government Regulations, 84
Commonwealth of Independent States (CIS), 196
Compound Growth Rate (CGR), 214
Corporate Social Responsibility (CSR), 145
Corruption, 84

Department of Economic Affairs (DEA), 141
Department of Industrial Policy & Promotion (DIPP), 123, 144, 213
Dicky-Fuller test, 150
Durbin-Watson (DW) statistic, 62

Economic Growth and FDI Nexus, 80
Economic Reforms in India, 55
Economic Survey, 101, 214, 217
Effect of FDI on:
  Exports, 183
  Growth of Indian Economy, 72
  Spillovers and Productivity, 221
Efficiency Enhancers (EE), 195
Environmental Management System (EMS), 9
Export-Led Growth (ELG), 89
External Commercial Borrowings (ECBs), 28

FDI Steering Committee Report's (2002), 28

Index

Foreign Capital Flows:
  Importance, 54
Foreign Currency Non-Resident Bank (FCNR), 155
Foreign Direct Investment (FDI) in India, 2, 21, 72, 78, 193
  and Economic Development, 152
  and Economic Growth, 30, 77, 97, 112, 214
  and Employment Generation, 217
  and Export Performance, 182-93
  Annual Inflows, 28
  Benefiting, 14
  Definition Issues, 198
  Determinant Factors, 155
  Determinants, 117
  Effects, 19
  Employment Generation, 211-20
  Factors Inhibiting, 83
  Features, 2
  in Global Context of Organized Retailing, 129
  in Multi-Brand Retail Business, 122
  in Retail Business Issues, 127
  Inflows, 154
    Analysis, 26
  in Manufacturing, 202
  Issues, 1, 7
  Opportunities for Organized Retail Business, 125
  Outflows, 198
  Performance and Potential Index, 194
  Policy, 153-54
  Potential Benefits, 9
  Potential Negative Impacts, 9
  Problems, 156
  Recent Trends, 212
  Role on Economic Growth, 67, 211
  Telecom Sector, 136-46
  Trends, 99
  Type of, 155
  Typology of Types, 5
  Why to Invite?, 3
Foreign Exchange Regulations Act (FERA), 153

Foreign Institutional Investor (FII), 20, 54, 58
Foreign Investment and Promotion Board (FIPB), 123-24, 141, 151
  Security, 151
Foreign Investment Entry Strategies, 124
Foreign Trade Performance Analysis (FTPA), 187-89
Foreign Trade Performance:
  Analysis, 187

Geetha, K.T., 77
Global Competitiveness Index (GCI), 195
Global Competitiveness of India's FDI, 195
Global Competitiveness Report (GCR), 15, 195
Global Depository Receipts (GDR), 58
Global Economic Prospects, 2010, 71
Global Mobile Personal Communication by Satellite Services (GMPCSS), 78
Global Retail Development Index (GRDI), 132
GM (General Motors), 13
Government Policy on FDI in Retail Business, 123
Granger Causality Test Based on ECM, 93
Granger Causality, 116
Gross Domestic Investment (GDI), 72
Gross Domestic Product (GDP), 72
Gross Fixed Capital Formation (GFCF), 198
Gross National Product (GNP), 214
Growth Competitiveness Index (GCI), 156
Gulf War of 1990, 26

Hannan-Quinn Criterion (HQC), 38
Hindustan Motors, 13
Human Capital (HC), 72

Impact of Capital Flows on Growth, 63
Impact of FDI on Macro Economic Variables, 73
Impact of International Capital Flows, 60
Impulse Response Functions (IRFs), 91
Index of Industrial Production (IIP), 61
Indian Economy:
    Current Status and Future Prospects, 103
Indian Iron and Steel Industry, 170-81
    Decomposition of Total Factor Productivity Growth, 173
    Functional Form, 173
    Profile, 172
    Ownership and Productivity Growth, 177
Indian Iron and Steel Sector, 172
Indian Machine Tool Industry (IMTI), 13
Indian Manufacturing Industry Output Growth, 147
Indian Planning Commission, 38
Indian Telecom Sector, 140
    Glance, 143
Industrial Development and Regulation Act (IRDA), 153
Infrastructure, 83
Innovations and Sophistication Factors (ISF), 195
International Monetary Fund (IMF), 20, 21, 27, 28
Investment Outlook, 194
Iyyampillai, S., 19

Japan Bank for International Cooperation, 212
Japanese Collaborations, 13
Johensen Cointegration test, 91
Just-in-time (JIT), 13

Kalaichelvi, K., 182
Kathuria, Vinish, 1
Kearney, A.T., 194
Keshava, S.R., 67
Kumar, K.S. Santha, 211

Labour Force (LF), 72
Labour Force Participation Rate, 38
Labour Laws, 84
Leeds University Business School, 213
Linkage Effect, 74
Low Developing Countries (LDCs), 52, 171

Market Fundamentalist, 20
Maximum Likelihood (ML) test, 92
Mergers and Acquisitions (M&As), 10
MLR Model, 41
Monopolies and Restrictive Trade Practice Act (MRTPA), 153
Multinational Corporations (MNCs), 2, 5, 77
Multinational Enterprise (MNE), 183
Muthu Kumaran, C.K., 52

National Stock Exchange (NSE), 175
Neo-Classical Framework, 36
New Economic Policy in 1991, 28
Newly Industrializing Countries (NICs), 1
Non-Resident Indian (NRI), 57-58, 155
Nunnenkhamp, Peter, 148

Overseas FDI by Indian Corporations, 108

Participatory Notes (PN) transaction, 20
Phillips Perron (PP) tests, 91, 116
Political Instability, 83
Potential Indirect Effects on Host Countries' Exports, 185
Prasanna, N., 26
Preethi, S., 77
Product Market Competition (PMC), 74
Public Private Participation (PPP), 47
Purchasing Power Parity (PPP), 103

Quality Assurance (QA), 13
Quality Control (QC), 13

RBI's Activities, 22

Index

Repo Rate (RR), 23
Reserve Bank of India (RBI), 20, 38, 68, 154, 198
Bulletin, 149, 214
Retail Trends in India, 122
Reverse Repo Rate (RRR), 23

Sachs, Goldman, 194
Sampathkumar, T., 170
Saravanan, G., 193
Saravanan, S., 192
Schwartz Information Criterion (SIC), 38
Schwarz Information (SC), 116
Secretariat for Industrial Approvals (SIA), 155, 198
Secretariat of Industrial Assistance's (SIA), 38
Sectoral Distribution of India's FDI, 160
Sectors Attracting Highest FDI Equity Inflows, 70
Sector-wise FDI Inflows, 202
Securities and Exchange Board of India (SEBI), 20
Shanmugam, M., 88
Share of Countries in Global FDI, 156
Sharma, Suman, 221
Srinivasan, J., 88
Statutory Liquidity Ratio (SLR), 23
Structural Adjustment Programme (SAP), 136

Tax and Tariff, 84
TEC, 180
Technical Efficiency (TE), 177
Technical Progress (TP), 177-80
Telecom Regulatory Authority of India (TRAI), 139-40
Telecom Services, 137
The Hindu, 21, 22, 23

Theory of Multinational Enterprise, 183
Total Factor Productivity Growth (TFPG), 177-78
Components of Foreign Firms, 179
Decomposition, 176
Total Secondary School Enrolment Rate, 38
Transfer of 'soft technology', 9
Transferable Development Rights (TDRs), 140
Transnational Corporations (TNCs), 106, 175
Trend in FDI and Broad Capital Indicators, 14
Trends in FDI Inflow, 115, 197
Trends in FDI Scenario in India, 196
Tripura Sundari, C.U., 112

Unit Root Tests Results, 62
United Nations Conference on Trade and Development (UNCTAD), 44, 68, 77, 78, 106, 194, 212
United Nations, 115
United States of America (USA), 21

VAR Framework, 38, 40
Vector Error-Correction Modeling (VECM), 91, 95

Wal-Mart's Plans, 125
Why India is Worried about FDI in Retailing?, 125
Why India Really Needs FDI?, 212
World Bank (WB), 20, 27, 28, 67, 68
World Economic Forum (WEF), 15, 195
World Investment Prospects Survey, 212
World Investment Report, 2005, 106

Regnl 655
28-11-73 ED